DOWN BY THE LIFFEYSIDE

DOWN BY THE LIFFEYSIDE

Colbert Kearney

SOMERVILLE PRESS

Somerville Press Ltd,
Dromore, Bantry,
Co. Cork, Ireland

ISBN: 978 1 9999970 69

Designed by Maurice Sweeney.
Typeset in Bembo Book.
maurice.sweeney@gmail.com

Printed and bound in Spain by GraphyCems, Villatuerta, Navarra.

For Mary

And we'll have little children and we'll rear them neat and clean
To shout 'Up the Republic' and to rally round Sinn Féin;
They'll emulate their oul' fella who England's laws defied
By letting off big guns against the Saxon Huns down by the Liffeyside.

Peadar Kearney

CONTENTS

PREFACE

This memoir was conceived many years ago in the wide-open eyes of my children as, listening to me tell tales of my childhood, they struggled to imagine a world as remote as any they encountered in their Ladybird Books.

I envisaged a sketchbook illustrating the life of a working-class family in Dublin in the mid-twentieth century; but almost as soon as I began to scribble some notes, the process took on a life of its own. The most obvious example of this in the early stages was the absolute impossibility of understanding my father without seeing him as the son of his own father and, to a less explicit extent, his mother. More generally, I discovered that there was a great deal of family material that, before I could recount it for others, I had to try and understand myself. In the process, I have learned much more than I set out to chronicle.

What follows is a memoir of my parents. Though, of necessity, I figure prominently, I have tried to confine my role to my relationship with the couple who are the central characters. I never addressed them as Con and Maisie: to me they were always Mammy and Daddy, or Ma and Da. I have given them the names by which they were known to their families and friends in order to support my attempt to recognise and record their existences independent of my own, although I should point out that Con always used his official name, Colbert, usually in its Irish form, and normally referred to Maisie by her given name, Mary.

Thanks to my agent Jonathan Williams and to my sisters Maura, Eileen and Eva for their unstinting support and assistance in writing this memoir.

INCHICORE

One thing I wish and that wish will come true: my sons will honour and respect me.
I know that & I'm happy in the knowledge. I care nothing about what anybody on
this earth thinks while they with your help will remain fit representatives of a great
name, to carry on. Swank? But it's true, & mark my words they who live shall see.

PEADAR KEARNEY (1921)

My earliest memories are of the small dark ground-floor room in 25 O'Donoghue Street, Inchicore, Dublin, where I lived with my nana Eva, my father Con and my mother Maisie, and my sisters Maura and Eileen from shortly after my birth in the summer of 1945 until we moved to Finglas in 1952.

Some thirty years later, as soon as they were old enough, I took my daughters over to have a look at this narrow red-brick house. They were incredulous as I described what had been behind the front door: one room downstairs, two bedrooms upstairs, an added kitchenette, an outdoor toilet, a small back garden. No bathroom: my bath was a metal tub placed in front of the fire. Nana slept in the front bedroom, which left Con and Maisie, my sister Maura and me crammed into the back bedroom and baby Eileen in the pram downstairs.

'You *can't* be *serious!*'

What would they make, I wondered, of the rooms in 3 Richmond Parade, North Circular Road, where Con's parents and older brother were living when he was born on 1 August 1918? Or of the fact that he never took me there as I had taken them to Inchicore?

An occasional addition to 25 O'Donoghue Street was Con's brother, Uncle Pearse, when on leave from the army, but permanently present in his own way was the man called Peadar Kearney.

He was Nana's husband and Pearse and Con's father. He had died before I was born but it was as if he was still up there in the front bedroom. This was because he was famous. Everybody had heard of him and his part in the fight for Irish freedom. I knew more about him than I knew about anybody else. He had worked in the Abbey Theatre and was with them in England when he had to come home for the Easter Rising. The British army had taken him away from Con and Pearse when they were little boys like me and interned him in Ballykinlar, County Down [*Image 3*]. De Valera came to see him before he died and he was buried in the Republican Plot in Glasnevin. He wrote the words of the national anthem that everybody sang before the matches in Croke Park and other songs that were played on the Walton Programme and that Con and Pearse and Nana sang at home. He was a great man whose name would go down in history.

(For as long as I can remember I always saw Con as the son of Peadar Kearney but even as a child I had concluded that his relationship with his father involved more than adulation; it took me many years to realise how complex the connection was, involving both admiration and rejection, the former proudly advertised, the latter implied in action but never given verbal expression. Among my earliest memories was the unsettling suspicion that while my Daddy honoured his father above all other men, he did not love him as he loved me; that Peadar Kearney had never hugged my Daddy the way my Daddy hugged me when he got home from work. Maybe one day, I thought, when I was big, I would understand the kind of love there was between my Daddy and the man he always called 'my poor father', never 'my Daddy'.)

Con and Pearse spoke of their father with a quasi-religious reverence, as did their mother and relatives, summoning up a poet-patriot of heroic achievement, Roman stoicism and absolute independence of mind; but their eulogies lacked any intimation of a loving father playing with his children on the floor, taking them for walks, helping them with their homework, introducing them to books, offering them advice and encouragement as they struggled through adolescence. Their Peadar Kearney had more important business to attend to and was, ironically, much closer to the stereotypical Victorian father: highly principled, sternly didactic, controlled and aloof, far removed from the rollicking spirit of his comical verse. He did what he thought was right with little or no regard for the opinions of others. Once a year he fasted for a week in the belief that his body would be forced to consume its own accumulated poisons. Con told me his father had never struck him or Pearse, preferring to punish their transgressions—never identified—by having them stand in a basin of water in the back garden. Years later Pearse was less discreet and more specific, recalling for his son Peadar an occasion when, having found him reading an English comic, he stuck young Pearse's head in a bucket of water.

His sons were well-versed in the compendium of song, speech and story that was the nationalist narrative of Irish history and it seems unreasonable to imagine that anybody other than their father had drilled them, that after his release from Ballykinlar Camp in November 1921 he commenced the educational programme he had planned while interned. But, for whatever reason, there was at least one aspect of the programme he did not fulfil.

Central—in principle—to the Irish cultural revolution was the revival of the Irish language: Con and Pearse, like all national school children in the Irish Free State, received half an hour's teaching every school day. If the object was to make all Irish students competent in Irish, the project was a dismal failure, partly because of the quality of the teaching and partly because, in the economic climate of the time, it was not generally felt to be a priority. Neither excuse applied in the Kearney household. Peadar championed the Irish language, was a fluent speaker and had taught it to fellow-nationalists, including his friend Sean O'Casey. Pearse and Con certainly acquired the prescribed respect for their native language but neither, to his great regret, ever acquired the ability to use it as a means of conversation.

The only Irish attributed by Con to his father was a kind of phonic mnemonic: 'Tommy McCullough made boots for me' for the title and refrain line of the song 'Tá mé 'mo chodladh 's ná dúistear mé' (I am asleep and let nobody awaken me). Neither he nor Pearse knew any more of the song than this. Both he and Pearse often quoted 'Éist do bhéal agus ná bí ag caint mar sin' (Keep quiet and don't say such things) but whether they learned it at home or at school is anybody's guess.

(In a playful imitation of fluent Irish Con would spatter out a line that for years I could not understand nor he translate. The only word I thought I could hear was 'galúnach', the Irish for 'soap'. Enlightenment came during my first few days at secondary school where the Angelus, like all prayers, was said in Irish; as I heard 'ionus go mb'fhiú sinn geallúna Chríost d'fháil', I realised Con had been half-remembering being taught (or overhearing) the same line in the same prayer, which is the Irish for 'that we may be made worthy of the promises of Christ', hardly a text his father would have chosen for an Irish language lesson.)

I don't know how old I was when it struck me as extremely odd that Con, without a hint of criticism or even irony, would recall how his father's wonder-dog, Jess, a super-intelligent Kerry Blue bitch, was monoglot in Irish, looking askance if addressed in English. (Jess was presumably named after the Kerry or Irish Blue Terrier registered by Michael Collins at the Irish Kennel Club on 21 January 1921.) She was never 'our dog', always 'my father's dog', accompanying him on his rural rambles and excelling at

badger-baiting. She also inspired his verses 'To a Dog' (1928) in which the
constancy of a dog is preferred to the fickleness of human friendship.

> *The yellowest dog in all the land*
> *Has more of a Christian soul*
> *Than the spineless crew that sought your hand*
> *On the scent of your dwindling roll.*
> *So whether you're down or whether you're up,*
> *Your Philosopher, Friend and Guide,*
> *Be he pedigree bred or nameless pup,*
> *Is faithful, 'till death, by your side.*

Though he could only manage the briefest and most rudimentary conversation in Irish, I was always aware of the importance Con attached to
the Irish language. Like his father before him, he always signed his name in
Irish, and as soon as I could sign my name, I did likewise. Both my parents
encouraged me to study Irish with special care and both glowed with pride
when (first for them, later for visitors) I could recite from memory a poem
from my Irish schoolbook about the 1798 rebellion:

> *Sínte ar thaob an tsléibhe, do chonaic mé an cropaí bocht.*
> *Bhí an drúcht go trom ar a éadan; bhí piléar trína ucht ....*

> Stretched on the mountainside I saw the poor croppy;
> The dew was heavy on his forehead and a bullet had pierced his
> chest.

LATER ON, when I was at Irish college, Con wrote me a letter in very basic
Irish, padding it out with 'an dtuigeann tú?' (do you understand?) at the
end of every second sentence. On my return he welcomed any opportunity
to have me speak Irish in the presence of his friends. But he never to my
knowledge blamed his father for not teaching him Irish. My sense is that
he would have considered any criticism of his father a form of blasphemy.

Peadar's cultural ambition for his children is evident in a photograph of
himself and Pearse from c. 1917 [*Image 1*]. Baby Pearse is in full 'Gaelic' dress:
kilt, cloak and Tara brooch. Peadar is wearing a Norfolk jacket, possibly the
'sports suit made from "Volunteer" material' he had worn during Easter

8

Week. It is unwise to extrapolate economic circumstances from posed studio photographs, but Pearse is positively plump and the proud father shows no sign of deprivation. The decision to be photographed professionally may even suggest a degree of economic comfort.

Less opulent is a picture postcard made by the photographer Hurley of Henry Street in 1921 [*Image 5*]. A three-year-old Con and his five-year-old brother flank their Slater cousins Maura and Kathleen. Pearse, in conventional attire, looks pleased with himself, as do the girls, but it is difficult not to suspect a deep and distant sadness in Con's listless stare, as if trying to imagine the absent father in Ballykinlar Internment Camp to whom this photograph will be sent. The text is written and signed by Pearse: 'Dear Daddy, Con & Pearse sends [*sic*] this Picture to you. We never forget to pray for you and all the men who died for Ireland. Pearse.' (Had it crossed Pearse's subconscious mind that 'you and all' implied that his father too had died for Ireland?)

Inherent in Pearse's words and Con's stare is the terror they had experienced some six months previously, on 25 November 1920, when—aged four and two—they were awoken in the early hours by loud banging on the door of 3 Richmond Parade. British soldiers and Auxiliaries had come to arrest their father, whose cool reaction suggests that he had been half-expecting such a visit. Before he was taken away to Ballykinlar Internment Camp, he urged his sons, Pearse aged four and Con aged two, to be brave and look after their mother. As the Auxiliaries watched in amazement, the children saluted and recited a prayer he had taught them: 'The Lord have mercy on the souls of the men who died for Ireland, for Sean Treacy, Peadar Clancy and Dick McKee.' For all their patriotic show, the raid must have left deep scars, conscious or subconscious, and perhaps explains their life-long unwillingness to visit the scene of their terror.

Even if Con had no conscious memory of that winter's night, he knew the story well enough but although he and I must have passed close by on our way to or from Croke Park, never once did he mention to me—or later to my sisters—that he had spent the first three years of his life just a stone's throw away. I distinctly remember driving with him down the North Circular Road and pointing to North Richmond Street as the setting of Joyce's story 'Araby', but even that did not prompt him to reminisce. Nor would I be surprised if he himself never stole a private glance at number 3.

Which makes me wonder why I never asked him about that terrible night even when it was in print in Jimmy Bourke's biography of his father, published in 1957. It was not due to any lack of interest on my part but to a telepathic connection that existed between us for as long as I can recall. There must have been at least one occasion when I was tempted to ask him about Richmond Parade but was prevented by an absolute conviction that it would cause him pain or embarrassment. There was never a time when I did not assume, instinctively, that there were aspects of Con's life that he chose not to disclose and that, for as long as he lived, I did not feel entitled to probe.

Pearse was equally unforthcoming. His son, my cousin Peadar, attended O'Connell Schools but was never told of the family connection with the nearby Richmond Parade. He seems to have pressed his father more than I did mine for details of his grandfather's life but was invariably deflected with the proverbial observation that 'a shut mouth catches no flies'.

IN THE early autumn of 1921 Peadar wrote a letter to Eva: 'How is Pearse getting on at school? He ought to be learning something now. Tell him I want him to hurry up and write me a letter. I'm sure Con will be catching up on him. . . .'

It is possible to detect in his letters from Ballykinlar that Peadar and Eva had noted differences between Pearse and Con, with the younger Con emerging as the quieter, the more academic, perhaps the more biddable. His references to his schooldays were undoubtedly edited with me in mind but probably accurate in their portrayal of a boy who delighted in all forms of learning and whose application and progress were admired by his teachers. He passed his primary certificate in 1931, but more impressive was the reference, dated 12 September 1932, his headmaster, Eddie Doyle, wrote for 'one of the cleverest boys with whom I have dealt'.

> Colbert Kearney has been a pupil of the above school since childhood and I have no hesitation in declaring him to be one of the cleverest boys with whom I have dealt. He completed the seventh standard course and received the Primary Certificate...before leaving. [His moral] character is excellent, being upright, honest and truthful. I most cordially recommend him.

It is notoriously difficult for bright pupils to maintain their commitment

10

while knowing that economic circumstances will oblige them to abandon the pursuit of knowledge and seek gainful employment; but his own deprivation, far from lessening Con's respect for further education, elevated it to the ultimate value, its absolute virtue expressed in one of his favourite sayings: 'education is no burden to carry'. The paper on which his headmaster had written the reference was flimsy but has survived where more durable academic parchments have perished.

The scarcity of childhood memories extended outside the home and only three incidents stand out. The first is set in the nearby Oblate Church and has Con's mother—no sign of her husband—turning to look back and up at the choir, proud of her younger son whose solo soprano floats above the congregation.

The second achieved its finest form at least thirty years later in the summer of 1976 in the Teachers' Club in Parnell Square at the launch of *My Dear Eva*, Peadar's letters to Eva from Ballykinlar. In the course of his remarks Jimmy Bourke (who, as Seamus de Burca, had published the letters) mentioned that Peadar had taken the young Con fishing in the canal. I had known this, most likely because Con told me when (while we still lived in Inchicore) he in turn took me up to the Grand Canal to fish for gudgeon, and I don't imagine anybody present gave this reference a second thought. Anybody but Pearse, who was standing up on the platform beside Jimmy. I can still see the look of stage-incredulity on his face as he shook his head and half-whispered, half-mimed: *He never took me fishing. My father never took me fishing.* People smiled at what they took, reasonably enough, to be a middle-aged man light-heartedly hamming up a childhood slight; but I knew my uncle well and what I picked up was not any form of personal resentment but absolute amazement that his father had ever taken either of his children on what, in the context of the average family, would have been a commonplace outing. I also recognised that I was witnessing that rarest of utterances: an extra-mural criticism of Peadar Kearney from within the family. (Pearse went further when he told his son Peadar that he had never sat on his father's knee.)

Con recounted the third incident for me when I was quite young, about fourteen. It featured a confrontation between his father and Joe McGrath, an old comrade in arms. Both had been interned in Ballykinlar until McGrath was released to accompany Collins to the London negotiations, leaving Peadar to complain to Eva in August 1921: 'The only real friends I had

11

here Dr Hayes and Mr McGrath being gone, I'm all on my owney oh!'
McGrath was a minister in the Free State government until he resigned in
1924 and began a spectacularly successful business career that made him
the Irish epitome of wealth: 'as rich as Joe McGrath'. Which gave a strange
energy to Con's story.

In my memory the meeting took place in Thomas Street and Peadar had
taken Con to the removal of an old comrade who had not prospered in the
state he had helped create. Nor had the many veterans who had come to
bid him farewell and who made way for the enormous chauffeur-driven car
that was nosing through the throng until the man in the back seat stopped
the car, got out and walked over to Peadar with outstretched hand. It was
Joe McGrath.

'How are you, Peadar?'

'Ask me arse.'

I was amazed that an impoverished house-painter had rejected the helping
hand of a former friend who was in a position to help him and his family.
(If the car was official, the meeting took place at the latest in 1924 when
McGrath was still Minister for Industry and Commerce and Con was aged
about six.) It may be that Con transmitted to me the confusion he himself
experienced then and still felt. If I asked him why Peadar had behaved as he
did, his answer did not prevent my question from bubbling up in my mind
for many years afterwards.

AS I have never heard Pearse linked to any other occupation, I presume he
left school in 1930 and became an apprentice house painter. I have Con's
own word that when he was sixteen—in 1934—he worked briefly as a
labourer on the new stand at Croke Park and found it hard-going. (This
was presumably the Cusack Stand, completed in 1937.) Why did he not
follow his brother's example? It is unlikely that the son of a house painter,
who was a staunch union man, would not have been given an apprenticeship. Did his mother urge him to look for something 'better'? Perhaps he
wanted to contribute as much money as he could get there and then, and
even a labourer got more than a first-year apprentice. Whatever the reasons,
he left Croke Park as soon as he found more congenial employment as a
mechanic in a garage in Pearse Street.

Although he must have guessed what was obvious to others—that he
was exceptionally intelligent and quick to learn—I never heard him express

regret or resentment at being deprived of a secondary education. As a son of Peadar Kearney, he considered himself culturally superior to his neighbours, but his upbringing had taught him that education, like so much else, cost the kind of money his parents, like most working-class people, did not have.

So different were Pearse and Con in temperament that it is tempting to see Pearse as his father's son, careless of domestic economy, with Con as Eva's child, imagining a better life. Pearse, who married almost a decade after his younger brother, was a free spirit, inclined to live for the moment: the life and soul of the party who loved the spotlight, content with sufficient for the day, willing to let tomorrow look after itself, easy come easy go, a man at home in a pub with a pint in front of him. Though Con liked his pint as an accompaniment to lively conversation, he was less forward than Pearse, generally more considered and cautious, very anxious that tomorrow would be better than today both for himself and for his family. Each accepted the other while acknowledging—maybe even appreciating—his different cast of mind.

But though far from identical, they were in some ways very close. For as long as I can remember I intuited that they were somehow bound by their strange childhood, by a faith in their father as a national hero that prevented them from ever disclosing any domestic detail that might sully his public reputation. With reference to their deceased parents, many Irish people use 'poor' to convey little more than sympathy for the relatively hard times they had endured; but the more I heard Con use it, the more I understood him to imply a considerable degree of anguish and suffering. In similar circumstances Pearse would throw his eyes up to heaven, bless himself semi-comically, leaving you in no doubt that as a child and youth he had witnessed what was—literally—unspeakable.

UP THE street from the garage where Con worked in 1934 was the Queen's Theatre, Dublin's premier venue for melodrama, then managed by his paternal cousin Lorcan Bourke, who had taken over in July 1932 on the death of his father, P. J. Bourke. Married to Peadar's sister Maggie, the larger-than-life P. J. was perhaps the last of the Irish actor-dramatist-managers, specialising in nationalist melodrama, raising the rafters with his stirring portrayals of such Irish heroes as Lord Edward Fitzgerald and Robert Emmet. It is unlikely that Peadar would not have been offered complimentary passes but there is no evidence that he, or his wife or children, ever attended the Queen's and the fact that Peadar's biographer—himself a son of P. J.—makes no reference to such visits is striking. But when Lorcan offered him a job in the Queen's, Con did not hesitate.

Lorcan must have seemed more uncle than cousin to Con and not only because of the twelve years age difference: by the time Con went into the Queen's—in late 1934 or early 1935—Lorcan was a name in the entertainment business, having managed the Masterpiece cinema in Talbot Street and been associated at different times with the Capitol and the Tivoli. In 1932 'slackness of trade' had obliged him and his partner to take the Queen's into liquidation, but he was back in business shortly afterwards because 'Lorcan left the Queen's in 1935 when it was taken over by the Elliman family and was managed for a time by Maxie Elliman'.

It is easy to see why the sons of the illustrious P. J. Bourke, bred to the business of popular entertainment, should have become drawn to the excitement of the theatre; but what could have tempted the thoughtful son of a house painter away from a secure trade and regular hours to a life where, behind a dazzling façade, the only certainty was uncertainty? And this during the Hungry Thirties when economic gloom hung over the western world, aggravated in Ireland by a trade war with Britain. Perhaps he had had enough grim reality in his personal life and could not resist the glamour of the theatre, however nebulous. And who knows to what extent he was emulating his father who had worked in the Abbey before the 1916 insurrection?

In later years I could see that he and Lorcan had an affectionate respect for each other quite distinct from that between Con and his other Bourke cousins, including his pal Kevin. My guess is that Lorcan probably thought he was rescuing an imaginative young man from the dreary routine of a garage and Con was flattered to be asked and happy to accept. On the other hand, if Lorcan had been a fishmonger in Moore Street, I doubt if Con would have been as quick to throw up his garage job. Very likely the glamour played a part, and when he had become inured to the extravagant costumes, the stunning sets, the glittering dancers (known as the Moonbeams) and the strains of Alex Fryer's orchestra, there remained the deeper appeal of a new young usherette called Maisie Brady.

CON HAD an extraordinary ability to learn 'on the job': I have seen him acquit himself remarkably well as painter, carpenter, plasterer, plumber, electrician, fixer of radios, mechanic, panel beater, as well as commoner domestic skills such as gardening, wallpapering, lino- and carpet-laying. By the time Maisie arrived in the Queen's, Con was working one of the gallery spotlights, with Kevin Bourke on the other. There were no strict lines of demarcation—everybody, especially family, was expected to chip in—and this suited young men like Con and Kevin, who were keen to learn as much of the business as they could. In order to survive, the Queen's had introduced cinema into a show that was now termed 'cine-variety', and soon Con was acting as projectionist. (In 1936 he was awarded the required City of Dublin Technical Schools certificate in Cinema Projection.)

I am not sure when or why Con left the Queen's but it followed the departure of Lorcan and the arrival of new management with whom Con had strong words. I got the impression from Maisie that Con thought Lorcan had been unfairly treated: he never had much time for his brother, Rick Bourke, who continued on as stage manager and whom Con considered 'a slippy tit' (sly) for not being more supportive of his brother. The new management, the Ellimans, had blocked a job

Con had got as a cinema operator (projectionist) in the Carlton cinema, which they also controlled.

The Hungry Thirties were about to give way to World War II and times were tough, especially in the theatre business. In or around 1939 Con found himself working with Lorcan in the Torch Theatre in Capel Street where every effort was made to keep the place afloat: patriotic melodrama, variety, films, anything that would sell tickets.

Crooning—the type of singing epitomised by Bing Crosby—was all the rage, partly because even the man in the street felt he could imitate this apparently effortless style. Always on the lookout for a turn that would bring in the crowds, Lorcan decided on a talent competition to discover the best crooner in Dublin. The heats would take place on Saturday nights and would go on for, say, eight weeks, each heat producing a contestant for the grand finale. There was more than a title at stake. The Torch Theatre was proud to advertise eye-catching prizes. The winner would walk away with £50 and 'a solid silver loving cup'. For the runner-up there was a two-week engagement at the Torch, for third place a one-week engagement.

On the first Saturday night Lorcan announced that six young men had volunteered to sing but by the time the fifth was reliving his time 'South of the Border Down Mexico Way', it was clear that the sixth was a no-show.

Everybody in the wings looked to Lorcan for a decision.

'Con, you're going on next.'

'I can't go on looking like this.'

'Of course you can. It's not a bloody opera.'

'And what am I supposed to sing?'

'Sing that thing you sang the other night in Cawley's. I'll tell the band. They played it a few weeks ago. Come on, don't just stand there.'

And so it was that, within minutes, Lorcan was back on stage as MC, amusing the audience while, in the wings, Con Kearney checked his hair, cleared his throat and ran through the words of whatever it was. Con had been among friends with a pint in his hand when Lorcan had heard him sing it; standing alone on the stage, almost certainly for the first time, facing an audience lost in the glare of the lights, was another matter. But he had seen hundreds of others do it and it was only a song and the boys in the band were on his side. He got through it, relieved when it was all behind him. Or so he thought.

The judging was the high point of the competition. Each of the contestants was brought back out in turn and invited to reprise a sample of their song to remind the audience of their performance. There was no jury, no hi-tech means of measuring the reaction of the audience. Lorcan simply asked for a 'let's hear it' for each of the singers and, turning one scientifically cupped ear into the auditorium, he quantified the response on an imaginary scale from one to ten, jotting the figures down on a piece of paper, which he then returned to his top pocket.

Con duly re-emerged, sang the first verse and retired, letting the magic of his singing cast its spell. He had barely got his breath back in the wings when he was surprised by the amount of the applause, at the very least the equal of anything any of the others had received. With growing anxiety he heard Lorcan list out the scores, all the competitors receiving high praise and flattering marks of either seven or eight. Until they came to tonight's winner who would go on to the grand finale: by popular acclaim and a mark of nine, none other than [*tantalising pause*] contestant number six, Crooning Con Kearney!

Among Con's confused feelings was the certainty that Lorcan was up to something. Before his reprise, every available member of the Torch staff had been directed down to the rear of the stalls and ordered to make as much noise as they could. When Con had asked him what he was up to, Lorcan had waved him away with a smile: 'Nothing! A bit of a laugh, that's all.'

As word of mouth spread news of the contest and the prizes (and of the mode of adjudication), audience numbers were up and, to the delight of the box-office, it was obvious that ambitious young crooners, who had most likely honed their talents in the local pub, were arriving with their own supporters primed to bring the house down when required. The event was established as a city-wide competition when Lorcan announced that among the following week's hopefuls would be none other than the celebrated Walter Bradley, aka Blackie Bradley, aka the Coombe Crooner. Until then the favourite had been a docker from East Wall whose support-ers had shaken the Torch to its foundations but, even before he appeared, Blackie Bradley was felt to be a dead cert. While the other winners (with one notable exception) were known only within their own immediate area, Blackie Bradley's rendition of 'Begin the Beguine' was legendary from the Liberties to Crumlin. Owners of pubs invited him and his friends to come on singing nights and have their drinks on the house, provided Blackie obliged the company with a song and an encore. (There was even talk of the Torch management banning him on the grounds of professionalism, but he and his team successfully insisted that no money had changed hands—only a pint to clear his throat—and that Walter Bradley was a full-time parking attendant.) An important part of Blackie's star quality—apart altogether from his crooning abilities—was the fact that his absent father had obvi-ously not been Caucasian and, at a time when blacks were seen in Ireland only on cinema screens, this lent him a cosmopolitan glamour none of the others could match.

The night of the grand finale arrived. Six contestants would sing but all agreed it was a two-horse race between the Coombe and East Wall, with the Coombe expected to win by a distance.

Earlier that morning Lorcan had sent Con over to Domigan's Wholesale Hardware, Toys and Fancy Goods Warehouses on Merchants Quay to buy a 'silver' cup for not more than half a crown. Con probably reckoned that Lorcan was correct in presuming that the winner would be much more interested in pocketing the cheque for £50 than in questioning the quality of the silver.

The house was packed with noisy supporters for the grand finale and it was obvious that East Wall and the Coombe were only concerned about each other. To nobody's surprise and despite the best efforts of the cast and crew, the applause for Con was audibly less than that for the East Wall crooner and Blackie Bradley, which was, in each case, thunderous. And, it seemed, equal: even Lorcan's sensitive ear could not come up with a clear winner and he was forced to have another general reprise before he could reach his verdict. Tension threatened the silence as Lorcan reappeared with what, after an almost impossible task, was his final decision.

In third place and winner of a week's engagement in the Torch Theatre ...East Wall's finest—

A shocked in-take of breath throughout the auditorium. Mumbles of amazement. A pretence of polite applause from the Coombe, relieved that their man had seen off the only opposition. Some coarse mutterings of East Wall discontent in which two words could be distinguished, one of them 'fix'. The neutrals wondering who, if not East Wall, had come second.

In second place, the closest second place imaginable in what was almost a dead heat...Walter 'Blackie' Bradley.

Two seconds of mute astonishment: ready, set, and then an explosive barrage of abuse directed at Lorcan by the Coombe. It continued as Lorcan appealed to 'your sense of fair play', begging them to 'get over your disappointment', 'respect the difficult decision' the judge had to make and 'show some fellow-feeling' for a young man with a great future before him. None of this could be heard; nor did anybody in the audience hear a word when Lorcan congratulated Con, presenting him with the trinket from Domigan's and the envelope. Curtain.

The police were not called. The Torch was not burned down, although the takings for the Crooning Competition were not enough to stem the tide. The final stage production was in February 1940; it operated as a cinema until it closed completely in 1941.

I was a child when Con first told me the story of the crooning contest and I wanted to know what about the £50. He smiled: there was no cheque. But what was in the envelope? Still smiling: a piece of blank paper. But why did Lorcan say there was a cheque for £50? His conspiratorial stare: that was hard to explain, but when I was bigger I would understand. I wondered how long I would have to wait for this enigmatic enlightenment in which a grown-up me would understand what then seemed mysterious. But, as ever, he was right: the time came when I could make sense of the whole story.

Peadar Kearney supplied the music for *The March of Freedom*, a pageant written by his future biographer and performed by the Collins Barracks

Dramatic Society in the Olympia Theatre in 1941 to mark the anniversary of the 1916 Rising. If Con was involved in any way, he never impressed it on my memory like the crooning competition. Which may be strange but no longer surprising: after all, we must have driven up and down Capel Street at least a hundred times but never once did he identify the surviving façade of the Torch.

At the outbreak of World War II, Con and Pearse had joined the army as a patriotic gesture for the duration of what in neutral Ireland was termed the Emergency. A newspaper included a photograph and the heading 'Sons of Famous Men Join Up'. Army life obviously suited Pearse, who remained in the service until the late 1940s; but, after his adventures in the theatre, Con found the regimentation tedious and left as soon as he could. The only military exploit he reported to me had himself and Pearse being frogmarched into some form of detention in Richmond Barracks. It was (probably) the day of the 1940 All Ireland football final between Kerry and Galway and there was a great deal of drink involved as the men listened to the radio commentary. Because Kerry, Dublin's regular nemesis, were playing, Con and Pearse supported the other side, Galway, with more fervour than their commanding officer, a Kerryman, could tolerate, especially in such a tight game, which Kerry won by a point.

IN DECEMBER 1940 Con signed up with Anew McMaster's travelling company as electrician and driver. Imagine what it was like for a young man who, it seems, had never been outside Dublin before, except maybe for army training. One whole year on the road with a famous fit-up company. Seeing Ireland. Moving from town to town to be greeted as exotic, artistic, cultural royalty. Watching the mouths of the audience open as the outrageously romantic and spellbinding McMaster filled the auditorium with Shakespearean arias.

And after the play and the striking of the set? Presumably cast and crew enjoyed a drink and basked in the admiration of the enchanted provincials. Did the local beaux court the actresses? The bolder girls try to catch the eyes of the actors? It would have been an unusual venue if there wasn't a whiff of romance in the air. And what about the good-looking twenty-year-old with the oiled black hair combed straight back? Was he thinking of Maisie Brady back in the Queen's?

The tour was interrupted by the war and, just when he wanted to save up enough to get married, he was out of a job. But not for long: swapping the romance of the stage for the financial security of the screen, he spent the next five or six years—say 1942 to 1948—projecting films. He worked for a while in the Savoy and also in the Pavilion in Dún Laoghaire where he passed the time between programmes by becoming, like his father before him, a proficient snooker player. He then moved into the Ritz in Ballsbridge where, as Maisie remembered, he made lots of extra money showing forbidden war newsreels and censored 'blue' films to private audiences. He also made slides advertising coming attractions and was particularly proud of the one for *Blood and Sand* (1941), a torrid tale of bullfighting and moral decline, starring the sultry Tyrone Power and *femme fatale* Rita Hayworth.

PEADAR KEARNEY died of phthisis or consumption at 5.30 on 24 November 1942, just short of his fifty-ninth birthday. A few weeks earlier Sean O'Sullivan had made a striking pencil portrait, catching his subject as the elderly soldier, erect, alert, lips clamped [*Image 8*]. If any emotion escapes his sidelong sardonic stare, it is probably resentment that official Ireland has taken so long before honouring his contribution. He is buried in the Republican Plot in Glasnevin in the same grave as Thomas Ashe, his friend and comrade, who died on hunger-strike in 1917, and Piaras Béaslaí, biographer of Collins, who died in 1965.

About a week before he died, Peadar received a visit from Taoiseach Éamon de Valera: Con remembered the tall figure climbing the narrow stairs while his entourage crammed into the tiny house and neighbours filled the street. Unfortunately, there is no record of the exchange between the man who would have followed Collins through the gates of hell and the man who had opposed Collins in the Civil War. My guess would be that Peadar was unlikely to warm to Dev but, both speaking Irish, Dev would have thanked Peadar for all he had done and Peadar would have insisted that no thanks were due to a man for doing his duty.

Jimmy Bourke describes Peadar as dying a good Catholic death:

> Father Traynor from St Michael's administered the last rights of the Church. Peadar was very happy. When Martin Walton called to see him, he was able to shout down the stairs to him. At 5.30 on November 24th, 1942, he went to join the men who died for Ireland. There was a slender 'bedside' Ruskin beside him.

John Ruskin, who had lost his Christian faith and proposed that Britain replace its exhausted Christianity with philanthropic socialism, had not necessarily been chosen for a deathbed table but his presence there, instead, say, of a New Testament or a prayer book, did not bespeak a paramount concern with a good Catholic death.

A week previously, when Jimmy had called,

> [He] looked ill, but he was vigorous enough and talked steadily for half an hour. 'I am resigned to the will of God,' he said, 'but I know this is not the will of God. I would like the doctor to tell me the truth,' and apparently the only doctor he trusted to tell him the truth was Dr Gaffney. He mentioned a priest friend of his whom he would like to see, but he had gone to Cork.

The saying 'Welcome the will of God' (in Irish 'Fáilte roimh toil Dé') is normally a simple statement of absolute faith, complete in itself and not allowing for the type of qualifier Peadar appended. He remained a man of his own convictions. Notice there is only one doctor he trusts, one priest he would like to see.

When he deemed me old enough to deal with such matters, Con told me his father had seldom gone to mass, and then only when he anticipated an anti-republican sermon during which he would stand up and walk out in very public protest. Nor would it be surprising if such a man had reservations about the Catholic hierarchy, whatever about the will of God. The hierarchy had always condemned the IRB and later the IRA because of their violent opposition to lawful governments. That so many members of the IRA managed to combine devotion to Catholicism with apparent disregard for the teaching of the church was probably due to sympathetic curates who heard their confessions and gave them absolution. Con told me his father had made it clear that he did not want any visits from the local clergy and specified a particular priest of whose political principles he approved. This was probably the 'Father Traynor from St Michael's' mentioned by Jimmy, as if it was Peadar's parish church; but St Michael's was some distance away on Bulfin Road.

Nationalist society, reared on political funerals to Catholic cemeteries, demanded a degree of piety in its heroes. In the early 1940s the vast majority of the people of Ireland would have thought less of Peadar Kearney had they suspected he was not a true believer. Peadar himself, the old IRB organiser, would have understood the need to observe the forms, especially when his meetings with representatives of the Irish Free State and the Kingdom of Heaven would be conducted in private.

WITHIN A year of his father's death, on 7 September 1943, Con and Maisie got married from Maisie's home, 11 Jarlath Road, in Cabra, and afterwards honeymooned for a week in Avoca, County Wicklow, returning to live with Eva in 25 O'Donoghue Street. There is no need to look for reasons why a twenty-five-year-old man and a twenty-seven-year-old woman, both in love, good health and employment, should get married, but there can be little doubt that the atmosphere in Jarlath Road would have been less festive had Peadar Kearney been there mingling with his in-laws.

I know less about Maisie's family than Con's, partly because they were less fascinated by their own past than the Kearneys but mostly because I was brought up by Con to think of myself as a Kearney rather than as a Kearney-Brady and, above all else, to be proud of my direct descent from Peadar Kearney. My Kearney grandfather had answered the call and played his part in the age-old fight for Irish freedom while, to their eternal shame, others had gone off to fight in the British Army during the Great War. Among those others—at best understood as simpletons deluded by British propaganda, at worst despised as anti-national knaves—was my mother's father. Con never said a word against Ben Brady but neither did he ever give him parity of esteem. Because he was Maisie's father, it was generously assumed that, like so many misguided others, he had joined the Dublin Fusiliers in a fit of youthful enthusiasm rather than as a consequence of any political conviction. Neither Ben nor any of his family ever showed any particular interest in Irish culture or politics, so that, to Con's way of thinking, they lacked 'national feeling'.

It is unlikely that Ben Brady was unaware of his son-in-law's attitude and this may explain why I saw so little of him, why he never to my knowledge took any interest in me. On the other hand, having fathered nine of his own, perhaps he had had enough of children.

I can recall him being in our house only once but, for a reason that remains mysterious, the image remains as sharp and clearly coloured as a digital colour photograph. We have very recently moved to Finglas: the sun streams through the front window onto pink-plastered walls and bare floorboards. My mother's father is on his knees at the hearth with a hammer and chisel, shaping firebricks to fit the grate. He works away without a word. He knows I am behind him, watching.

I was about six at the time. Looking back, I wish we had been close enough for him to tell me his story; but in those days there was no way I could have listened sympathetically to an Old Tough and remained a true Kearney. He was a fine figure of a man, a thick white mat of the famous Brady hair crowning a listless face that had seen the horrors of hell on earth. (Or so the oral and photographic evidence has led us to believe. Cyril Griffith junior, a son of Maisie's sister Eileen, trawled all the army archives in a vain search for any record of Ben. It may be that, like many others, he enlisted under a false name.)

I am aware of meeting Maisie's mother only once. She is an old woman with long grey hair, lying in bed although it is daytime. Almost certainly it is 1948 and I am around three years of age; if so, she was dying and Maisie had brought me upstairs to say a last goodbye to her beloved mother.

Elizabeth Mary Rafferty (b. May 1887) had grown up in the north-inner city where she was known as Lal. I wish I had had more time to get to know her, partly because Maisie frequently referred to her mother's ways and quoted her old inner city sayings, even more because Con thought the world of her, insisting she was the precursor (and by implication 'only begetter') of Maisie, honouring her as 'the heart of the rowl', the supreme accolade for outstanding humanity and good-humoured generosity. Con and Lal took an instant shine to each other: he delighting to recall how, when he left Maisie home, Lal would always rustle him up a supper that could well have been somebody else's breakfast. She must have seen that, for all his high-falutin talk, Con had the makings of a good husband for her daughter.

Ben's innate contentment contrasted with the aspirations of his siblings. One of his brothers was an insurance collector who somehow ended up in Malta as some kind of honorary consul. Another was an assistant wine-taster in Gilbey's, noted (with a hint of mockery) for his refined deportment. One sister became a nun and spent her life teaching in South Africa; she visited us in Cappagh Road around 1957. The sister I knew best was Auntie Maisie who was a regular visitor to Cappagh Road and always brought a bag of Lemon's sweets: despite losing a hand in a printing works accident, she was an accomplished knitter.

Ben worked first as a van driver for Arnott's and then as a boilerman in

Grangegorman Asylum. The Bradys were economically more comfortable than the Kearneys. I remember (in my early teens, I think) being struck by the superior tone Maisie adopted when remarking that there had always been a 'croft' of water on their table at mealtimes. Only later, when I read in the Oxford English Dictionary that 'croft' was a nineteenth-century corruption of 'carafe', did I understand her choice of tone. We never, to my knowledge, had a jug of water on the table at dinnertime: anybody who wanted water got it themselves from the tap.

MAISIE WAS born on 27 July 1916 in 111 Seville Place (where the family had the whole of the top floor) and went to school in Marlborough Street. They left around 1922 amid mutterings of discontent, Ben believing the house had been left to an aunt when it should by right have gone to him.

They spent about a year in Marino—15 St Aidan's Park Avenue—before moving to 25 Linenhall Street, off North King Street, in order to be closer to Grangegorman Asylum. Maisie remembered this house as 'a dog's box' to which Ben had added an extension, 'using the best of Grangegorman tradesmen and materials'. She also remembered that 'Annie Geraghty and I were counting the days till we were fourteen and could go to work in Dowling's sweet factory in Liffey Street for twelve shillings a week'. She did start there but Ben thought the work (labelling and packing Lucky Lumps) too hard for such a gentle girl and convinced Lal to keep her at home to help with the children, which she did for years, serving her apprenticeship as a mother.

However happy she was at home, a teenage girl must have felt some twinges of envy when her older sister spoke of her work in the Queen's Theatre. Lal, who had lived in Dominick Street, had been a friend of Maggie Bourke—sister of Peadar, wife of P. J—in nearby Nelson Street, which may explain why Lorcan had taken on Eileen around 1930 when she was sixteen, young enough to make the attentions of her future husband, Cyril Griffith, slightly scandalous. Maisie remembered Eileen rhapsodising about 'this beautiful young fellow' who worked at the Queen's and whose head had been 'split open' during a hurling match in the Phoenix Park. (His name? Con Kearney.) Maisie did not hesitate to say yes when (probably in 1935) a man called Charlie Wakefield came to the door and told her she was wanted at the Queen's.

All Maisie's four brothers were talented woodworkers and French-polishers, once highly prized skills for which popular demand was falling.

Joe, the eldest, a handsome charmer and a champion cyclist, was the apple of all Brady eyes but that did not stop him running off to England when a love affair went against him. Despite frantic efforts to find him—ads in newspapers, announcements at masses—he disappeared for years, not even coming home for his mother's funeral. Eventually (in the mid-1950s) he was located in Nottingham and, enabled by a small lottery win, Ben visited Joe and his English family and some years later Joe returned to Dublin for Ben's funeral. His reappearance haunted me for years, not because of anything that happened between us and despite Maisie's best efforts to shield me from what had shattered her. A compulsively inquisitive ten-year-old, I was alert to the opening and closing scenes—Maisie's girlish excitement at the prospect of seeing her long-lost brother again and her muffled tears as we made our way home to Finglas—but the drama of the central action remained a dark mystery until I eventually collated scraps of evidence from overheard conversations.

At the time, Maisie's sister Eileen was living in Jarlath Road, having lost the house in Whitehall as a consequence of her husband's bankruptcy. The sisters had always idolised Joe and could not wait to see him again. Having embraced both of them, he had stood back and gazed at them.

'My, how you've changed! All these years I've been telling my friends in Nottingham about my two beautiful sisters in Dublin. And look at you now. My, how you've changed.'

It is not difficult to imagine the effect this had on Eileen and Maisie. In their single days they had indeed enjoyed a reputation for beauty. They were now older, of course, and were no longer the sylphs they had been before the wear and tear of family life had left their mark; but to have this thrown up in their faces by their own flesh and blood was more than Maisie could take and she tore into Joe, letting him know how much he had changed from admired paragon to the unfeeling wretch who had broken his mother's heart, first by disappearing without so much as a word of explanation and then by not coming home before her death. She concluded with a withering jibe that was never forgotten by those who witnessed it.

'I notice you didn't bring that oil-painting of yours over from Nottingham for us all to have a good look at her.'

This was Maisie at her best, one of those moments when you suspected that her powers of vituperation reached back through the oral centuries to some considerable satirist. Her brother's response, if he had one, is not recorded in the annals.

Paddy (Patsy) was next in line: when his woodworking skills were no longer in demand, he took a job in Grangegorman. His younger brother Peadar was luckier inasmuch as he found well-paid work as a wood-turner when ten-pin bowling was introduced into Dublin. The youngest son, Bennie, emigrated to New York where he made a good living as a French-polisher.

The next of the girls after Maisie, Teresa, was my godmother; she never fully recovered from the death of a boyfriend during the TB epidemic and later emigrated to Canada. After her came Annie, who, with her friend Patty Barnes, used to visit us in Inchicore and who, like her baby sister Bridie, later made her life in London.

Maisie seemed much closer to her sisters than to her brothers. I recall several visits to Whitehall where Eileen and her family lived (about a hundred yards from Maggie Bourke) in a house that seemed palatially opulent to me.

My favourite visit was to Broombridge Road in Cabra West, not because of Maisie's brother Patsy but to revel in the warmth of his wife's personality and generosity. Maureen McManus was a woman of contagious vitality, a storyteller of genius who, while spellbinding an audience, was (or seemed to be) unaware that she was involved in anything other than casual conversation. (As I walk through the hall into the kitchen, she is there in her pinny, already turning to the gas stove as she asks 'Would you like your Antie Maureen to make you a few chips?')

Con's ideas of the sexes were those of his time and enabled him to enjoy the company of the Brady women (including Maureen McManus) while remaining somewhat aloof from their brothers. Women were not expected (or, in this case, did not desire) to take an interest in politics and thus could not be faulted for any lack of 'national feeling'. Men who failed to support the idea of an independent Gaelic Ireland enjoyed no such immunity. None of the Brady women had any interest in sport and were consequently exempt from the charge of preferring soccer—the 'foreign' game that was by far the most popular among the Dublin working class—to the native Gaelic games Con supported.

WHEN WE were growing up, my sisters and I would have been more embarrassed to seek details of their courtship than our parents would have been to supply them. Bits and pieces rose to the surface of conversations and inevitably we tried to link them together, using the evidence of our own eyes and ears to imagine the connections. There is little that is historical in my account of their lives between their first meeting and their marriage in 1943; inevitably my guesswork is directed by what my sisters and I observed of their later life. When we were young, it would have seemed ridiculous to think of them as figures in romance, but time taught us to recognise the happy-ever-after of their life-long love affair.

I imagine Con fell in love with her beauty, her high spirits and her invincibly good nature. Her family nickname was 'Large-heart' and the longer I knew her, the more I came to regard her emotional intelligence—the milk of human kindness—as the supreme human virtue. Not that she was saintly or even demure—she was quick to spark and had a sharp tongue—but though she might in passing disparage absent people, she could never hold a grudge against them face to face. She had an enormous sense of compassion, especially for poor or neglected children. She was pained by cruelty or suffering but would have killed if necessary in defence of her family.

Besides his handsome looks, I imagine she was drawn to Con's unassertive intelligence, his caring nature, his decency and trustworthiness. And maybe 'the little mother' in her sensed the anguish and confusion of his life as the son of Peadar Kearney.

Neither would have been short of admirers, but from the beginning, whatever about their eyes, they had hearts only for each other and their very different lives fused into the most complete union I have ever known.

In this 'story' of their togetherness, there are only the two of them. No remarks by them or others conjured anybody from either's past haunting their early rendezvous, no anonymous competitor lurking in the wings, waiting to cut in. I find it unlikely that Maisie—or any other an attractive girl of eighteen—didn't have boyfriends before Con; but my guess is that, against all odds, she was his only serious girlfriend. Maisie, less discreet than Con, used to joke about his friendship with the Bourke girls, going so far as to call Patsy 'your girlfriend'; but my sense is that this was an expression of her possessiveness (and a proud affirmation of his attractions), rather than an imputation of infidelity with any of his first cousins.

(Many years after Con's death I attended the funeral of a relation. Walking into the dining room for 'the afters', I noticed this same Patsy Bourke deep in conversation in the far corner. As I scanned the room for my sisters, I was aware in my penumbral vision of a figure rising and moving in my direction.

27

It was Patsy, her smiling stare reminding me of ecstatic faces in religious paintings. She was still three or four strides away when she stretched out her hands towards me. *Colbert!* I was taken aback: she had never been quite so dramatically affectionate before. I asked her how she was, but she was not listening. Instead, her head inclined, her eyes penetrating mine, she sighed: *Colbert, when I saw you walking through that door I was looking at Con Kearney*.)

I have always been to some extent aware that the union between Con and Maisie was a marriage of different minds but it occurred to me only recently that they had both 'married out'. It was the norm for women at the time to follow their husbands' directions in extra-domestic matters such as religion, politics and education. Maisie always seemed happy to defer to Con in such matters and never criticised or contradicted him in the presence of their children. But she remained a Brady in having little or no interest in the fight for Irish freedom or the part played in that conflict by Peadar Kearney.

SHORTLY BEFORE they got married, Con called into the Queen's to collect Maisie and was congratulated by one of the managers, George Wilde, who expressed the hope that Maisie would be resuming her job after the honeymoon. Almost certainly intended as a generous gesture to both (and an unprompted compliment on Maisie's work), it was not taken as such by Con, whose response was more principled than polite: 'If I couldn't support my wife, I wouldn't be marrying her.' He had been imbued by his father with a particularly pure form of independence that, given the least hint of the possibility of what might be seen as subservience, demanded—even glorified—the biting of hands offering food.

Had it been Lorcan, Con would have been more diplomatic, less inclined to fear the humiliation of kindness *de haut en bas*, but the thrust of the response would almost certainly have been the same. It was partly due to the convention that most women, especially those in the middle and upper classes, stayed at home after marriage to keep house for their husbands and children. But there was probably another reason why he felt so strongly on this subject, one which—like so much of his sense of himself as a husband and father—looked back to his own upbringing.

Although Eva had been 'tenderly reared'—it was often recalled that she 'had gone to school in a hackney'— and maintained to the end an aura of gentle refinement, the circumstances of her married life were anything but comfortable and she was obliged to go out to work as a nursing assistant. Her husband revered her as 'the lady' but relegated all domestic duties to her while he devoted himself to 'the cause'. When he withdrew from political action and worked as a painter, he was unable to support his family, spending (by his own account) half of 1923 on the dole. Rather than repeat the grim drama of his own childhood, Con would lavish on his children the paternal warmth he himself had never known: he would never draw the dole but would work day and night (and forego any indulgence) to ensure his wife was never obliged to leave her home in order to augment the income it was his duty to supply.

I am only aware of two wedding photographs. One is a colour-tinted picture of the couple cutting the cake in Jarlath Road [*Image 12*], the other a formal foursome of the happy couple, flanked by best man Kevin Bourke and bridesmaid sister Eileen, outside the front door [*Image 13*]. It was wartime and they were working-class, with neither family in a position to subsidise any extravagance.

When Cyril Griffith had married Eileen shortly beforehand, he had hoped that it would be a double wedding, which he would pay for, but Con would not agree to the offer. His sense of independence did not allow him to be beholden to anybody, least of all, perhaps, a brother-in-law who was comfortably middle-class. The most historically interesting contribution to Con and Maisie's wedding breakfast came from Cyril, who supplied sufficient sawdust (in short supply like almost everything else during the war) to maintain fires on which food could be prepared and kettles boiled for as long as the festivities required.

Being engaged to sisters, Con and Cyril had socialised together and the fact that Cyril owned a car meant they could go outside the city on excursions. This must have provoked mixed feelings in Con, who cycled to and from his work in the cinema and who, while happy to benefit from such a luxury as a private car, must often have wished he had the material means to treat Maisie as Cyril treated her sister. Cyril's father was a leather merchant who had anticipated the outbreak of war (and the consequent shortages) by stockpiling leather at pre-war prices and could afford to buy a house in Whitehall as a wedding present for Cyril and Eileen.

I got the impression from both Con and Maisie that, though in monetary terms Cyril Griffith was a better 'catch', Lal preferred Con. She had, for example, two little china flower baskets that her grandmother had given to her mother and which she proposed to give, one each, to her future sons-in-law; but when Cyril said he wanted both or none, she gave both to Con.

WEALTH WAS the last thing on their minds when Maisie became pregnant and on 30 June 1943, gave birth to a baby boy, who was—almost inevitably—called Peadar. Infant mortality rates were high in those days in Dublin. There had been a growing epidemic of gastroenteritis since 1940 which, unfortunately for Con and Maisie, peaked in 1943 when 1,223 deaths were recorded in Ireland, among them baby Peadar's. Neither ever tried to express their desolation to me. Sporadic details emerged of Peadar's illness—as a child I was amazed to overhear Maisie describe how Peadar had been 'fed through the toe', presumably some kind of drip—but the traumatic effect on his parents was for a long time kept to themselves.

Years later Con told me how he and Kevin Bourke had collected the little white coffin at the hospital and taken it by taxi to Glasnevin Cemetery where they handed it over to staff who would, in line with standard practice, inter the child in an unmarked grave with no relatives present. (Years later still, Maisie's sister Bridie told me that Cyril Griffith had paid for the taxi.)

Why did I not ask my father if he or anybody knew where baby Peadar was buried? Most likely because, while telling me about (and reliving) the journey with the little white box, he also transmitted one of those signals requesting me not to exacerbate his pain by asking him to reveal more than he had chosen to relate.

While we were living in Finglas—a period of some thirty years—the road into town took us past Glasnevin Cemetery but never once was there any reference to baby Peadar's burial. The cemetery itself could not be avoided: there were family funerals, visits to Nana's grave and much was made of Peadar Kearney's grave in the Republican Plot. But no mention of their first-born.

I would be amazed if either Con or Maisie knew where baby Peadar was buried. Far from being criticised as callous, parents of dead infants were encouraged to blot out as much of the memory as they could. This practice was extended to their children, whose innocence was to be preserved for as long as possible, using all means available, including lies and prohibitions, but preferring silence. (When they were both dead, my sisters and I located the grave and marked it.)

Peter Michael had been born in the Rotunda and had died seven weeks later, on 20 August, in St Kevin's Institution, the latest name for what had begun as the infirmary attached to the workhouse known as the South Dublin Union. It never lost all its associations with 'the sick poor' until it was demolished and replaced by St James's Hospital in 1971. Con and Maisie could not have avoided speculating how better would have been Peadar's chances of survival had he, like his cousin Michael—son of Cyril and Eileen, born in June 1944, and a victim of the epidemic—been treated in a hospital catering for the better-off.

If the move from O'Donoghue Street to the ground floor flat of 54 Eccles Street—a house owned by Mamie, a sister of Cyril Griffith—was an attempt to put their terrible loss behind them, it seemed to work. Maisie had been so heartbroken at the loss of Peadar that (as she told my sister Maura many years later) she did not want to get pregnant ever again; but on 25 July 1945 she gave birth to another boy and this one survived to tell the tale.

(Before working on this memoir it never occurred to me to wonder if the Con and Maisie who had returned from their honeymoon to Inchicore were, to some extent at least, more happy-go-lucky than the parents I knew. It is unlikely that they escaped unscathed from the death of infant Peadar, but I never heard anybody even hint that either of them 'was never the same again'; nor did it ever cross my mind that they might be nursing a secret sorrow.)

SHORTLY AFTER my birth I was taken to be baptised in the nearby Catholic church on Berkeley Road. The course of the ceremony was diverted when, in an aside, the priest explained that he could not possibly christen me Colbert because it was not a saint's name, but would christen me Cuthbert instead. Conditioned to expect unquestioning obedience from his flock, the priest had already resumed his script when Con interrupted to inform him, again, that my name was Colbert. If the priest was shocked or offended, he managed to conceal it, condescending to explain that, yes, I could be *called* Colbert but I would have to be *christened* Cuthbert because, *as he had already explained*, Colbert was not a saint's name. But he had seriously misread this particular member of his flock, who calmly announced: 'Well, if you won't christen him Colbert, I'll take him to somebody who will.' Without further ado the priest christened me Colbert.

Much of the excitement of the situation has been lost in the social changes of the intervening years. Even the youth of today will have gathered that, as a pillar of what was in effect the established church, the priest enjoyed the kind of power and prestige not even a modern cardinal could expect; but few of those born since 1960, many of whom name their own children after international film stars, pop singers or herbs, could imagine the affront to my father in the proposal that I be called Cuthbert. The priest might just as well have suggested Egbert or Norbert or, for that matter, George or Henry, for to the culturally sensitive ears of the time these names were all essentially (if not always etymologically) English. If the priest was tempted to point out that Colbert was not a Gaelic name, he wisely held his tongue, not wishing to be told that, notwithstanding the origins of the name, the death by execution of Con Colbert in 1916 had made it more Irish than the Irish names themselves.

From Con's refusal to do as he was told and, even more outrageously, his slightly veiled threat to have the child christened in a Protestant church, the priest inferred a rather dangerous type of anti-clerical republican, many of whose predecessors had been condemned and threatened with excommunication if they did not mend their ways. He therefore cut his losses by seeming to surrender to the heretical bully in order to gain the greater prize of claiming the child for Mother Church.

Con would never have taken me to a Protestant church because, for all its faults and for all the failings of some of its clergy, he believed the Catholic Church was our church, the Protestant overwhelmingly that of the oppressor. Nor was Con the dangerous type the priest had imagined, his face half-hidden by a cap, a hand inside his trench coat clutching a Webley revolver.

The older I got, the more fully I appreciated his courage and the range of dramatic skills he displayed. He was not physically aggressive, but he had inherited from his father an absolute unwillingness to bend the knee.

And then there was his choice of part. He could have sought the sympathy of the priest by imploring him to make an exception, listing sentimental reasons for his choice of name. He might also have sought to trump the priest's theology by pointing out that he himself had been christened Colbert. Even after all these years it is difficult not to conclude that he chose the right role, that the priest would not have been impressed by pleading and would have drawn the line at being lectured by a working-class man of no standing or education. No, the masterstroke was putting the pressure back on the priest, making him realise that any insistence on his rights or dignity could easily lead to the ultimate failure and he would be responsible for sending a soul, which had come to his church for baptism into the One True Faith, into the arms of the heretics, who would not care what his name was.

The Eccles Street flat glowed in their shared memory: here for the first time they were in a place of their own by themselves, making their new life together, Maisie doing all in her power to make the flat a haven for Con when he arrived home on his bicycle from his work in the Pavilion, Dún Laoghaire or the Ritz, Ballsbridge. And whenever Maisie recalled those early days in Eccles Street, she always referred to the many happy hours Con spent taming and improving the back garden, which was at their disposal.

The idyll ended when, out of the blue, Mamie Griffith dropped in to tell Maisie that, while she was not putting any pressure on them—she and Con could take their time—she wanted them to look for other accommodation. When I was old enough to ask her why Mamie Griffith had given them notice, Maisie's reaction was characteristic. She flared in sudden rage, as if she had only just that minute been told to leave. 'There was no reason,' she rasped; 'bad luck to that hoppidy one!' (Mamie Griffith walked with a limp.) But why do you think she did it? 'Because she was a dry old bitch that no man would marry, despite all her money, and she couldn't bear the sight of a happy couple with a lovely new healthy baby.'

Con's reaction was different but equally characteristic. Having cycled home from work to be told of Mamie's order, he promptly got back up on his bike and, 'in a cold fury', peddled over to O'Donoghue Street in Inchicore to ask his mother if we could move back in with her, which we did the following day. It was not his nature—both his parents despised 'bad' language—to indulge in coarse abuse, and certainly not of a woman, no matter how deserving; but neither was it his nature to forgive and forget. Mamie Griffith was beneath his contempt and it is even possible that her behaviour coloured his attitude to her brother Cyril.

Memory of the expulsion from Eccles Street helped shape one of Con's dreams: a house they would own, not rented from the corporation or anybody else but a 'purchase house', such as the Bourkes and Cyril Griffith had, a house from which nobody could expel them, leaving them in Con's ideal state, 'under a compliment to nobody'.

Well wrapped up for our flight into Inchicore, I was carried over to the cramped two-bedroom, two-storey house in which we would spend the next five years. In many respects mine was a conventional working-class childhood in which, as the only grandson on the Kearney side, I was 'spoiled' by loving parents, a proud grandmother and an unmarried uncle who arrived occasionally on leave from the army. But, all unknown to me, there was another crucial element.

I was the sole beneficiary of baby Peadar's death. Years afterwards—when to do so could no longer be seen as tempting fate—Con and Maisie would recall (he with a wry smile, she sighing nostalgically) how obsessively vigilant Maisie had been to ensure I did not follow my brother to Glasnevin. I was cosseted, protected, attended, inspected and cared for as if my life was more important than the lives of those around me, cuddled as if I was one of those princes on whose well-being the prosperity of a million subjects depended and not the happiness of a young couple trying to get over their broken hearts.

THERE IN O'Donoghue Street my brain stuttered into action, forming memories of which splashes still remain on the vast blank screen of the vanishing past.

Maisie's warm, soft embrace as she lulls me with the swaying strains of 'The Castle of Dromore' or 'You are my Sunshine' or bounces me over and back on 'The Good Ship Lollipop'.

Waves of heat from the big red fire with inglenook seats on either side.

The slither of the weatherboard across the threshold as somebody comes in the front door.

Nana's bony arms, not soft and warm like Maisie's, but loving. And constantly singing, no less. *Colbert and Nana were sailing, all in a big, big boat.* We were headed for America, for Washington D.C., in an improvised song that would end when the president came down the steps of the Capitol and took us to the White House where we were guests of honour at the top of a huge long table.

I loved the musical adventure without ever understanding any of the details. I had no idea who the president was—it was Truman—but I saw the Capitol and the White House as they appeared on pennants Auntie Katie had sent. This was Nana's older sister, who had emigrated to New York whence she sent gifts for me that were almost beyond the imagination of post-war Inchicore: pearl-handled pistols in fancy holsters and a buckskin-fringed cowboy waistcoat. To the best of my knowledge the extravagant gifts stopped when Nana died and contact with Katie was lost.

In my earliest memories of Con, I am no longer a baby. According to

Maisie, he had no real interest in his children until we began to speak. He must have been very keen for me to start because I was taken to a specialist in Merrion Square who charged them 5 guineas—an enormous sum for a working man—and told them not to worry, that I would talk in my own good time and once started would be hard to stop.

WHAT DISTINGUISHED life in 25 O'Donoghue Street from that of the average working-class family was the cult of Peadar Kearney, a cult so internalised by the occupants as to seem natural. It was like believing in God, an attachment of vital importance but limited to allocated hours. My favourite rituals were the social occasions in the house when his patriotic songs were sung, among them lively ballads such as 'Whack-fol-the-Diddle', 'It's a Grand Old Country Every Time' and 'Sergeant William Bailey' and the haunting 'Down by the Glenside', which was then (and would remain until the Northern troubles quietly censored such explicit nationalism) his best-known work after the national anthem.

Oddly enough the song that that moved me most was not one of Peadar Kearney's and was called 'Ireland, Mother Ireland'. I can still recover something of my confusion as Con cleared his throat and stared at the floor before, in the respectful silence, he raised his head and began:

> Oh, land of love and beauty, to you our hearts are wed;
> To you in lowly duty, we ever bow the head;
> Oh, perfect loving mother, your exiled children all
> Across the sund'ring seas to you in fond devotion call.

Much of the surface meaning was beyond me but the bowing of the head and the word 'devotion' were enough to make me wonder why Con was singing a hymn at a party. I knew there were other kinds of mother, that Mary was the Mother of God, and that countries were often called mother. (In 'Whack-fol-the-Diddle' Peadar Kearney had imagined how surprised 'Mother England' would be to discover that Ireland would be peaceful and civilised when free from English oppression.) But you could not see, only imagine, a country as a mother. There were lots of statues and holy pictures of Mary the mother of Jesus but none of them showed her as a real mother, who made dinners and put clothes out on the line, like Maisie.

No such confusion was attached to the great men who fought for

35

Ireland—Lord Edward Fitzgerald, Robert Emmet, the Fenians, the Invincibles, the rebels of 1916—and slowly I began to understand something of what Nana and Con meant when they described living people as 'an out-and-out Major Sirr' or 'a proper Lord Norbury' or, worst of all, 'a right Carey the Informer'.

I remember Nana—a frail lady in spectacles with rectangular rimless lenses—quivering with intensity as she chanted Peadar Kearney songs or told me how proud he would be to see me growing up a patriotic boy who would always be faithful to Ireland. When eventually I was big enough to be taken into town on the bus, she pointed to the house in Thomas Street where Lord Edward had been arrested by the cowardly Major Sirr, and to St Catherine's Church, in front of which Robert Emmet had been executed, having made his great speech from the dock before being sentenced by Lord Norbury.

She was anything but a wizened fanatic, my gentle Nana, who at Christmas and Easter—and on many occasions in between—lavished as much as she could afford on me. It was years before I began to imagine what Nana had endured 'for Ireland' and why she made me promise never to point Aunt Katie's guns at anybody.

Outside the house the older forces continued to rule. As soon as babies were old enough, there was no shortage of girls willing to take them out in their prams for walks. Marie Farrell from across the road was my first love, asserting her proprietorial rights over me even when I was big enough to get out of the pram and try skipping with the girls on the car-free street.

The boys my own age included Raymond Courtney, a large boy from next door who impressed himself on the memories of all who heard his foghorn voice call on me through the window early in the morning. Then there was Tommy Murphy, who lived up at the Ring Street end of O'Donoghue Street: all of Tommy I can remember are the two green 'candles' that dangled perpetually from his nose. Most memorable of them all was Monty, not his Christian name but the nickname inevitably applied in the years after the war to a boy whose surname was Montgomery. Monty was by some way the youngest in a family in the corner house across the road. The long back garden was a junk yard because the Montgomerys had a horse and cart and dealt in anything—from scrap to coal—that offered a profit. They were the 'roughest' on the street but stayed within the pale of acceptable behaviour.

Inevitably it was courtesy of Monty's father that I shattered my record of exemplary behaviour, sitting with Monty on the cart as Mr Montgomery shook the reins and took us off on a magical mystery tour all the way into Townsend Street and back home hours later, covered in coal dust and nodding with exhaustion.

WITHIN A few years of moving back to Inchicore Con had given up being a cinema operator and had turned to house painting. Why would such a skilled, reliable and conscientious operator choose to leave a job that involved working in a warm room twelve months of the year in favour of one that had him toiling away outdoors in the cold, if not the rain, climbing high ladders up to fascia boards and gutters, thinking himself lucky to avoid 'the knock' when, at the onset of winter, bad weather made outside work impossible? I always assumed that my sister Maura and I were the reason, that he decided the cinema hours—mostly afternoons and evenings—were unsuitable for a married man with young children. Perhaps he found the long periods of inactivity in the tiny operating box increasingly tedious. Jimmy Bourke recalled that Con had no qualifications as a painter but was 'an out-of-work projectionist, whose father and uncle were painters.' The uncle was Frank Behan, father of Brendan and president of the painters' union from 1948 until his death in 1967, who supplied Con with the necessary union card, which enabled Pearse to get him a 'start' on a corporation building scheme, probably Ballyfermot.

Con had an encyclopedic knowledge of Forties' films, as his children learned when hundreds of them were revived on television. He was also sick and tired of them and never again to my knowledge went to the cinema for pleasure. Somebody—probably Maisie—convinced him to accept invitations to *How to Marry a Millionaire* (1953) at the Metropole and *Doctor in the House* (1954) at the State cinema in Phibsborough where Maisie's sister Teresa worked as a cashier. He enjoyed *Doctor in the House*, somewhat to his surprise, as his years as a cinema operator (combined with 'national feeling') had not given him a high opinion of British pictures.

Once, when I could hardly have been four years old, he took me on his crossbar to the Ritz in Ballsbridge. My recollection is very hazy but I am convinced it was after he had left the Ritz and that whatever he did in the operating box was as a favour for a friend.

On the good side, painters worked in gangs and were notoriously talkative, so the time flew on a fine day painting windows in one of the new housing schemes.

My earliest awareness of Con's time as a painter involved his overalls. On at least two occasions—before I had begun school—I accompanied Maisie down to the Dunlop Laundry in Mount Brown to complain about the treatment of Con's overalls. Although, given the occupational hazards of the job, some painters were less than fastidious about their appearance at work, there was no way Maisie was allowing her husband appear in less than spotless overalls.

FOR MOST of the twentieth century Ireland suffered acute unemployment but the Fifties were particularly grim, with hundreds of thousands forced to take the boat for England. One autumn day in the early Fifties Con was painting away when the foreman told him he was being moved outside to paint railings. The implication was not lost on Con, who knew that his place would be taken by a relation of the foreman, an inferior painter who was then on outside work and was being brought inside so that he would not get 'the knock' when winter weather brought a halt to outside work. Knowing there was no point in trying to dissuade the foreman, Con quietly put down his brush and announced he was quitting the job on the spot. On his way to the hut to 'draw his cards', he called on his brother Pearse (who was working on the same job) to explain why he was leaving. Pearse expressed his disgust at the foreman's behaviour and quit in solidarity with his brother.

Pearse too was a married man but more impulsive than his brother. Had Pearse been similarly mistreated, he would not have hesitated to quit or to subject the foreman to a tirade of abuse. The sensible course for both men was to think of their families, suppress their feelings of righteous indignation and consider themselves lucky to have a job at all. Had they been asked—then or later—why they had not taken the sensible course, they would have replied that their 'pride' left them no alternative.

This pride was central to their inherited sense of themselves as Kearneys and, at its core, was a moral imperative to stand up for their dignity, irrespective of the cost, disdaining both the strong oppressors and the weaklings who buckled before them. This elitism was obviously not based on wealth or social prominence, but on their connection through their father with the noble and unselfish men and women who had disdained material wealth and given their lives for the freedom of Ireland. Pearse and Con were brought up to revere the old Sinn Féin virtues of patriotism, independence and self-reliance, a reverence they sought to pass on to their own children.

THE IDEOLOGIES that informed life in 25 O'Donoghue Street were clear but essentially moderate. We were Irish nationalists, gratefully respectful of those who had fought for the liberation of Ireland from British imperialism. We too were willing to make sacrifices for the survival of Ireland, but they stopped short of joining the IRA. Con could not help himself admiring the courage and commitment of those who continued the armed struggle, but he supported the policies of the Fianna Fáil party.

We were also Catholics but while we might have suspected Protestants of being less Irish than we were, there was nothing theological involved. Those who had enforced English rule in Ireland had been overwhelmingly Protestant. Unionists in the mid-century were seen as almost always higher up the social and economic scales than Catholics. The early republicans—Wolfe Tone, Lord Edward Fitzgerald and Robert Emmet—came from the Protestant tradition, but the vast majority of their foot-soldiers were Catholic.

Con and Maisie fulfilled their duties as Catholic parents, attending church themselves and bringing their children up in the faith. It is possible that they were both devout but neither had any interest in doctrine. My sense is that they were pragmatic, turning to prayer in search of omnipotent favour concerning a hope or a fear for the future.

I was an Irish nationalist and a Catholic before I knew it, having absorbed the basic tenets so soon and so quietly that they pre-date memory. I was never aware of any indoctrination. Nothing illustrated Con's brilliance as a teacher more than his disdain for direct instruction or chastisement. Not only did he eschew physical punishment, he never raised his voice or be-rated us. The worst I ever endured was a fleeting glance of disappointment, invariably followed by a smile of forgiveness and renewal.

It is not that we were brought up in a super-libertarian free-expression atmosphere. There were very strict rules, many of them conventional enough—finishing one's food, for example—but others would strike a twenty-first century child as cruel and unusual punishments from the early Victorian age. It was absolutely unacceptable to answer Con or Maisie (or Nana or indeed any adult) with a simple 'yes' or 'no'; good manners demanded 'yes, Daddy' or 'no, Mammy'. To say 'no' to a request from either of them or Nana was unthinkable: I have no idea how I discovered the enormity of this transgression because I have no memory of ever having committed it but, had I done so, I would have expected the sky to darken, the heavens to rumble and lightning to raze Dublin to the ground. (To this day I cannot hear a child dismiss a parent's request without initial shock, followed by wry amusement.) Marginally less offensive was to refer to Daddy as 'he' or to Mammy or Nana or even my sister Maura as 'she'. *Who's she? The cat's mother?* (I must have picked up these rules quickly. I remember being surprised that Maura, two years younger than me, had to be instructed in something that had for me become instinctive.) The ultimate betrayal of our code was dishonesty—lying or stealing or cheating—but, because this was generally condemned by church and state, the taboo did not seem in any way unusual. Not that it was less forceful: to this day I fear that if I tell a lie, a guilty blush will burn my cheeks.

This social system—smacking of the barracks and not significantly different from that found in houses in which Henry Newbolt was recited rather than Thomas Davis—was instilled without the least hint of physical force and consequently was made to feel as natural and sensible as not putting a finger in the fire.

Con was purer in his pacifism than Maisie, who had grown up in a large family and who, much more than her husband, had to balance the protection of children from themselves with the seemingly endless chores of running a house. Occasionally, when the need arose, she would raise her voice to threaten us with bizarre forms of discipline—most memorably to 'dig my ten knuckles into you'—but she always settled for a slight slap on the girls' legs. I was spared such indignity, presumably because I was her only boy rather than because of my perfect behaviour.

But Maisie's eruptions were infrequent, short-lived and quickly regretted. More generally she was the nurturing, loving mother, sacrificing her own demands and desires for us, stretching her budget to feed and clothe us as best she could, a mother hen who lived and would have died for her chicks.

If Maisie was physical warmth and loving sustenance, Con was a combination of best friend and God Almighty, the creator of all things in 25 O'Donoghue Street. There was nothing he could not do, could not fix. If he has a treat for me, he would never dream of simply giving it to me, preferring—like a stage magician in the Queen's—to use dramatic delay and suspense in order to heighten the pleasure (and, in the process, increase my belief in his superhuman powers). Rather than simply produce a big bar of

Cadbury's chocolate, he would make it appear from beneath a cloth where previously there had been nothing.

TODAY, SUNDAY afternoon, he is down on the floor with me. He has shown me a lump of lead—about the size of a sixpenny bar of chocolate—and is about to do something amazing with it. Unknown to me he is going to transform it into small discs that I can use for The Mowl, a game boys play on the street, throwing ha'pennies (or tokens) into the shore (the opening on the pavement containing the stopcock) and then trying to win the other boys' ha'pennies by landing on them.

He invites me to touch the lump of lead to prove that it is real. Then he covers it with a cushion and begins to weave his spell. I watch his every move as he wobbles his hand over the cushion, chanting *criss-cross the maggot's a*. ('A' was the polite remnant of the censored 'arse'.) I follow his eyes as they dart wildly all around the room and up at the ceiling and am startled when he stops and stares silently at the cushion for what seems a long time. I cannot believe that magic has happened right in front of me but I know from the look of uncertainty on his face that it has. Or has it? He peeps under the cushion, looks at me, peeps again, then whips the cushion away to reveal not the lump of lead but a dozen or so discs better than any coin or token. He calls them *leadeners*. I can only stare at him in wonder.

The lead and the *leadeners* came from the nearby Inchicore Railway Works where Con (who had friends everywhere) knew somebody. My *leadeners* did not last long: they were quickly 'borrowed' by bigger boys who could make more effective use of them than I could.

I was obviously a soft touch, tenderly reared by parents who wanted more for me than would be the lot of the other boys in the neighbourhood. Like most sissies, I longed to be a *gurrier*, even as I knew such an achievement was beyond me. My mother did not help by buying me underpants, a refinement unknown to working-class boys in those commando days. Inevitably my effeminacy was discovered and I retreated into the house to a chorus of *Ding-dong! Ding-dong! Colbert's got his knickers on!*

Maisie thrust refinement upon me but it still remains a mystery how I could have cultivated certain sensitivities in a community where all toilets were outdoor and not usually flushed after urination. How did I acquire the temerity to complain that Uncle Pearse (whom otherwise I idolised) had made the toilet smelly (presumably after a night drinking Guinness)?

Or learned to ask Monsie Ward in the corner shop for what I called 'bum-bum paper', the soft tissues in which fruit was presented on the counter and which I preferred to the default toilet wipes, squares of old newspaper?

AMONG THE regular visitors to our house were Maisie's younger sister Annie and her pal Patty Barnes, both of who were unmarried and working in Cahill's Printing Works in Parkgate Street. I was sent to bed shortly after they arrived but I remember how much Con and Maisie anticipated and enjoyed their company and, presumably, their tales of the single life Con and Maisie had so recently forsaken. Among the glamorous elements in their lives was the holiday Annie and Patty had taken in the Isle of Man.

On Saturday nights Con met 'the boys'—friends such as the Bourke brothers, Noah O'Leary and Francie Black—in Cawley's of Essex Gate, off Dame Street, and I have a patchy memory of a party when they arrived in O'Donoghue Street to drink and sing, Francie Black producing an unforgettable performance that years later I identified as 'On with the Motley', an English version of the prologue to *Pagliacci*. Unforgettable because I had burst out crying when he let fly with the stage laughter.

My other memory of social life also features a song. Maisie took me (and Maura in the pram) over to the Behans in 70 Kildare Road, Crumlin. There were no children for me to play with and I felt rather as if I was moving among a cast of dramatic characters. The climax was the excitement which greeted the arrival of Brendan—obviously a favourite and the lead actor in this non-stop play—who just happened to be on his way to France and had dropped by to pick up his entire luggage, a toothbrush.

(France! I am not sure what the word meant to me; whether I had visualised the map of Europe or whether France was a country across the sea where young Irish exiles had found fame in brigades that achieved victories such as that celebrated in Thomas Davis's rousing poem about the battle of Fontenoy. From the radio I had gathered that modern France was the most mysterious country on earth, the capital of wine, women and song, whatever that meant. And Brendan Behan was going there with only a toothbrush in his top pocket.)

But the inevitable singing had begun and he was prevailed upon before he left: his rendition of 'My Lagan Love' was—to my expert ear—more operatic than anything I had ever heard in a house, even Francie Black's 'On with the Motley'.

I HAD heard of people who had been to England, but not to France. Pearse had worked for a while in Liverpool and Annie and Patty had gone on holidays to the Isle of Man. Mag Harding too had been to the Isle of Man.

Mag Harding and her husband Tom lived across from us in a house of gold. Our west-facing house was rather gloomy, because the added kitchenette blocked out some of the morning light, and I can remember looking with envious awe out our front window at the blinding blaze of gold that was Mag's window. When her curtains were pulled back, they were held in highly polished brass clips that are (in my memory) so enormous—some four inches deep and ten across—and reflect so much of the early sunshine as to conjure up an El Dorado on the other side of the street.

Nor was her golden window her only glory. Mag had returned from the Isle of Man with a utensil so exotic that those who had not seen it in action could not credit the claims others made for it. It was a whistling kettle and such was the aura of magic surrounding it that Mag, rather than inviting neighbours into her house to witness a demonstration, took the kettle on a tour of O'Donoghue Street. I cannot readily imagine an appliance that would cause a similar excitement today: a robot that cleaned the house from top to bottom, maybe. Maisie certainly prepared as if for a very important visitor, tidying the room and clearing the hobs on the gas stove.

Suddenly I was told to sit down and not to move. Mag had been spotted crossing the road holding her exhibit aloft. Once inside, she directed operations, urging Maisie to take it easy and get out of the way so that she could fill the kettle at the sink, place it on a hob and light the gas. Then all they could do was wait.

Not easily managed when all conversation was forbidden. It was alright for me—I was used to being silent in the presence of adults—but for Maisie it was a form of torture and inevitably there were false starts, Maisie's eyes widening as she detected a hiss, only to be dismissed by a shake of Mag's head. But eventually there was something and this time Mag pursed her lips with proprietorial restraint. And yes, the little hiss grew to a sizzle and then to a rising squeal that no ordinary kettle had ever produced, no matter how long left hissing on the hob. Maisie's eyes widened wider and her mouth opened in awe as she heard a low whistle begin to fill the room.

'Jesus, Mag, I can't believe it.'

'It's hardly started. Just wait.'

At this point the squeal had become a shriek and was spreading out into a terrifying scream. Who knows how long Mag would have let nature take its course if I had not started to cry? The gas was knocked off and I was hushed and the women celebrated with a cup of tea.

Mag features in another vignette. Given the absence of tape-recording and the considerable changes wrought on our accents by education, social mobility and the media, we can have little idea what we actually sounded like in those days. Little, but, thanks to Mag Harding, not none at all. Mag was no posher or more pretentious than anybody else, which is presumably why a brief extract of an exchange between us lodged in my memory. It went something like this:

Mag: You're getting to be a big boy now, Colbert.

Me: I'm going to school in July.

Mag: Not *skewel*. School!

Or that is how it might be written, had Mag been middle-class or in some significant social way different from her neighbours. I presume my parents would not have allowed my accent to be noticeably 'lower' than that of my peers. In fact I suspect they would have sought to keep my accent, like theirs, slightly higher. In the absence of a tape-recorder, we can only guess at the possible distinctions between Mag's 'school' and her 'skewel'.

I COULD not wait to start school and loved it when I did, which was on 2 July 1951, less than a month before I turned six. (Was this late? Had I not started the year before because an age threshold of five was strictly applied?) From Con—and to a lesser extent from Maisie—I had acquired a huge respect for education in general and reading in particular, so much so that I always found the school reading curriculum frustratingly easy until I came towards the end of primary school.

Scoil Mhuire Gan Smál was an impressive two-storey granite building that had been completed in 1939 on the site of the school Con had attended. Mr Doyle, who had given Con the glowing reference, was principal and went out of his way to welcome the son of Con and grandson of Peadar Kearney. My teacher was Miss McDonald, who seemed fine to me.

But not to Monty, who was not a goody-goody and who had been brought up blissfully unaware of the duties owed to the men who had died for Ireland or indeed to anybody else, even the father and mother who let him run as wild as a child could in Inchicore. He was seated towards the back and went along with this school business—making chalk marks on little slates—for half an hour or so, then decided he'd had enough, stood up and headed for the door. When asked by Miss McDonald where he thought he was going, he replied 'home'. Told by Miss McDonald to sit down and not to be so silly, he paid no heed and continued on his way. When Miss McDonald moved over to the door to block his exit, it dawned on him that he was trapped inside the classroom, the prisoner of a woman unlike any he had known. His eyes welled up, which is where Miss McDonald—who, though old enough to know better, had most likely never encountered a colt as unbroken as Monty—miscalculated, telling him not to be such a cry-baby. Such slights on manhood were taken very seriously in Monty's family, and the more she repeated the word 'baby', the more enraged Monty became, his red cheeks glistening with tears and snot and glowing with an intensity that could end only in the kind of heroic explosion he had witnessed during heated discussions in his own backyard: *I'll tell my brother on you and he'll be straight down here with a fucking crowbar!*

I have no idea what happened next and can only presume that shock shut down my mind temporarily.

I got a prize that year. For what or when—Christmas or the end of the year—I can no longer remember. The prize itself I still have, thanks to Maisie, who preserved so many records of our childhood that would have vanished years ago had they been left to us. It was a plastic horse with a red body and blue legs [*Image 18*]. The legs hung loosely and independently from the body and the hooves were flat supports, rather like small skateboards. The point of this construction was that when the horse was placed on a plane—such as a tray—and the tray inclined slightly downwards, the horse walked. For me the miracle of the whistling kettle was only in the ha'penny place: I was mesmerised for hours as I watched my wonder-horse—without winding up or human contact or attachment of any kind—walk.

(It occurs to me that this horse, whose cleverness is in simple obedience to the laws of nature and the inclination of an off-stage hand, represented me, especially when compared to Monty who got the real horse, sitting up there beside his father, each with a sack over his lap, coated with coal dust and without a care in the world.)

THE RELATIONSHIP of mutual adoration between Maisie and me did not always include understanding, not on my side anyway. I am thinking of the day she took me with her to Frawley's in Thomas Street. I cannot recall what it was she went to buy but let us say it was a pair of socks for me.

Frawley's was a large clothes and fabric store directed at the lower end of the market and priced accordingly. All or most of the assistants were male and their attire—suits and ties—identified them as men of some status, experts who were to be respected. Goods such as socks, vests, shirts and jumpers were generally displayed in trays on the tops of counters (that contained more stock beneath) and the price—invariably something-and-eleven or something-and-six, eleven being one penny short of a shilling, sixpence being half a shilling—was advertised on a small white placard.

Maisie entered the shop and moved along the aisles, refusing to acknowledge the greetings of the assistants as she passed into their sections, scowling disdainfully at the articles on sale. It was clear to me that she had seen nothing worth buying and so I was confused when she began a second tour, again receiving and again ignoring the greetings of the assistants, this time pausing at various counters—including that containing a wide variety of socks—frowning at them as if she found them repellent, then moving on.

At which point my confusion had developed into a bored frustration that was building towards exasperation. What was Mammy up to? I thought we had come in here to buy something. We had been all over the shop twice; if what she wanted wasn't here, why didn't we try somewhere else? I could not understand what was happening.

But the assistant could, which is why, like an experienced predator, he had stood off during my mother's first two passes at the sock counter, and why, when she approached it for the third time, he abandoned the study of his nails and came up alongside.

'Can I help you, missus?'

Why doesn't she answer him? It's rude not to answer people. Why isn't he annoyed that she is acting as if she hasn't heard his question? But eventually his inexplicable patience is rewarded when, having fingered a sock as if it was something she had picked out of the gutter in O'Donoghue Street, my mother inquired: 'How much are these?'

Agh! Was ever any human being as mortified as I was? Having to listen to my own mother ask such a stupid question? When the price was clearly written in the tray in front of her eyes? Obviously not the assistant, who seemed used to dealing with customers who either could not or would not read the marker.

'One and eleven a pair.'

'Ah, stick them up your jersey.'

Just when I thought things could not get worse!

Minutes later, open-mouthed, I watched my mother buy the socks she had scorned at first sight, at the price clearly indicated by the sign and pronounced by the assistant. By the time he handed her the paper bag containing the socks, she and the assistant were the best of friends, discussing the weather and hoping to see each other again soon.

It was years before I understood what had taken place. The assistant had seen it all before and not only had Maisie done it before, she would do it again. The price of the socks meant nothing to me but for her it was money she could ill afford. The buying of the socks was a commercial transaction that demanded a ritual interval during which she could consider it carefully. Her economic circumstances did not allow for impulse purchases; but even the buying of the bare necessities could be savoured, resisted, deferred and finally enjoyed.

It took me a long time to realise that, though she deferred to Con in certain matters—notably politics—Maisie was not mentally inferior to him, merely different, that her way of speaking was not an imperfect version of Con's but, again, different. I had always enjoyed her way of expressing herself, finding it more striking and amusing than Con's, but I was at university before I identified it as related to the old oral culture of Dublin city, a style that in the hands of James Joyce (and of the man with the toothbrush who sang 'My Lagan Love') would delight me as much as my favourite English masters of language from Shakespeare to Evelyn Waugh.

Who can say for sure why some moments in time remain rock solid in the memory while the vast majority of our works and days quickly fade and are soon forgotten? Perhaps that day in Frawley's is among my clearest yesterdays because for me it marks an emergence from the innocence of an absolutely happy childhood, a quantum of awareness of Maisie as distinct from me.

There is a matching moment involving Con, and this has an equally dramatic setting: our last Christmas in Inchicore in 1951, when I was six and a half (and fractions mattered).

My first memory of reading and writing involved the children's crossword puzzle in the *Sunday Press* that Con shared with me after Sunday mass. I'm not sure if he entered the fashion competition (which carried the biggest prize) but in the case of Spot-the-Ball he allowed me to believe he took my advice when trying to work out where the ball had been in a photograph of a football game before it was erased. The one competition I am (reasonably) sure he entered was the children's crossword competition where the successful entrant might win a bicycle. Sunday after Sunday we filled in the blanks and following Sunday after following Sunday felt the disappointment of not winning. (I continue to believe that, having cut out the completed crossword, he actually sent it to the *Sunday Press* and was not merely stringing me along.)

I resented the persistent injustice of it all: if my entry was correct—and the following Sunday's paper agreed that it was—where was my prize? I found it very hard to accept Con's explanation that all the correct entries were put into a hat and the winner picked out by an honest man wearing a blindfold.

Nor do I think it would have bothered either of us had my name been picked out, although Con would certainly have known it was cheating. I have a memory of being able to manage some degree of reading before I started school—but I would not have been able to do the crossword unaided at the age of, say, five. Con would have been capable of concocting a specious defence—that, though he had read out the clues and kept prompting me till I had hit on the correct answer, technically I had been the first to say the words that fitted the blanks correctly—but he was too intelligent to believe it himself.

But not too morally fastidious to submit a forged entry in the hope of winning a prize he could not afford to buy me. Not just then; but as the photograph in the back garden shows [*Image 21*], having set his sights and mine on winning a bike, he was not about to disappoint me and so, by scraping and saving, the price of a bike—actually a trike—was found.

CON AND Maisie ensured that none of their children would ever be in a position to write a misery memoir. We were always warm, well-fed and well-clothed, even if heavy overcoats served as eiderdowns on our beds during cold winters and the favourite Sunday dinner of my early childhood was roast rabbit. We were taught to look after our clothes, which were made to last as long as possible. (If, later on, any of us got an article of clothing as a present, Maisie would urge us to 'put that up' and reserve it for 'special occasions'.) We did not have to be told that while we were better off than some of our neighbours, we were not as well-off as some of our relations.

Back to Christmas morning 1951. I am asleep in bed. Hoping to catch a sight of the man we called Santy Claus, I must have stayed awake longer than usual the night before because Con has to wake me and remind me what day it is.

'And I think Santy came for you.'

'What did he bring me?'

'I think he brought what you asked him for.'

'An annual!'

Annuals were the big thing that year. There had been yearly editions of comics for ages—printed stories with illustrations—but later arrivals such as *The Dandy* (1937) and *The Beano* (1940) had changed the emphasis from print to cartoons and established Desperate Dan and Dennis the Menace among the best-known characters in the Anglophone world. When *The Eagle* appeared in 1950, everybody was taken by the superior quality of the illustrations and the up-to-date appeal of 'pilot of the future' Dan Dare and his efforts to save earth from the threats of the Mekon, a green creature from Venus with an enormous head and a withered body. The fame of Dan Dare was exploited by the makers of Horlicks (a malt drink alleged to facilitate sleep by curing a non-existent disease they named 'night starvation') who in July 1951 sponsored a Radio Luxembourg series based on his adventures.

'Did he bring me *The Eagle*?'

'Oh, I think what he brought you is better than *The Eagle*.'

Better than *The Eagle*? I could not have explained why I kept the question to myself: it was as if a warning buzzer had gone off in my head. But warning against what? Yes, there were some people who preferred *The Beano* to *The Eagle*, mostly those who had never heard Dan Dare on Radio Luxembourg but ....

'*The Beano*?'

'Better than *The Beano*.'

Was I dreaming this? No, I was awake: I could feel Daddy's breath on my face, see his eyes moving as he looked into mine.

'*The Dandy*?'

'Much better than *The Dandy*!'

'What is it?'

'I couldn't say for sure—you'll open it yourself—but I think it's the *Radio Fun Annual*.'

But the *Radio Fun Annual* was not .... That warning buzzer again. His eyes waiting for me to smile, just like he waited for me to think of the right answer for the crossword, nodding when I said one word but asking me to think of another like it. He knew everything, but maybe that did not include children's things like annuals. My father would always want the best for me and it wasn't his fault if Santy had got it wrong. As I knew for absolute certain Santy had.

'Come on, son. Get up and I'll carry you downstairs.'

The more certain I was that under the Christmas tree I would find not the *Eagle Annual*—with its glossy paper and perfect colours—but the *Radio Fun Annual*, the harder I hugged him. It was not that I blamed Santy when I tore open the wrapping paper and identified the *Radio Fun Annual 1952* with the cover featuring a British soldier—plumed helmet and red jacket—sitting on a black horse. My doubts about him, sown by overheard remarks by older boys, were confirmed. (How come my father knew what was inside the wrapper?) But this too I kept to myself.

That is what the buzzer was telling me. It was not what I wanted, but my parents had done their best and I had to be careful not to hurt their feelings by showing how disappointed I was. When they asked me was I happy with my presents, I would tell them of course I was. It was their Christmas as well as mine and Maura's.

And now there was baby Eileen, born on 2 January 1951 and in strange circumstances. Maura and I were too young to notice any change in Maisie's shape or, in a culture that protected innocence, even to be told that she was about to have a baby. Con explained Maisie's absence in the maternity hospital with a story that had her off in Scotland. (Why Scotland, I have no idea. England might have been ideologically contaminated, America too far away.) During Maisie's absence I was amazed to see Con sawing about four inches off the legs of a new wooden chair. I have forgotten whatever explanation he gave for destroying a perfectly good piece of furniture but it all made sense when Maisie, having arrived home from Scotland with baby Eileen, sat on the shortened chair and pronounced it perfect.

There were now six of us in that tiny house, and Nana had to have a bedroom to herself. Four of us squeezed into the back bedroom that looked out at the garden and down on the tarred roof of the kitchenette. Con and Maisie slept in the big double bed along the back wall. (Because I am asleep when they go to bed and still asleep when they get up, I have no memory of them actually in bed—apart from a single instance when, awoken by some noise, I cry out and my mother comes over to comfort me.) Along the partition wall—between the door and the fireplace—is my bed; between the fireplace and the window is Maura's cot. There is no room for baby Eileen who sleeps in her pram downstairs, obliging Maisie to scurry down the stairs if she begins to cry. Con and Maisie applied to the corporation and early in 1952 we moved to Finglas.

FINGLAS

Finglas was the newest of the public housing 'schemes' built by Dublin Corporation to re-house (among others) those living in substandard conditions in the inner city. Remarkably few of those re-housed were grateful to Dublin Corporation: city-dwell-ers—even those who, like Con and Pearse, were only second-gener-ation—combined an intense pride in their native places with a deep suspicion concerning the cultural, social and moral standards obtaining outside-the-walls.

Kathleen Behan would not of her own free will have left the security of Russell Street in 1937 to take her chances 'out in the country where they eat their young'. (Her son Brendan Behan had referred to Crumlin as 'the Wild West'; Ballyfermot was known as 'Little Korea'.) Ten years later Eamonn Dunphy's mother chose to live with her labourer husband and two sons in a single rented room (without electricity) in Drumcondra rather than slide down the social ladder by accepting corporation accommodation in an inner-city flat or a suburban estate.

As the newest, Finglas was considered more remote and proportionately more unruly than other corporation estates such as Cabra or Ballyfermot. Most Dubliners were familiar with Glasnevin Cemetery, but few had crossed the Tolka Bridge that marked its northern border and had continued a leafy mile into *terra incognita* to discover the old agricultural village of Finglas, the single street sloping steeply up to the Catholic church, beyond which the two main pubs, O'Neill's and O'Donnell's, faced each other.

I must have been all eyes as the 40 bus turned west at the village, pass-ing what I would soon learn was the Holy Faith Convent on the left and the picturesque Protestant Church and school on the right. At that point, marked by an enormous tree, it seemed we were entering into a vast Arcadia, vacant apart from grazing cattle. But not for long: a mile from the village the bulldozers had begun transforming the ancient fields into sites for hundreds of identical houses into which would swarm thousands of urban aliens. Three roads were ready for occupation, Cappagh Road, Mellowes Road and Mellowes Avenue, the latter two consisting of blocks of new houses facing one another, Cappagh Road of a single line of houses confronted by hedges and trees behind which were fields that stretched all the way over to Cabra West.

We were number 262, the first house on the last block of Cappagh Road. Beyond us were the foundations of a block that had never been built, beyond them a row of agricultural labourers' cottages, the farthest shrewdly converted into a shop to attract the newcomers who would otherwise have to make their way to the village. Across the road from the shop was the bungalow we called the Egg Farm, where hens and pigs were kept. A quarter of a mile farther on was Cappagh Children's Hospital, a name with which most of the migrants were familiar from radio programmes such as 'Hospitals' Requests'. Beyond that another infinity of fields it would take us years to explore.

Con and Maisie must have found it hard to leave Nana alone in O'Donoghue Street and relocate to an alien environment, part of a social experiment in which hundreds of young families from various areas and circumstances were pitched into vast estates which inevitably—given the absence of social facilities—got the name of being 'rough'.

There were other more immediate disadvantages. Maisie would have to push the pram a mile down to the village for her shopping and Con would have to cycle even longer distances to work. I would have to leave Scoil Mhuire Gan Smál, where my family was known and respected, and take my chances where nobody had ever heard of us.

But there was no choice. A husband and wife and three children could not fit in one bedroom. Would Eamonn Dunphy's mother have held out if, instead of two boys, she had had a girl and a boy (or, as in our case, a boy and two girls) in a culture in which the sexes were segregated with Talibanic rigidity?

And so Finglas it was.

Much to my delight. Whatever reservations Con or Maisie had were lost on me. Although it was wintertime when we moved, I saw the new house as Hockney saw California: an enormous south-facing front window opening on a bright new world, extravagant volumes of light replacing the gloom of O'Donoghue Street. Nor did it matter that the colours were muted, comprising the pale pink of bare plastered walls and the beige of floorboards. Nor that the nearest swimming pool was the corporation facility over near Cabra, the water as grey as the concrete enclosure. Our new house was not without its own exotic features: a bathroom, a front garden and a side-entrance.

Even more overwhelming was its sheer size: three bedrooms—an enormous expanse for Con and Maisie in front, the larger of two at the back for Maura and Eileen, the smaller 'box room' that was all mine. For me, six years of age, my head filled with stories of adventure, the new house offered the excitement of change and infinite possibility.

Con—with a wife and three children to look after—was less starry-eyed. The move from Inchicore had been forced on him and, in retrospect, I suspect he was never fully *at home* on the Cappagh Road. Yes, he more than fulfilled his duties as man of the house, paterfamilias, our Daddy, going out to work in the mornings before we even got up, coming back in the evenings to help us with our home exercises, play games with us, read his paper and listen to the radio; but he never became part of any local community or circle, never established a close friendship with any of the neighbouring men. He continued for some time to meet 'the boys' in Cawley's on Saturday nights. (Francie Black lived in a 'purchase' house on the Ballygall side of Finglas and used to give Con a lift home in his car.)

In this, Con was not unique. A handful of men became involved with organising Gaelic games street leagues or with church projects and they and/ or others established themselves as regulars in the village pubs, especially at weekends; but the majority maintained closer ties with the inner city communities they had grown up in than with their new neighbours in Finglas. Con did become a member of the Men's Sodality and attended meetings in the church but it strikes me now that this was less an expression of religious enthusiasm than a means of ensuring that no hint of heterodoxy would attach itself to his children and endanger their prospects. He was too much his own man ever to join a group, religious or secular.

THE CLEAREST proof of his state of mind is that within two years of arriving in Finglas he moved to Limerick, the plan being that the rest of us would follow when he had arranged accommodation. The Bourkes had taken over the City Theatre, with Lorcan's son Jack as general and Con as stage manager, his responsibilities to include electrics and film projection, by then a necessary part of a popular theatre programme.

Aged eight and a child of the time, I neither sought nor was given an explanation for this sudden change of direction, which I now believe reflected Con's suspicion that as a house-painter he was unlikely to realise his core ambition of bettering himself and his family, socially and economically, during a period of economic stagnation and high unemployment. (By now there were four children, Eva having arrived in July 1953.) Both Lorcan and Con hoped the City Theatre would provide an escape from the uncertainties and vicissitudes of a tradesman's life. Instead of cycling long distances to work out of doors for strangers, Con's employment would be indoors, varied and more autonomous; his skills and experiences would be valued by his relations and he would enjoy the status and remuneration that went with 'management'.

I must have mastered the art of selective suppression at a very early age because I have no memory of my grief during his absence and only the vaguest sense of the joy that overwhelmed me on his return. Of the interval, one episode survives as clearly as if it had happened yesterday.

It is a dark, wet and windy late afternoon and Maisie is shepherding us from the Finglas bus up along Lower Abbey Street, across O'Connell Street and into the GPO. It would be difficult to find a contemporary correlative for what we were about to do. Skyping a loved one in Antarctica would not even come close. We were phoning Limerick.

In those days nobody in a corporation house had a phone. I cannot even remember where the nearest public phone-box was but I presume it was frequently vandalised and 'out of order'. (It would be more than another twenty years before the government began to encourage people to get phones by promising prompt installation.) To ensure that the expedition into the city centre was not in vain, the time of the call must have been arranged by letter between Maisie and Con.

Inside the GPO Maisie would have given the number to a clerk behind the desk who would have communicated it to a telephonist and, when the connection had been made, directed Maisie to the appropriate booth.

Even then the atmosphere was supercharged. Overwhelmed by excitement and fear of forgetting the clerk's instructions, Maisie took it out on us, hissing at us to keep quiet until, to all our amazement, Hermes waved his magic wand and produced a crackle in the hand-piece she could just about recognise as the voice of her husband in the outer space that was Limerick.

Eventually I was given the big black hand-piece and, instructed by Maisie, told Con how well I was doing at school and how I was helping Maisie in the house and, in response to his parting statement, how much we all missed him. Or that is what I assume happened: I have no actual memory of any such exchange. But what is as distinct in my mind now as it was then is the cold terror that gripped me when I noticed Maisie's face as she prepared to take us home. Seeing my mother on the verge of tears was frightening enough but I could understand that, like me, she had found the sound of

Con's distant voice upsetting; what threatened to unhinge me was the set of her face, hard and white, as if she was angry.

(Educated by television soaps, a modern child would look for signs of female jealousy and male infidelity. Nothing in my reading had given me such terms of reference nor had I ever known an unloving glance to pass between Con and Maisie and so it remained a mystery tinged with fear. I would be amazed if Con had given Maisie any reason for anxiety; but a wife with young children does not need much of a reason to be anxious when her husband is 125 miles away and back in the theatre atmosphere in which they had both spent so much of their carefree youth and witnessed so much frivolity.)

Before long Con was back with us and we were not moving to Limerick. His decision made, he had contacted Pearse, who had arranged a painting job, which Con took up on his return.

Why had he changed his mind? It was not the nature of the work, at which he excelled and which he preferred to house painting. There was no compatibility problem with Jack Bourke, with whom he remained on affectionate terms. I suspect at least part of the problem was the nature of show business life and especially the hours. It must quickly have dawned on him, as it had when he worked as a cinema operator, that he would not see much of his children except at weekends: by the time they got home from school, he would be going to work and they would be fast asleep when he returned. It may also be that the late-night socialising he would have enjoyed when single did not appeal to him now when whatever money he earned was earmarked for his home and family.

Each of my parents always insisted that the other was less capable of leaving Dublin but I am convinced that neither of them was keen on the move. Con had toured Ireland with Anew McMaster but, apart from her honeymoon in nearby Wicklow, I am not aware that Maisie had ever been outside Dublin. Con would have been attracted by a move that promised access to a better life for us all. The move for Maisie would have involved an enormous upheaval, uprooting herself and her children just when she was settling into Finglas, leaving the neighbours she had just got to know. Had Con asked her to move, she would have done so; but he never did. I suspect that Maisie was instinctively opposed to living 'down the country' and that Con (less willing to reveal similar reservations) was happy to accommodate her. The job had attracted him despite the location and he was sufficiently perceptive and intelligent not to risk his happiness by pressuring Maisie to live where she did not want to live. His brief sojourn in Limerick had taught him—if he had not known it already—that he could not envisage life without a contented Maisie and their children and that no increase in wages or esteem was worth more than the bond they had forged together. Maybe in the course of that phone call he had heard in her voice what I saw in her face: that she wanted him back in Dublin, soon.

Blithely secure, I would probably have embraced a move to Limerick, just as I had the move to Finglas, as an adventure that would involve new places, new friends, new possibilities, plus the continuing assurance of Con and Maisie and my three sisters.

PERHAPS THE Limerick experiment modified—or helped to modify—Con's lack of enthusiasm for Finglas. If he never felt at home in the community, 262 Cappagh Road was his home and he used his considerable range of skills to make the most of it. Shortly after our arrival he had begun the necessary decoration: papering the front room, painting the other rooms, the ceilings and woodwork, laying down lino on the floors—all done with professional care and precision. Then there was the clothes line to be strung up, pelmets to be attached to walls and curtains hung, extra shelving to be put up in the kitchen. When they had saved enough money, he extended the kitchen, building and equipping it, even moving the gas and electrical fittings himself.

One small part of this make-over lodged itself in my memory, not so much because of the skill involved as because it preserved an early vignette of our relationship as it began to take its characteristic form.

We are in the bathroom, Con and I. I am probably about eight. The room is tiny, not much more than the length of a standard bath, hardly six feet wide. We are cramped into the space beside the bath, some of which is taken up by the sink, and I am given the important task of ensuring that nobody barges in the inward-opening door. Thrilled to be considered grown-up enough for such a post of responsibility—to be helping rather than merely looking—I take my assignment very seriously, reminding myself not to ask silly questions. There is no need for me to say anything: if Con needs my help or advice, he will ask for it.

He is at the final stage and the trickiest. He had painted the walls the previous day and they are now dry enough to take the burgundy dado line that will finish the job, breaking the monotony of the blue-green walls. An awkward task, but not beyond the scope of a DIY non-specialist today, who would carefully apply two parallel lengths of masking tape, the gap between them equal to the desired depth of the dado line, then apply the burgundy freely in and above and below the gap, letting it dry before removing the tapes.

But Con is not using masking tape, presumably because he hasn't any of what was not then a standard item of a house painter's paraphernalia. Using a yellow wooden rule and a spirit level, he has made scarcely visible pencil marks to show him the line and the depth of the dado. Then, while kneeling, bending or squatting in the bath, using only his left forearm to help prevent shaking, he pulls the tiny brush along, over and back, leaving behind a rich red line that is not only delightful in itself but, as he had promised, adds life and lustre to the rest of the walls. Spellbound, I stare.

But what is this? Just as Con is adding a little more body to where the lines meet in the corner beside the window, I notice—back at my end, near the door—a tiny scallop of red beginning to dribble below the line. I know I have told myself not to say anything unless he asks me; but my entire body is bursting, unable to bear the idea that all his careful skill has been undone by one little slip. 'Daddy! Daddy! Daddy!' He turns, registers my consternation, follows my finger to where the fresh paint is threatening to run. But there is no panic in his face, or even disappointment. He is smiling, his eyes drawing me into his so that instinctively I lean towards him, expecting a secret whisper. But he says nothing; there is no need; a raised cautionary finger says it all. 'We can handle this.' *We!*

I maintain guard on the door as he rests his brush on the paint tin, damps his rag with turps and returns to the run. It is just as well he has his back to me so that I cannot see what I would probably be afraid to look at: the desperate measures he is taking to undo what has already happened.

Ten seconds or so later he drops his hand, pulls back to review his effort, then picks up his brush, raises his left forearm for balance, applies three slow strokes, turns: 'What about that?'

With my back to the door, I am not even sure where the run was. Only when I get as close as I can to the wall can I discern a shadow of the recovery. I am thinking two thoughts. What incredible skill to have removed almost all trace of the accident; but what an awful pity the accident had occurred at all. Poor Daddy. It was so unfair.

He is staring at me again, smiling as if he knows exactly what I am thinking, beckoning me into a hushed conference.

'Now you know and I know what has happened here; but nobody else knows. You know and I know that if you put your nose up against the wall over there you'll see where I retouched it. But we're the only ones who know. Nobody else will notice a thing. Everybody else will think it's perfect. Wait and see. So, not a word to anybody.'

His prophecy was fulfilled when Maisie was invited to inspect her new bathroom. 'O, I love the line in the middle. Really beautiful. Of course you had Colbert to help you. It's a credit to the pair of you.'

And when Maisie had concluded a closer inspection and returned delighted to the kitchen, Con smiled at me and I smiled back at him. He was right, of course. He was always right. I was prouder than ever that he was my father and I could hardly contain my rapture to realise that he no longer saw me as a child but as a big boy, big enough to be his helper and, even better, to share his secrets, man to man.

CON'S MAIN source of pleasure and fulfilment was his wife and children but when weather, work and domestic duties allowed, he got stuck into the back garden. Compared to Inchicore, it was a vast wilderness—some twenty-five metres long—but he soon transformed it into a source of vegetables throughout the year: winter cabbage, new potatoes, onions and beetroot, salad ingredients such as lettuce, scallions and radishes, herbs such as parsley and thyme, Brussels sprouts for Christmas and other things I have forgotten.

Presumably he inherited his horticultural skills from his father, who was even more aware of the economic advantages. When I was not elsewhere engaged with my pals, I often watched Con at work and must have sometimes asked him why he was doing whatever he was doing in that particular way, inviting him to explain such mysteries as growing seeds from packets before thinning out the shoots and transplanting the stronger into patches that afforded them ample scope for growth. But in my recollection I am more filled with admiration than with any desire to emulate him. (And yet, years later, when I acquired a back garden myself, I immediately began, with unwarranted confidence, to re-enact his transformation of the garden behind Cappagh Road and with inexplicable success.)

Con's horticultural skills were rare, if not unique, in our part of Finglas; most of our neighbours, displaced from the inner city where such gardens were rare, had an ingrained antipathy to anything that smacked of agriculture.

The man of the house immediately behind us on Mellowes Road was known to us as 'the gravedigger'. (Name courtesy of Maisie, who always preferred a descriptive title to an arbitrary name.) For whatever reason—most likely the fact that he spent his days digging and filling graves in Glasnevin Cemetery—he was fascinated that a working man would squander his spare time as Con did. Characteristically curious, gregarious and loquacious, he eventually made his way down through his knee-high prairie, leaned on the metal railing, nodding in fascination, waiting until Con raised his head and caught his eye, then: 'You like the oul' gardenin', wha'?'

Conventional manners dictated that Con should immediately cease what he was doing and respond to what was obviously an invitation to social intercourse. But all the gravedigger got was the briefest of mumbled agreements: the last thing Con wanted was a long chat with somebody who had nothing better to do than winkle out details of his neighbour's life and opinions. The gravedigger was surprised and disappointed but, given the long walk he had made from his kitchen window, was not going to give up just yet: 'I do often look out of an evening and see you there, working away, happy as Larry. [*Pause for response, which does not come.*] I suppose you could say that gardening is your hobby, wha'?'

(It would take an essay in social history to detail the aura of polite contempt with which he invested the word 'hobby'. Back in those days working-class men did not have hobbies. Pigeon-fancying was a pastime, as were frequenting the bookie shop or following a team or playing football. A hobby was essentially alien, middle-class, childish, encountered in comics or films. Stamp-collecting was a hobby, or train-spotting, or making boats in bottles.)

If the gravedigger was attempting to provoke Con into a defence of horticulture, he was wasting his time: all he got was another nod, another mimed and mumbled agreement. He gave it up as a bad job, confirmed in his suspicion that his tongue-tied neighbour was not a real man, not like him, who, prior to negotiating the return journey to his kitchen, nailed his colours to the mast: 'My hobby is knocking them back!'

OUR NEIGHBOURS in the adjacent attached house were the O'Neills. Mr O'Neill was rather clerical in his demeanour, balding prematurely and long-sighted enough to carry spectacles. He worked in Williams and Woods jam factory at a time of high unemployment, and it was his wife's boast to Maisie that she had no fear of him being let go; that, on the contrary, 'he could be working night and day, night and day' if he wanted to. With the result that, in the privacy of our house, Mrs O'Neill—not to be confused with *The Other* Mrs O'Neill four doors farther up—was never referred to as anything other than Night'n'Day. She was a 'country-looking' woman with a slightly nasal delivery and inevitably she and Maisie became neighbourly close.

To explain what I am about to recall, it may be that (perhaps like the gravedigger's wife) Night'n'Day got fed up looking at Con pulling vegetables in the back garden (or hearing Maisie praising the lovely heads of lettuce he had grown) and decided that Mr O'Neill could do likewise.

One fine evening in late spring he set to clearing a patch—about two metres square—but even I suspected his method, having a vague notion (perhaps acquired telepathically from Con) that skimming off the sods and tossing them in a heap farther up the garden was a quick fix that would haunt him later on when he expanded the patch.

When the patch was dug, raked and de-stoned, he emerged with a packet of lettuce seeds and came over to the railing beside where Con had some weeks previously sown a line of lettuce seed that he was subjecting to a preliminary thinning, as he explained when asked by Mr O'Neill, who expressed his gratitude for Con's brief tutorial on growing lettuce but seemed less than convinced of its efficacy. It obviously struck him as a waste of time that Con sowed seeds in a row that he would then thin out with a view to transplanting the sturdies in a bed with room enough around them to develop into heads. Applying his brand of common sense, Mr O'Neill put on his spectacles and, using the handle of his rake, made a series of holes one foot apart from each other, into which he placed a single seed, none of which survived. The only reason I recall the episode is that it marked my first awkward effort in my mother's footsteps: I nicknamed him Single-seed.

My substantial contribution to the garden was made while Con was at work. When we arrived on the Cappagh Road, there was nothing between us and Cabra except hedges and fields where herds of cows dropped count-less smelly fly-infested pats. It was my duty after school to go with bucket and shovel and collect a load of this disgusting slop to fertilise the garden.

I found it unpleasant and vaguely humiliating, but it would never have occurred to me to refuse—or even question aloud—a request from Con that for me had the force of an instruction. In my own mind I might resent that

I alone on the Cappagh Road was condemned to such slavery—or that my sisters should be exempted simply because they were girls—but even such thoughts reminded me that it was little to ask in return for all I was given.

(Years later, I am fourteen and yet there I am in the field with bucket and shovel, trying to ensure that no drop of this green scutter splashes on my good clothes. Good clothes? Yes, within a couple of hours I will be on my way to Irish college in Connemara for two weeks of what must have seemed to my sisters suspiciously like a seaside holiday. As resentment begins to coagulate in my mind, I suddenly see that the point of this shit-shovelling is to reassure my sisters and remind me that being the eldest and the only boy does not exempt me from helping out at home.)

Not all my horticultural labours were performed in such a slow and sullen manner. Every now and then it was as if manna had been spotted falling—or about to fall—and then it was a frantic rush to grab bucket and shovel and get there before anybody else.

Up to the mid-Sixties the horse continued to hold out against the van as an engine of delivery. For example, Johnston, Mooney and O'Brien used horse-drawn carts to deliver their daily bread, and for a gardener like Con, horse manure was highly prized. So, Maisie and my sisters were trained to spot the steaming brown-green buns on the road and send me sprinting into action. (I don't know when I was demobilised. It was probably when we moved to Cappagh Avenue in the very early Sixties, by which time no farmers would have risked their cows anywhere close to the corporation houses.)

Collecting manure was not my only contribution to the back garden where Con had planned a central path, using stones from the garden as hard-core. All it needed was a coat of concrete and that was where I came in.

As we were among the first to move to Finglas West, there was a lot of building going on. At the bottom of Cappagh Road a big mixer was kept going full-time filling up dumpers, which then ferried the concrete away to where it was needed. Using ball-bearing wheels and assorted pieces of wood, Con made me a little cart. The procedure was to position myself close to the chute that fed the concrete into the dumper and, when the dumper pulled away, to nip in and shovel up the inevitable spillage. Making garden paths and the like was obviously more popular than fertilising, so that there were often several boys in quest of the mixer's droppings and it was every boy for himself. Con would presumably have approved of this competition as likely to 'make a man of me'. Always feeling myself the least tough of the competitors, I often found it a little daunting and preferred it when I was there by myself and a wink from the driver warned me that he was about to pull out sooner than his employer would have preferred, leaving me with enough concrete to fill my cart. This duty was mercifully short: in no time at all the path was finished and I could concentrate on shovelling shit.

DOMESTIC SCENE of a winter evening. The fire is lit. Maisie is in one of the armchairs, darning or sewing. Maura and Eileen are kneeling on the floor, minding baby Eva. I am sitting at the table doing the sums for school tomorrow morning. Con has come over to have a look. I hope he won't find any mistakes. He taps the numbers lightly with my pencil as he follows my calculations. I hold my breath until he goes through the final sum and congratulates me: all correct. Such was my faith in his infallibility that I see no reason why I should have to wait until the following day to award each of my sums an extravagant tick with my marker. Which makes for an embarrassing moment when Mr Feeney does the sums on the board. One of mine is wrong, not the way it was done—after all, my father had checked it—but because in my enthusiasm I had taken it down wrong from the board.

Among the clearest memories of my time with Mr Feeney was listening to his account of the Battle of Clontarf, how, on Good Friday 1014, King Brian Boru, having driven the Danes into the sea, was in his tent thanking God for the victory when an escaping Dane, Brodir, found him and killed him. The other boys hung on his every word. I was flabbergasted that a teacher should have missed so much and my dissatisfaction must have been clear on my face: Mr Feeney came over to me and asked if anything was wrong with me. Wrong with me!! He was the one who was in the wrong. Some gentle questioning elicited that my father had given me the *right* version of what had happened at Clontarf. And would I like to tell the class what had actually happened? They'd all like to hear it.

'Well, take the death of King Brian ....'

Con's account had been as carefully set, dressed and choreographed as any play or film. It was as if we had been there when Brodir pulled open the flap of the tent and saw the saintly greybeard clutching the bejewelled crucifix. Brodir had tried to sneak up on Brian but at the last minute Brian had shifted sideways and Brodir's sword had cut deeply into the little altar at which Brian was praying. There was a great deal of gasping and swashbuckling as Brian defended himself against the much younger man, but eventually Brodir knocked the sword out of Brian's hand and, cowardly scoundrel that he was, killed the unarmed king.

The kindly teacher asked the class to give me a clap. I could not understand why he had been so impressed with my version. I was merely telling what had happened, exactly as Con had told me. At the time I had only to hear a story or a song once to have it by heart.

Though he was happy to lose himself in the isolation of gardening or DIY, Con liked nothing more, when the curtains had been drawn, than to surround himself with his family in the front room, playing games, telling stories, singing songs or inspecting our home exercise.

I think I enjoyed the family singsongs more than my sisters did. There was a lot more Irish music on the radio in those pre-TV days and, with Con, I listened to programmes such as *The Ballad Maker's Saturday Night* and *Take the Floor* as enthusiastically as I followed *The Adventures of Dan Dare, Pilot of the Future* or the serial editions of *Robbery Under Arms* and *The Coral Island*. Even back in Inchicore I could learn a song before I had understood the meaning of all the words. Sentimental songs such as 'The Stone Outside Dan Murphy's Door' and 'The Moon Behind the Hill' still take up increasingly valuable space in my memory. Con knew at least a hundred songs. Maisie's favourite was 'Teddy O'Neill'. I recall feeling that such emotionalism was the mark of *real* music and pride prevented me from admitting that I preferred the jauntily comic 'Courtin' in the Kitchen', just as I preferred Peadar Kearney's 'Down by the Liffeyside' to his 'Down by the Glenside', which was featured regularly on the Walton programme on Saturday afternoons.

I had a special affection for 'Follow me up to Carlow', partly for the verve with which it celebrated an Irish victory over the English but mostly for the hint of bad language in the opening words of the chorus:

> *Curse and swear, Lord Kildare, Fiach will do what Fiach will dare,*
> *Now Fitzwilliam, have a care; fallen is your star low.*
> *Up with halberd, out with sword; on we'll go for, by the Lord,*
> *Fiach MacHugh has given the word: follow me up to Carlow—*

Besides, one of the verses was as ferocious as anything you would read in a comic or see in the cinema:

> *From Tassaggart to Clonmore, there flows a stream of Saxon gore*

O, great is Rory Óg O'More for sending loons to Hades.
White is sick and Lane is fled, now for black Fitzwilliam's head
We'll send it over dripping red, to Queen Liza and her ladies.

I had no idea what 'sending loons to Hades' meant. All my attention was on the dripping head of 'black Fitzwilliam', whoever he was, and I was pretty sure, given the relish with which his fate was celebrated, that he was an agent of the English queen and richly deserved whatever he got.

For as long as I could remember I was conscious of a powerful, if vague, sense of loyalty 'to Ireland', of inheriting from Con an awareness of my place in the world that he had inherited from his father and mother. I grew up with the assumption that England had taken unlawful control of Ireland and treated her people, especially the Catholics, like slaves, driving them off their lands and depriving them of their god-given right to education and self-determination. The Irish people had never surrendered, and our history was a series of rebellions, all of them (alas) heroic failures until the War of Independence had finally driven the English out of the Twenty-six Counties. Con's father had played an important part in this liberation, and not only with his rifle: he had written the national anthem and many songs that inspired the fight for freedom. My favourites were his rollicking satires on the English, especially 'Whack-fol-the-diddle'—

I'll sing you a song of peace and love,
Whack-fol-the-diddle-and-the-di-dol-day
To the land that reigns all lands above,
Whack-fol-the-diddle-and-the-di-dol-day;
May peace and plenty be her share,
Who kept our homes from want and care,
O God bless England is our prayer,
Whack-fol-the-diddle-and-the-di-dol-day

—and, most especially, 'It's a Grand Old Country':

Now how often we've been flattened out
Our history books can show,
And Mother England battened on
Our misery and woe;

68

She slaked us and she baked
Till the snivellers cried 'amen',
But the world knows that Ireland rose
From out the dust again.
(Chorus) For it's a grand old country every time,
With its trees and rivers, rocks and soil and clime;
We're God's own people & we'll shout from tower and steeple:
It's a grand old country every time!

I acquired from Con the assumption that to be *truly* Irish was to be a fervent nationalist. This was not an unusual position in those days; but I knew no other family in Finglas so committed to this faith. Con insisted on buying Irish whenever possible; even if the article cost a little more, it was an investment in our own economy that would eventually pay off. Although I played soccer on the road with the other boys, my loyalty was to our own Gaelic games. I accepted Con's belief that the ultimate proof of our independence would be the revival of the Irish language and this—and the guarantee of his admiration—spurred me on to learn it myself. And I never dreamed of questioning his opinion that Fianna Fáil was the only political party worthy of government.

Fianna Fáil advertised itself as the Republican Party, which seemed logical, given that it was founded by de Valera, who had led the Republican opposition to the Free State during the Civil War, but there were others who claimed to be Republican and who loathed de Valera as the traitor who had imprisoned and executed members of the IRA during World War II.

Con allowed me to grow up believing that his father, a close associate of Michael Collins, had, after a brief and soon-regretted period as censor in Maryborough Gaol, taken the Republican side during the Civil War. There is no doubt that Peadar soon lost faith in Cumann na nGaedheal but the evidence suggests that, far from supporting Fianna Fáil, he maintained a disenchanted distance from all forms of parliamentary politics.

When Peadar died in 1941, Brendan Behan, then in Mountjoy Gaol for the attempted murder of a policeman, was bitterly disappointed not to be allowed attend the funeral of his uncle and 'very dear friend'. Though hardly a model of consistency, it is unlikely that such a hard-line member of the IRA would have thought so highly of a man who owed any allegiance to a government that, in Behan's eyes, had betrayed the ideals of 1916.

Many of those who had fought on the Republican side during the Civil War became prominent members of Fianna Fáil, which became the party of those who balanced—to varying degrees—a commitment to democratic politics and a desire to 'recover' the Six Counties, as they tended to call Northern Ireland. Con would not have been unusual in choosing parliamentary politics while preserving a residual admiration for the idealism of those who, like his cousin Brendan, had emulated his father by sacrificing themselves 'for the cause'.

It was government policy to name roads in the new housing estates after the heroes of the struggle for independence, the choice often indicating which of the Civil War parties was in power at the time. Two major roads on the north side of Dublin were Collins Avenue and Griffith Avenue, heroes of the pro-Treaty Fine Gael; behind Cappagh Road were Mellowes Road and Mellowes Avenue, commemorating Peadar's IRB friend Liam Mellowes, who had been executed by the Free State during the Civil War.

Before we moved to the Cappagh Road a small estate of private houses had been built on the other side of the village, which I got to know well because it was less than a hundred yards from my school in Ballygall. Friends of mine lived on McKee Road and Clancy Avenue. In June 1951 a memorial to Dick McKee (born on the Phibsborough Road) had been unveiled by Éamon de Valera in Finglas village opposite the Catholic Church.

In a state still recovering from the divisions of the Civil War, modern Irish history—apart from Easter Week—was not included in the school curriculum and my guess is that very few of my pals (or most of their parents) had any idea who these men were whose names featured in their addresses. On the other hand, I cannot remember a time when I did not know that they were Peadar's friends, who had been 'kicked to death in Dublin Castle'.

What intrigues me now is my inability to summon up any clear memory of Con reminding me of this connection. I must have passed the McKee memorial at least a hundred times with Con and it is possible, maybe even probable, that he did make comments that I have forgotten; but my present inclination is not to fault my memory or Con's failure to transmit such ideas with his customary efficiency. I think it is more likely that he tempered his pride in his father's friendship in what he considered to be my best interest.

Early in the 1950s the IRA began to reorganise and, with a view to expelling the British from Northern Ireland, to plan a campaign of raids across the border. The territorial claim, enshrined in de Valera's 1937 Constitution, had the support of the majority of the Irish people, even those opposed to the illegal military action of the IRA. Con's position was similar to that of many who voted for Fianna Fáil (a party that had interned and even executed members of the proscribed IRA). He agreed with their political objective of restoring the integrity of the country, admired their courageous dedication 'to the cause' and, wanting it both ways, would have preferred if the Irish government had somehow helped rather than hindered them.

But he had more immediate concerns. In 1955 he turned thirty-seven. His life had been far from easy, thanks largely to his father's political commitments. He made no secret of his pride in his father's contribution to the struggle for independence, but he chose not to follow his example. He was essentially a family man, dedicated to the care and development of his children, willing to do all in his power to enable them to better themselves. Convinced that education offered the only escape from the limitations of working-class life, he helped and encouraged us to apply ourselves at school.

IN 1955 I turned ten and was already showing signs of scholastic ability. No hot house flower, I revelled in all types of play—football, cowboys and Indians, excursions into the surrounding countryside—but I enjoyed school just as much, my instinctive delight increased by Con's admiration. I was his eldest surviving child, his only son, and it was natural that he should take a special interest in me, transmitting to me—as well as a respect for learning—his other values, notably his family pride and his nationalism. He was characteristically thoughtful and cautious and, as I came towards the end of my primary school days, he was on the look-out for anything that might distract me from the further education that he hoped lay ahead. It was one thing for a child to give precocious performances of patriotic zeal in song and story, quite another to progress from there to the kind of activity that, for example, had led his cousin Brendan Behan to spend years in confinement. And that is why, I suspect, he moderated the tone of his lessons in patriotism, why the names of McKee, Clancy, Clune and Mellowes remained names on roads rather than models to emulate.

I was too young to notice any such complexities or to gather (as he would) that in the economically depressed mid-Fifties there was a revival of support for a reorganised and re-armed IRA. Which is why the events of one Easter Sunday are seared into my memory.

It was probably Easter 1956, the fortieth anniversary of the Rising. We had just attended mass, wearing our Easter lily badges in memory of Easter Week, as we had for as long as I could remember. Even as we came out the church door, we could detect an unusual buzz in the air outside. Members of the congregation were pushing over towards the corner shop where some kind of fracas was taking place. Presuming it was a personal row, I was surprised at the urgent way Con shepherded me through the throng in order to see what was happening.

Half-a-dozen uniformed gardaí were scuffling with two or three young men. I had no idea what it was all about, until one man beside us told another that the young men were the IRA selling Easter lilies.

I am not sure to what extent I could interpret the situation; the gardaí had justifiably assumed that the badge-sellers were member of the proscribed IRA and were attempting to arrest them or at least confiscate their badges. For this they were being roundly booed and barracked by many of the mass-goers, some of whom were politically motivated, others merely manifesting the traditional Dublin working-class antipathy to any police activity.

I was beginning to become anxious as I sensed the possibility of a fight in which Con and I might be injured. And then Con's protective fingers dug into my shoulders. *Leave them alone! Leave them alone!* My heart pounding, I looked up and back, shocked to discover that it was my father who was shouting at the policemen.

I was suddenly adrift at the precipitous edge of my world. It was as if he could not fully control himself, he of all people. The familiar part of him, represented by his protective grasp on my shoulders, wanted to rush me away from this social disorder; but some necessity—a revelation to me, frightening but at the same time thrilling—obliged him to side with the IRA against the upholders of the law.

I will never forget his eyes. All other elements of the scene have been obscured by time: how long we stayed; if I questioned him on the way home; if he made any reference to his shouting. Only the haunted eyes and the clenched hands remain as pressing as if that Easter Sunday had been yesterday.

Another vignette can be safely dated Sunday, 6 January 1957, and located to the right of the fireplace in the front room of Cappagh Road where Con's armchair was situated beneath the radio. The year had begun with news of the deaths of two IRA men in a cross-border incursion and such was the reaction that both are commemorated in ballads: the conventional 'Sean South from Garryowen' and Dominic Behan's more sceptical 'The

Patriot Game'. Con has arrived back from mass with his copy of the *Sunday Press* and I stand beside him as he reads a detailed account of the disastrous raid on Brookeborough RUC barracks. His general reaction is one of pity for the brave but poorly equipped boys who took on the still considerable might of the British Empire. Almost as if accusing the RUC and the British Army of not playing fair, he explains how flares had been used to expose the retreating IRA.

Con was anti-English to the extent that he took pleasure whenever Mother England was bested in politics or in sport. The Fifties was a good decade to be against the British Empire. We knew very little about the EOKA fighters in Cyprus or the Mau Mau in Kenya or President Nasser and his supporters in Egypt or whoever was shooting at the British Army in Aden, but we assumed their cause was just and their methods fair, and we hoped they would be victorious. Being a stamp collector and familiar with the vastness of the British Empire, I was less optimistic that we would live to see the happy day of its demise; on the other hand, Con seemed confident that the end was nigh, and I hoped for both us that he was right, as he usually was.

I HAD to wait some thirty years for Con's clearest statement of his early hopes for me. We were in The Willows pub in Finglas, celebrating a major promotion I had recently received, when somehow we got round to discussing the what-ifs of my career. Was there anything I had ever wished to become, apart from an academic? I mentioned that when I was aged about ten, too young to know what the words meant, I convinced myself that I wanted to be an electrical engineer; but no, not really.

'Of course, you know what I always wanted you to be.'

I could hardly believe what I was hearing.

'No. Not a clue.'

'Go 'way, you chancer. You must know.'

'Honestly. I never had any idea you ever wanted me to be anything in particular.'

It took him a while to believe I was not trying to cod him and the longer his sardonic stare continued, the more I was tantalised by what I was about to hear.

'An army officer.'

'You're joking!'

'To join the cadets and become an officer.'

I was flabbergasted. I had grown up in the Sixties and while never one to go on peace marches or sloganise about love-not-war, I would have found the life of an army officer deeply unattractive, physically, mentally, emotionally, culturally.

Had there ever been anything else in our lives that placed us at such odds to each other? All we could do was smile, me that Con had nursed such a hope through many early years, he that I had never picked up what he thought he was signalling clearly.

Pondering our exchange before I nodded off that night, I began to appreciate the logic of Con's point of view. A Sam Browne belt would have fulfilled so many of his hopes for me, would have been—albeit at a remove—the closest he would ever get to realising the forlorn dreams of his own youth.

It would satisfy the patriotic imperative and trump better-paid professions such as medicine or law: I would serve my country in the national army, the official title, Óglaigh na hÉireann, derived from the Irish version of the Irish Volunteers, of which my grandfather had been a founder-member in 1913. It would also satisfy the socio-economic imperative. Captain Colbert Kearney could expect benefits unavailable to the working class: security of employment, professional status, and the respect traditionally reserved for gentlemen. And this at a time of peace, not long after a world war in which Ireland had remained neutral, when the element of risk must have seemed very low. (Although, had Con's dreams come true, I would have entered the Cadet School about three years before the Niemba massacre of Irish U.N. troops in the Congo).

There was one aspect of the puzzle that took a little longer to tease out. Why was he so certain that he had conveyed his preference to me and I so certain that he had not? It was an extraordinary, perhaps a unique, breakdown of communication between us. A man who eschewed physical violence, he was equally disinclined to use mental or intellectual force. A subtle teacher, he would encourage, cajole and show by example, but never simply instruct, correct or dismiss. He would have considered it unacceptably coercive to say, for example, 'it would make me very happy if you became an army officer', an abuse of his position to put that degree of pressure on a child—apart altogether from considerations of its likely effectiveness.

BY FAR the most powerful and popular institution in Ireland in the first three-quarters of the twentieth century was the Catholic Church. The 1937 Constitution guaranteed freedom of worship and forbade the establishment of any one religion but recognised 'the special position' of the Catholic Church. In those days before ecumenism, the Church brandished its authoritarianism with pride, boasted of its infallibility, demanded absolute obedience and dismissed freedom of conscience as an absurdity that had caused the Protestant churches to disintegrate. The vast majority of politicians, like the vast majority of those who elected them, were practising Catholics and it was hardly surprising that they should legislate in a manner of which the Church approved. The Church controlled the education of Catholics by acting as managers of the national primary schools and by building, owning and staffing most secondary schools.

(In a 2008 BBC television programme 'Inside the Medieval Mind', the presenter constantly advised his audience that they would find it difficult if not impossible to apprehend the religious beliefs of that distant age, which included such bizarre fantasies as hell and purgatory and the power of relics, holy water, the invocation of saints, visiting shrines, indulgences, prayer and fasting to effect changes in this world and the next. I had to smile: I had grown up in that same world and such beliefs were the norm throughout Irish society, even among university students of the early 1960s.)

While the Church wielded its power not only with impunity but also with the approval of the majority, it never quite achieved absolute control, even among Catholics. Popular history described how the Catholic clergy had suffered with the people through the dark days of the Penal Laws—most famously the Father Murphy of 'The Boys of Wexford' who led his flock during the 1798 rebellion in Wexford, was captured and his body burned on the rack—but the Catholic hierarchy had, especially since the French Revolution, forbidden the faithful to join secret societies or to use violence for political ends.

The Princes of the Catholic Church had long enjoyed a social prestige that rivalled the secular aristocracy and they still lived in palaces and wore purple and fine linen. They never forgot the threat posed by the atheists of the French Revolution, and by the time I went to school the arch-enemy was godless Communism. In the meantime they had sided with the employers against the 'socialist-led' workers in the 1913 Lockout and threatened members of the IRB and those who took part in the War of Independence.

It is hardly surprising that Peadar Kearney, guilty of sin on several counts, had little time for them.

Such a conservative church was bound to be more popular with the middle class than with the working class, especially the Dublin urban working class where memories of 1913 lingered and where there was an innate tendency to resent such arms of the state as the police and the priests, almost all of them from 'the country', the priests mostly from better-off families and now living—on the contributions of their parishioners—in houses and in a style their parishioners could never aspire to.

Like my sisters after me, I was brought up as a devout Catholic, attended a primary school where Christian doctrine was Catholic teaching, made my first communion and confirmation with the rest of my class and subsequently became an altar boy. The whole family attended mass (not necessarily together) and even when—aged about sixteen—I had ceased to believe, I still absented myself from the house on Sunday mornings and went for a walk. Why? Not so much to avoid an argument with Con or Maisie, who by then had guessed my situation and accepted it, as to avoid setting my sisters an example they might find dangerous to follow. It was one thing for me, an intellectual follower of James Joyce, to break ranks, quite another for my sisters, who were still at convent school.

I am not sure I ever had such conscious thoughts: it is more likely that I acted instinctively, having intuited from Con that anybody with any ambition kept his doubts or his apostasy to himself. A teacher who did not toe the Catholic line could be fired by the local parish priest, who could count on the support of his parishioners. Anybody, from civil servants to doctors to shopkeepers, risked being blacklisted if they advertised their freedom from Catholic control, with the result that very few did, keeping their criticisms to themselves and a trusted circle of friends.

None of our neighbours could have doubted that Con and Maisie were anything other than 'good Catholics'. As well as going to mass and confession and receiving communion regularly, Con turned up at the men's sodality. Within the house they would check that we said our night prayers before getting into bed and I recall a period—in the mid-Fifties when Father Peyton's Rosary Crusade reached Ireland—when the family knelt down in the front room to say the Rosary together, Con urging us to straighten our backs when we slouched over a chair.

Yet even in those early years I noticed that his religion was a private matter, that at mass he paid little attention to what was happening on the altar, preferring to lose himself in a silent rosary or pursue his own meditations. And the more familiar I became with the priests I served at mass, the more I observed that my father's attitude to them was distant, with none of the awe or subservience they generally inspired.

In retrospect, I suspect that, as with his sympathy for the IRA, he did his best to conceal whatever reservations he had about the Church in order not to hinder his children's prospects of advancement through education.

HOW DIFFERENT was this lovingly anxious father from the man who worked with Brendan Behan during the early Fifties for CIE, the national transport system? I doubt if he ever wished to emulate the outrageous behaviour of his cousin, but here he was, a relatively young man working at a trade with a reputation for merriment. And besides, there were no children present to be led astray by his example.

My only actual memory of those days features a cradle suspended from the Loopline Bridge to enable the men in it to paint the underneath of the bridge. It was a cold grey day shortly after we moved to Finglas—the 40 bus started from nearby Eden Quay—when Maisie brought my sisters and me over to Butt Bridge and across the road where she pointed to men in overalls in a wooden box hanging above the murky waters of the Liffey. It was only when one of the men waved back that I recognised Con and was horrified to see him in such a dangerous position. All the way home on the bus I was praying that I would see him again that night; when he arrived home for his dinner, I wanted to make him promise never to get into that box again.

In later years he recounted some incidents from those days, with details edited to suit my understanding. Con and Brendan got on well enough to feature in several stories set in pubs, one of which lodged in my memory, presumably because so much seemed enigmatic when I heard it first. The pub was Tom Crilly's of Townsend Street, not far from Tara Street Station (where the CIE pay office was located) and the Queen's Theatre. It enjoyed a certain reputation (which lingered long after it closed) based on its arrangement with the local working girls known (after the Queen's dancing troupe) as Crilly's Moonbeams. Con and Brendan were joined on this occasion by Pearse.

As often happened in stories that even hinted at such risqué topics as prostitution, Con represented himself as a relative innocent compared to his more widely travelled brother or cousin, but this could have been to some extent for my benefit. Pearse and Brendan were seated in an almost empty saloon as Con stood at the bar while the barman pulled the three pints. Con had paid and was about to take the drinks over to the table when the barman leaned forward and muttered: 'Would yiz like a drop of the chat?'

A decade later Con would mime his reaction, shaking his head, not quite sure what was being offered in such a place in such a hugger-mugger manner but instinctively convinced he did not want any part of it. (In 1950s' Dublin, 'chat' was slang for 'breast'.) Back at the table with Pearse and Brendan, having checked that he could not be overheard, Con whispered that there was something funny about your man behind the bar. What did he mean? Drawing them in still closer and speaking in even more muted tones, he repeated the barman's offer. The others paused, nodded, asked: 'What did you say?'

'I said no. What do you think I—'

The furtive whispering was blown away as Pearse stared incredulously as his younger brother and Brendan jumped up and roared at the barman.

'Yes! Three glasses and may the giving hand never falter.'

The 'chat' in question was a mixture of the dregs of all the wines, including sherry and port, sold in the pub, which was offered free to customers to get them so drunk so quickly that they would stay on the premises and buy more drink. (Con did not imply that it might also boost the demand for Moonbeams.) The grimace of revulsion on his face led me to believe that much and all as he loved to chat over a pint, he would never subject himself to such a vile concoction and I never asked him if he had drunk his glass or passed it over to his less fastidious companions.

IT IS interesting to speculate how Con would have fared had he, like me, had three daughters and no son. Doubtless he would have accepted his fate and made the best of it, devoting his loving attention to his daughters, but he would never have experienced what became the social highlight of his week: taking me to Croke Park on Sunday afternoon. (Eventually, when I left Dublin, I was replaced by my sisters Eileen and Eva and—who would have thought it possible?—Maisie.)

We would have been noticed by our Cappagh Road neighbours as we headed off around lunchtime with our sandwiches, not merely because of my age but because most men in Finglas, like most of the inner city working class, were soccer supporters and travelled in large numbers to watch Shamrock Rovers, Drumcondra, Bohemians, Shelbourne or St Patrick's Athletic. When boys played ball on the road or on the green, it was always soccer. It may well be that some of those who packed Croke Park for the big matches wished that Con had waited a little longer before taking me with him into that cauldron of competitive devotion. I don't know exactly how young I was—no more than seven—when, in my earliest memories, I am within the protective fork of Con's legs, submerged in a nether world of shoes and turned-up trousers and coat pockets, inching our way through the bottleneck of Jones's Road towards the turnstiles. Excited but never afraid, I had an absolute trust in my father almighty and a general hope/belief that the men around us, who had no qualms about elbowing other adults out of their way, felt a duty of care to a child, even if some of them thought the father mad to be putting him at risk on an occasion like this.

Having lifted me over the turnstile, helped me up the steep steps and down the terraces of Hill 16, he ushered me across to 'our' place by the wall between the terrace and the pitch. And was transformed. No longer the anxious father of four, he became a Dublin man—'Dubs' had yet to be invented—his own identity almost entirely merged in a motley host united by semi-hysterical pride of place and fanatical team loyalty. Croke Park was where he let off the considerable amount of steam that must have built up behind his serene self-control, the theatre where his part demanded that he raise his voice, clench his fist and come as close as he ever came to cutting loose. Having sung the national anthem with pride and gusto, we were, literally, ecstatic: transported into a world that was divided in two between Jackeens and Culchies, leaving us in heroically paranoid isolation against the other thirty-one counties.

Even I was sometimes left open-mouthed by the degree of his passionate involvement, caught between fear and excitement at the sound of my father abusing the referee or the opposition with a verve that in other circumstances would have led to physical violence. On the other hand—lest I give the impression that the Hill was in any way like the thuggish terraces we see on televised soccer matches—I should point out that, for all the passionate involvement and rhetoric, our section of Hill 16 was decorum itself. Anything more impolite than 'bloody' was considered unacceptable and if an instinctive 'fuck' slipped out in the heat of the moment, there was an immediate murmur of disapproval—*language, please, child present*—followed by a muttered apology from the sinner. Although Hill 16 was generally associated with the true-blue Dublin supporters, anybody was free to go anywhere and supporters of opposing teams stood shoulder to shoulder, shouting their conflicting reactions but never, in my experience, provoking so much as a push.

I got to recognise the regulars through their shouts of encouragement and mutterings of disappointment. There were two with whom Con would always chat. The first was the actor Mícheál Ó Briain, whom he knew from the Abbey Theatre, a native speaker from Spiddal in Connemara whose English, so flat and distinct, was in contrast to the predominant Dublinese. The other was a ballad-maker, who sold his wares, octavo sheets on which recent events—always with a strong republican slant—had been gestetnered into song, charging (I think) sixpence. He was the last of the ballad-makers, a small sweet-voiced man called Jimmy Hiney (which I assume to be another form of Seamus Heaney) and I recall the mixture of affection and embarrassment that overcame Con when the ballad-monger recognised him. All business was forgotten and Jimmy Hiney came over to us, smiling happily, proud to shake the hand of a son of Peadar Kearney, insisting on presenting us with a copy of his latest composition and recoiling with outrage when Con reached into his pocket. As the last of his kind left us to ply the trade that would not survive him, Con would shake his head wistfully. At the time I presumed he was feeling sorry for a man who was scraping a living, a man to whom he would have preferred to slip a few pence rather than accept his generosity; now I wonder if he saw in the little man's doomed struggle a version of his own father's attempts to make a living as a poet of the people.

Con began bringing me to Croke Park at an early age partly because he saw it as his parental duty to introduce me to the mysteries of identity, to transmit the nationalist fervour he had inherited from his father. It was patriotic to follow Gaelic rather than 'foreign' games. (Gaelic games were organised by the GAA, the others by what he always termed 'the soccer crowd' or 'the rugby crowd'.)

It is not surprising that a father would derive a variety of pleasures from the company of his young son, especially a father who as a child himself seems to have experienced little paternal indulgence and, besides, who knows to what extent Con's desire to share his world with me was sharpened by the pain of having lost his first-born before he could begin to walk or talk?

But the fact remains that when first I was taken to Croke Park, and for many years afterwards, I tended to be the only child on our part of the Hill. Many of the other men around us must have had sons about my age but, for whatever reason, they did not bring them. Perhaps the men wanted a complete get-away from family life and/or looked forward to breaking their journey home with a few pints in the local, which was not what today would be termed 'child-friendly'. Perhaps the sons did not want to come, preferring to spend the weekend with their own pals. Or maybe the other fathers thought Hill 16 on the day of a big match was too turbulent for children.

We generally arrived in time for the minor match and before the mayhem that preceded the national anthem and the senior game. And there was another important reason for getting there early. We had to claim a place down by the wall where Con, because I was too small to see over the wall or over the shoulders of the tiered supporters, would hoist me up beside one of the stanchions that supported the wires that gave me something stable to hold on to. This was, of course, against regulations and an affront to the ground staff who made several efforts to dethrone me. I remember one particular soul who, clad in the uniform of the cartoon Irish nationalist engagé—mac, beret, a pioneer pin that betokened abstinence from alcohol and a frown that betokened immunity from frivolity—came charging up the side-line, wagging his finger threateningly and revealing the badge that identified him as a *maor* or steward. What the poor man had not learned was that in the eyes of Dublin men he represented everything they despised about Croke Park officialdom: he was not only a Culchie, he was an uppity Culchie, dressed in a little, brief authority that he thought he could impose on us in our own city. He was met with a barrage of abuse that began with righteous indignation—*leave the child alone, you bully*—but soon descended into ridicule—*go 'way you Russian spy*—and, inevitably, as he recognised the imperviousness of these feckless Jackeens to law and order, he retreated.

A paradoxical form of patriotism dominated. All who attended Croke Park would have claimed to be nationalists but, that matter agreed and set aside, there were sub-national niggles—ancient and modern—to be nourished. I was initially appalled to notice the pleasure experienced by people from third counties when things were not going Dublin's way, but I soon learned to rejoice in this oppression and to emulate Con in composing battle cries based on the assertion that it always was, and always would be, us-against-the-rest.

Few enough of 'us' were far from rural roots—Con's paternal grandfather had been born in Louth, his grandmother in Meath—but it was remarkable how quickly those born in Dublin accepted the vagary of a beneficent Fate that had given them as their birthright a sense of superiority to the rest of humanity. (Years later I was pleased to recognise the same easy arrogance in the classical Athenians who considered the rest of humanity—with their strange ways and even stranger speech—'barbarian'.)

There was never any question in those days of Maisie (or any of my sisters) coming to Croke Park. Most working-class women stayed at home, rearing children for whom (before the arrival of the fridge or pre-packed meals) they shopped almost daily for fresh produce to be cooked that day. Epidemics of tuberculosis and polio—recalling the fate of her first-born from gastroenteritis—obliged Maisie, like most other women, to protect her children by feeding them wholesome food. Economics obliged her to watch every penny she spent, weighing quality against cost, always with an eye out for a bargain, always counting the days until payday on Friday. Trips into town to buy clothes were not without an element of pleasure but it was a pleasure paid for in bus fares.

Nor was it simply a matter of jumping on a bus into town and flitting from shop to shop before hopping on a bus home. In those days before legal contraception, most women in Finglas went nowhere without a pram and there was room on a bus for only one pram, which meant that a woman with a pram (and maybe one or two older children in tow) might wait half an hour for a bus only to find that, while there were plenty of vacant seats, the pram space beneath the stairs had been taken and there was nothing for her to do but wait for the next bus and hope that it was pram-free.

Nobody living in a corporation estate had a car. A taxi was an extravagance reserved for special occasions—birth and impending death—and, since nobody had a home phone, calling one involved getting to the nearest public phone in working order. Not that anybody missed having a car or a phone or calling a taxi any more than they missed flying to the Mediterranean for their summer holidays.

SOCIAL VISITS, like our annual excursion to the seaside at Portmarnock, were major undertakings and expensive, involving four bus journeys, two there and two home. On several fine afternoons Maisie took us on the long walk over to Auntie Maureen in Cabra West. Even more physically demanding were those summer Sundays when Con and Maisie led us all the way over to Pearse's house in Raheny, a walk of at least two hours that had my sisters complaining, but halved the cost of buses.

On at least two occasions Maisie brought us over to her sister Eileen in Whitehall and I recall a couple of visits with Con to his Aunt Maggie Bourke in Whitehall and his Aunt Maura Slater in Fairview. (It may be that on at least one of these Con ferried me on the crossbar of his bicycle.)

Visitors to our house in Finglas were rare. Kevin Bourke and his family were regulars at Christmas time, but they had a car. Maisie's Aunt Maisie came several times. I only recall Nana coming over to us once; I can still see her sitting by the fireplace with Maisie and Mrs O'Neill.

I am over at the front window, at most ten years of age. Why I am indoors and not out playing, I have no idea. For as long as I can remember, I have been a compulsive eavesdropper on adult conversation, adept at making myself invisible, listening for references to matters considered unsuitable for my tender ears.

Shortly after Nana's arrival I was dispatched to the village for a Baby Power. On my return Mrs O'Neill had joined the company around the fireplace and it was obvious that a serious discussion was dropped while Maisie dispensed the whiskey, pouring most of it into Nana's glass, despite her protests. As I retired to my off-stage perch by the window, Maisie turned to me.

'Colbert, go out into the kitchen and get your Nana a cup of water and let the tap run.'

I was disappointed to be called on-stage and perplexed at Maisie's request; but I would no more have questioned my mother than I would have refused Nana anything. And so I went out into the kitchen, let the tap run for ten seconds, turned the water off and—

'Agh, Colbert, that's not nearly long enough. Let it run for ages. Your Nana likes it ice-cold, don't you, Nana?

'Love it. Good boy, Colbert.'

How long afterwards was it that my suspicions were confirmed—that the point of the task was to get me out of ear-shot so that the adults could continue their furtive whisperings? Probably when I saw my sisters being sent on the same errand in similar circumstances.

Not long afterwards I visited Nana in Inchicore. I cannot imagine a ten-year-old today being allowed make the four-bus journey—setting out on the 40 from Finglas into Abbey Street, then the walk across to the 21A stop in College Green, returning in the dark of night—but Con and Maisie trusted me and I saw no problem. In the room where I had spent my early childhood Nana intrigued me with her talk of Peadar Kearney and of my inheritance as a Kearney. Kind and loving as ever, she fed me the chicken Maggie Bourke had sent her to keep her strength up. I had no idea Nana was dying: in my eyes she was simply 'old', although she was nearly ten years younger than I am as I write this. I knew she had had a hard life as Peadar's helpmate during the fight for Irish freedom but, as she never complained, this was more a matter of pride than pity for me.

MAISIE'S DAY began when she went downstairs to prepare Con's breakfast and pack his lunch while he got ready to cycle to work. She then turned her attention to Maura and me, calling us from our beds to the kitchen where she placed hot porridge breakfasts in front of us and then hurried us out to school, the sponsored programmes on the radio reminding us how long we had left. Then it was the turn of Eileen and Eva; while they were too young for school, they had to be washed and fed and dressed. After a preliminary tidy of the front room and kitchen, Maisie would grab a breakfast—generally a mug of tea and a slice of bread—wash and dress herself, put the baby in the pram and (in the early years before the new shops at the beginning of Cappagh Drive were built) make her way down the best part of a mile to the village to do the basic shopping. In time bread and milk deliveries were arranged and vans selling vegetables began to call regularly but though the walk to the shops was a trudge, especially in bad weather, it offered an escape from the house and a chance to talk to somebody other than the immediate neighbours.

How women related to each other was a mystery. There were hints at the time, and even more later on, that they were not all models of Catholic motherhood. *The Other* Mrs O'Neill, who lived at the far end of our block, emerged as the most colourful. Every Thursday she sent a child down to ask if Maisie could spare her a few pence until the following day, payday. She regularly repaid Maisie's kindness with an ox-tail her husband had acquired in the course of his work in an abattoir. Maisie was anxious that as little as possible be said regarding these transactions but there were other matters (both relating, I think, to *The Other* Mrs O'Neill) that were top secret. I suspect that this interesting woman had come from or had connections with the East Wall dockland area because she sometimes gave Maisie the loan of a newspaper called the *News of the World*. I discovered a copy in the sideboard when I was old enough to sense that some of the photographs were not what you would find in the *Sunday Press*, but not old enough to know why the *News of the World* was banned in Ireland and therefore much appreciated.

Many years later, Maisie recalled for me how shocked she had been to realise that *The Other* Mrs O'Neill was practising contraception, then both illegal and immoral. Maisie had (by her own account) been too shy to press her further on the matter and had been delighted when another neighbour asked her what she had told the priest in confession. 'Nothing', *The Other* Mrs O'Neill had replied. 'Why should I bring it up? That's none of his business.'

I suspect *The Other* Mrs O'Neill was far from unique in her attitude to the Catholic Church. It was her church, which she would defend against its enemies. She accepted it as her duty to follow its rules and regulations, provided, of course, they did not fly in the face of common sense, as did the proposition that she should year after year accept as a gift from god a child that she had to feed and clothe.

BY THE summer of 1955 I had more on my mind than women's gossip. I was an authority on Gaelic football, supplementing what I picked up on Hill 16 with what I garnered from Con and from radio and newspaper reports. I knew everything about the Dublin team, names, clubs, positions, styles of play. And I loved them all. Danno Mahony was like a boulder guarding the goal. Cathal O'Leary was an army officer, long and lean, who could rip defences apart with his solo runs. Ollie Freaney was a bit of a mystery, a solicitor who always looked as if he had just got out of bed, a shambles of a man who ambled all over the park, 'winding up' the opposing players; but he could kick frees over the bar from anywhere within range. Kevin Heffernan was the brains, in some ways an unlikely-looking genius, but you could sense panic in other teams whenever he got his hands on the ball. My own favourite was Des Ferguson, small and brave, his blond hair as beguiling as his nickname, 'Snitchie'.

On Sunday 25 September we made our way to Croke Park. Whatever about Con, I was supremely confident my beloved Blues would win the All-Ireland, if only because I loved them so much.

No previous visit to Croke Park had prepared me for the tense anticipation that had begun at the sight of the extraordinary crowds converging from all directions. Even the hawkers inside the turnstiles seemed more ebullient than usual, the men urging us to wear our team's colours, the women advertising ripe William pears. It was head down for me as I laboured up the steep steps behind Hill 16, head up as we made the summit to be overwhelmed by the unearthly perfection of the green pitch under a vast canopy of blue sky, as if God and his angels and saints were wearing our colours.

I was unable to imagine we could be beaten by a team of countrymen; but some instinct suggested that all precautions should be taken—just in case—and so with this in mind I addressed myself to God up there in his upper upper stand.

'O God, I realise your constant concern to guard all Mankind against the wiles and schemes of the Devil won't leave you much time for the game this afternoon but, as you must know, it means an awful lot to me and my Daddy and we'd both be eternally grateful if you could keep an eye on Croke Park and make sure Dublin win. Amen.'

Time has kindly erased much of what followed, leaving only nightmare flashes.

Compared to Dublin in their stylish sky blue, the Kerry players looked a bit hicky in their green and gold but, from my perch on the wall, I couldn't help noticing that they were bursting out of those jerseys and socks, that their eyes were the eyes of men possessed, that they were superhumanly fit and fast and strong, their midfielders soaring like birds, their forwards not bothering to work the ball in close to the goal but belting over points from unlikely distances.

We got a goal but they still beat us by three points.

Shocked and heartbroken, still unable to accept what I had seen with my own eyes, I accompanied Daddy down the silent steps, my faith in God shaken, my faith in my fellow human beings shattered by the traders' cries. *Wear your winning team's colours! Get yizzer ripe Kerry pears!*

We won the All-Ireland three years later but I was far from Croke Park and could only imagine Con's jubilation as the final whistle went and he looked forward to the Manhattan as never before.

It had become a ritual that after a good afternoon in Croke Park we would head out to the Manhattan Bar in Raheny in the certain knowledge that Pearse would be perched on his stool at the end of the counter to our left as we came in the door.

'Well, will you look what the wind's blown in. What are you having, brother? And how is the quare fella? Come over and let me have a look at you.'

I revelled in Pearse's company, delighted in the insouciance with which he lived the life of the bar. At that time of day, between five and six, there would be few in and everybody knew everybody else and acted accordingly, amusing themselves by exchanging jokes and light-hearted jibes, anything to maintain a high level of merriment. Pearse was a natural in this milieu; Con never quite achieved his brother's unselfconsciousness, but there were occasions when, if Dublin had won an important game, he came close.

'What's the news?'

'Divil a bit.'

In charge of the bar was the owner, a rather dour Northerner with no detectable sense of humour who insisted, for example, on general silence for the six o'clock Angelus and brooked no blasphemy or coarse language. He tolerated singing but only in the knowledge that the singers would go home for their tea and would not be there for the rest of the night. It was inevitable in those days that, after a few pints, somebody would strike up a song and this of course was meat-and-drink to the Kearney brothers who would contribute a medley of their father's broadsides against Mother England.

The three of us were in our various elements. Con was delighted to be with his brother. For all their apparent differences, I intuited that there was between them an unbreakable bond that had been formed in the mysterious recesses of their childhood. Pearse grinned with glee as he saw his brother loosen up. I was in heaven, the only child present, allowed to witness my two favourite men laughing away without, it seemed, a care in the world. When the fun was under way, Pearse would pause and turn to Con and me:

'I love this. All the Kearneys together.'

I loved it that I was included, that I was one of them. Pearse had a son but he was even younger than me and not interested in football and pub chat. Even so, it made me, the quare fella, special in some vague but deeply flattering way.

ANOTHER EXAMPLE of father and son together in the grown-up world. The scene is the Queen's Theatre in Pearse Street, the time late December 1955 or early January 1956, the show the Irish-language pantomime performed by the Abbey Theatre company, which had relocated to the Queen's when their own theatre burned down in 1951. It is entitled *Ulysses agus Penelope*, the prize-winning entry in an open competition, written by a teacher from my school, Mr Watters. He has brought boys from his class along and I recognise them sitting in the front of the circle.

They could not see me because I was high above them in 'the gods', the gallery of curved wooden benches to which the public was no longer admitted. At each side was an eyrie containing a spotlight. They were carbon arc lamps and Con had done his best to explain how an electric current was passed through two slightly separated carbon rods and the resultant flare projected down to the stage through a lens and filters. I could never relax as the rods got closer and closer, my whole body clenching in fearful anticipation of the sudden blinding blaze.

Presumably Con had been hired for the Abbey pantomimes because he had operated the self-same spot long before the august Abbey ever thought they would have to slum it in a variety theatre such as the Queen's. There was a shop beside the theatre, run by a woman who obviously knew Con from his Queen's days and who always asked for Maisie.

I frequently accompanied him over the next ten years, until the Abbey returned to its new theatre on the old site, and I am struck by how little he told me about his youthful adventures in the Queen's, when he met and fell in love with Maisie, and where he was on one spot and his pal, Kevin Bourke, on the other. The only story he imprinted in my memory was his retort to the manager who expressed the hope that Maisie would return after their honeymoon.

It would have been pitch dark when we got the bus into Abbey Street and made our way across the river to Pearse Street. Sometimes, instead of heading up the steps to the gallery, we went down the alley, in the stage door and onto the stage where Con chatted with actors and checked if there were any changes in that night's show. I must have stood open-mouthed, unable to absorb all the details of costume, lighting, back-drops, flats, cables, curtains. Even more amazing were his light-hearted exchanges with the actors and actresses: I was seeing stars and they were joking with my daddy! All this was hidden from the audience on the far side of the curtain; but because Con was 'in the business', I was allowed into the heart of the mystery.

When the curtain rose we sat silent in our spot booth, me following the action on the stage, checking the laughter from the stalls and the circles, turning to watch Con as he tracked the actors with the spot, at the end of each scene throwing the light up on the ceiling above the proscenium while closing the aperture and leaving the theatre in blackout before the next episode began or the house lights came up for the interval.

Looking back, I wonder if we were even more together in our own covey

IMAGE 1 (above):
Peadar Kearney
with Pearse in full
'Gaelic' dress.

IMAGE 2 (left):
Peadar at the grave
of Wolfe Tone in
Bodenstown, Co.
Kildare.

IMAGE 3 (above): Internees at Ballykinlar Internment Camp in Co. Down during the War of Independence. Peadar Kearney is third from the left (with cap and pipe) in the second row from the front.

IMAGE 4 (right): Peadar Kearney when he worked on and off in the Abbey Theatre before the 1916 Rising as a property manager and painter as well as being available for walk-on parts.

IMAGE 5 (above): Con and Pearse flanking their Slater cousins, Maura and Kathleen, in a picture postcard sent to Peadar while he was interned in Ballykinlar.

IMAGE 6 (left): Con and Pearse photographed around 1930. Con's teacher said that he was 'one of the cleverest boys with whom I have dealt'.

IMAGE 7: Peadar and Eva Kearney (née Flanagan). She was 17 and he 30 when they first met; they married in 1914.

IMAGE 8: A pencil portrait by Sean O'Sullivan of Peadar just a few weeks before his death on 24 November 1942.

IMAGE 9: Eva with Pearse and Con. It is possible to detect in Peadar's letters from Ballykinlar that he and Eva had noted differences between Pearse and Con, with the younger Con emerging as the quieter, the more academic.

IMAGE 10: Eva maintained to the end an aura of gentle refinement but circumstances obliged her to go out to work as a nursing assistant.

IMAGE 11: Masie Kearney (née Brady) before she met Con. She remembered her sister Eileen rhapsodising about 'this beautiful young fellow' who worked at the Queen's Theatre.

in the empty gallery than we were in the tumult of Croke Park, especially during those long silences as I feasted on the glamorous world from such a privileged position.

I was company for him during what he knew would, when the show had settled down, become relatively dull and repetitive. But it was more than that; I loved what was happening on the stage which, perhaps because it was in Irish, was much more literate and sophisticated than the traditional English language pantomimes. (In passing: despite the paucity of his Irish, he could follow the action and the cues as if the performance was in English.) If he did not regale me with stories of his own adventures as a young man, perhaps it was to prevent me from being seduced by the glamour that had taken him away from his steady nine-to-five in the garage. He would not have wanted me to work as a stage electrician in the fragile world of theatre. He had other hopes for me that involved staying on at school, far away from the spotlights.

After the show we wrapped ourselves up against the cold before rushing over to Eden Quay for the Finglas bus. There must have been nights when I nodded off: I have a dreamy memory of leaning against his shoulder, only half-noticing as he disengaged his arm to snuggle me into his warm overcoat.

(A decade later he got me a holiday job on the Abbey panto, so that I must have experienced, however unconsciously, something of his excitement when Lorcan had lured him over to the Queen's three decades earlier. My duty during rehearsals was 'to make myself useful' about the stage; during the run I was up in the fly loft, assistant to an old-timer responsible for the lowering and raising of back-drops using ropes. There were the inevitable adventures, most notably the night, well into the run, when my elderly superior was so 'tired' he fell asleep in his chair. Leaning on the rail, I had noticed a celebrated actor standing on his mark, checking his costume and looking up, wondering why the back-drop had not yet descended now that the front curtains were about to sweep back and reveal him against a brick wall. Suddenly the red light was flashing and, with my mentor in another world, it was up to me to save the night. Instead of lowering the back-drop slowly and carefully, I literally let it fly so that Tír na nÓg descended like a rocket, its lethal metal batten narrowly missing the head of the celebrated actor and before hitting the stage with an impact that was heard throughout the theatre. Years later an even more celebrated actor, hearing how close I came to killing his fellow-player, lamented that I had 'missed my chance'.

But the show went on without loss of life and I enjoyed every moment of my weeks in the Queen's. Con obviously stayed out of my way as much as possible: a stranger would never have guessed from our eye-contact that we were father and son.)

THE ECONOMIC catastrophe of the Fifties affected the people of Ireland in many different ways. As ever, the well-to-do were largely insulated against any sudden drop in their standard of living while, at the other end of the scale, the poor were wide-open to poverty, desperation and unemployment. Towards—but not at—the bottom of the heap were many strong-minded working-class fathers and mothers who worked hard and lived sensibly, denying themselves in order to shelter their children from the down-turn. I was among the lucky few who had such parents; for me the Fifties were a golden age.

It helped that I was also lucky at school at a time when the average national school teacher used a degree of physical violence that would land him in court today and instilled in many of my contemporaries a sense of school as a prison sentence with their fourteenth birthday as their release date. Mr Feeney was far from average and developed in me the love of school I knew would gladden the hearts of Con and Maisie. I was instinctively interested in everything he had to say, but I still looked forward to the games we played in the yard during the breaks. No odium was attached to being top or bottom of the class; outside the classroom it meant little or nothing. Terry Cooney and I were top of the class but we remained good friends. I was not the biggest or the strongest or the fastest—and certainly not the toughest—but I made the football and hurling teams and on Saturday mornings joined the others on the two-bus journey over to the Fifteen Acres in the Phoenix Park where we pulled on the coarse green and black jerseys and lined out against another primary school. One day a press photographer asked our trainer, Headmaster Devlin, to nominate a boy to be included in his newspaper's *Stars of the Future* series; more a nod to my performance in school than an expression of confidence in my future as a hurler, he chose me.

There was only one cloud in the sky. Shortly after making my first communion in 1953 I touched the communion wafer with my teeth. I believed literally what I had been told in the preparation for first confession: that any touching of the wafer was one of the most terrible sins against the Body and Blood of Christ, the Son of God. So overwhelmed was I by shock, guilt, shame and fear that I could not bring myself to mention it to the priest in confession and so I compounded my original sin with a string of sacrilegious confessions and communions for the following seven years.

Among the other teachings that I believed literally was the Last Day. Nobody knew when God would declare the End of the World—it might be hundreds of years or tens of seconds away—but it would happen: there would be all sorts of tempests and earthquakes and wars, and then God the Father would judge the living and the dead in open court, welcoming the pure into Heaven, sending the venial sinners to Purgatory for a period of purification, and damning the mortal sinners to an eternity of agony in the fires of Hell.

There could be no doubt as to what awaited me, especially on those nights when I feared that the End of the World had already begun, when I could hear a mighty tumult getting louder and louder as it approached, causing the very house to tremble as it arrived overhead. In fact I was hearing the sounds of a plane landing or taking off from nearby Collinstown Airport; but the interval between the first growing growls and the final fading into silence were clammy.

Eventually, inspired by a retreat priest at secondary school, I confessed everything, was congratulated for my courage rather than berated for my wickedness, and walked away, probably the happiest I have ever been or will ever be.

Why did it take me so long to see sense and safeguard my immortal soul? I can only guess that the initial panic was so awful that I instinctively tried to deny it, though there was little chance of erasing such a terror from my mind, not when I continued to go to confession and communion once a week.

Nor can I explain why I did not confess my terrible secret to Con and Maisie, who would have assured me that my touching of the wafer was an accident and consequently no sin at all. They would have urged me, for my own peace of mind, to make a good confession as soon as possible, Con accompanying me to the chapel to give me confidence. (If shame was a primary factor, it is interesting that the good confession took place a hundred miles from Cappagh Road and to a stranger I was unlikely ever to meet again.)

But if Con and Maisie were as carefully protective of me as I believe they were, why did they not notice the anguish on the face of their beloved son who, for seven years, trudged through the valley of the shadow of death? Because it was not written there. Of one thing I am certain: nobody around me had any idea one of the greatest sinners in the history of the church walked among them. Apart from those anxious moments in bed, where nobody could see me, I continued along the primrose path: I was as cheerful as ever at home, as attentive and hard-working at school, going to Croke Park and the Abbey panto with Con, playing games, collecting stamps and reading everything I could get my hands on, sleeping soundly when the fears faded and I nodded off.

How to explain such apparent equanimity in the face of what I believed would be eternal damnation unless I changed my ways? I can only surmise that Con and Maisie created in 262 Cappagh Road an environment of absolute loving care that was proof against the threats issued on behalf of an imagined regime that itself claimed to prize love above all else: I loved and trusted Con and Maisie more than I feared God the Father. Whatever the means, I was enabled to square the circle and live contentedly in circumstances that should have left me catatonic. And the world went on.

P. J. Bourke's of 64 Dame Street was Ireland's premier costumier and dress hire business. Con's cousin Jimmy was general manager and the costume departments upstairs were mainly staffed by other Bourke cousins, Peadar, Kotchie, Peggy and Patsy. In charge of dress wear was Brendan Nannetti, grandson of Joseph Nannetti (1851-1915) who had a successful career as a trade unionist and nationalist politician—President of the Dublin Trade Council, city councillor, Lord Mayor of Dublin, Home Rule MP—but who is remembered today for his encounter with Bloom in *Ulysses*. By the mid-Fifties Brendan, an elderly, very gentlemanly bachelor with a club foot, was no longer comfortable working alone and Lorcan, seeing the need for a more energetic presence, thought of Con. He was shrewd enough to know that, with his characteristic adaptability and pleasant personality, Con would fit the bill and, besides, it would be less demanding and more rewarding than painting. Con agreed to join Brendan Nannetti in dress wear with a view to taking over when Brendan retired.

It was an imaginative move for a house painter with no experience of dealing with customers, never mind fitting them for morning or evening wear, but I suspect it worked out even better than anybody anticipated. Brendan welcomed Con, who in next to no time was engaging customers with his easy charm and learning to gauge with a glance dimensions that would be confirmed by the tape. As Brendan quickly prepared for retirement the lion's share of the work was left to Con; but he was happy to take it on, so much so that when Brendan left, Con preferred to run the department by himself rather than look for an assistant who might not prove as congenial as Brendan.

Measuring people for suits may not sound like the most exciting employment—and I am sure there were moments of tedium and customers who were hard to stomach—but we must remember that in those days very few people owned their own dinner jackets: even those who regularly went to formal functions rented a suit on each occasion, providing Con with a wide variety of customers, from bankers to rugby players, professors to university students, politicians to actors. He enjoyed meeting new people and catching up with old friends: he revelled in a friendly joust with a politician or, his favourite of all, an exchange of gossip with actors and entertainers.

The move into Dame Street coincided with a brief revival of the Bourkes' involvement with theatrical production in Dublin in St Anthony's Theatre on Merchant's Quay. I cannot say for sure that Con was involved in the production of Jimmy's *Family Album*, which opened on 19 October 1955, but his contribution to Jimmy's *The Boys and Girls are Gone* (October 1956) was noticed in Terry O'Sullivan's 'Dubliner's Diary' in the *Evening Press,* which included a photograph of Con hanging a picture of his maternal grandfather [*Image 29*]. O'Sullivan admired the set and was informed by Jimmy that it was the work of Colbeard Ó Cearnaigh. It captures him as I remember him from those days: a handsome man, the right side of forty, smartly dressed, black hair sleeked back, smiling. (Although the smile is surprising in the circumstances: he generally assumed a semi-frown of seriousness when faced with a camera.)

Con also stage-managed Jimmy's dramatisation of Charles Kickham's *Knocknagow*, performed in March 1957, which I attended; I can still see Jimmy's younger brother Peadar getting the laughs as Barney 'Wattletoes' Broderick. The other production I recall was Boucicault's *Arrah-na-Pogue*. I cannot find a date for this production, which was probably later in 1957, but it must have felt like a last hurrah for Con and his Bourke cousins and anybody else who could recall earlier days in the Queen's and the Torch. My clearest memory is of the opening of Act II where the curtain goes up to reveal Shaun the Post, played by Lorcan, in the gloom of his prison cell, sitting at a table, his hands fettered. The melodramatic mood is suddenly shattered when Lorcan's ad-lib—*This is not the lord mayor's chain, you know*—brings the house down.

Why? Because when Robert Briscoe was elected first Jewish Lord Mayor of Dublin in 1956, his fellow Fianna Fáil counsellor, Lorcan Bourke, was appointed his deputy. As Briscoe seemed to spend most of his time visiting the U.S., Lorcan was forever in the papers performing mayoral duties and wearing the mayoral chain, with the result that many people thought he really was Lord Mayor, an error Lorcan made no effort to correct.

The last I can recall of this series was less of a family affair. When Jimmy's *Mrs Howard's Husband* ran for a week at the Gate in early 1959, the Gate craftsmen remained in charge of carpentry and electrics while Jimmy's own team were in charge of stage management and wardrobe, with properties in the hands of Colbeard Ó Cearnaigh, who was (unknown to me then) following in the footsteps of his father who had been properties man in the earliest days of the Abbey. The tune used during the performance was 'Down by the Liffeyside', here called 'Fish and Chips', and acknowledged as the work of Peadar Kearney.

P. J. Bourke's must often have struck Con as a pleasant change from dangling under a railway bridge over the Liffey or trying to keep warm while painting a soffit first thing on a March morning. Best of all, in dress wear he was effectively his own boss, entrusted by Lorcan (and his other cousins) to manage all matters related to dress wear. If he was busy, the time flew; in between customers he could read his paper without having to keep an eye out for the foreman.

Bourke's of Dame Street bought him back into the centre of the city he loved, in those pre-EEC days a relatively small and intimate city dominated by small business people whose primary objective was to make a living rather than a profit. I was always amazed at the number of people Con knew with varying degrees of intimacy, from a slight nod to a big wave to a crossing the road for a chat. How did he know such a person? From his days in theatres or cinemas or painting jobs or the likes. His was a generation when personal friendships were maintained with mutual favours, some hovering on the edge of legality. A man in need of paint would wonder if he knew anybody in the way of getting him a can. A man unsure he could afford to hire a dress suit for a dinner dance would be advised by a friend to drop into Bourke's and ask for Con Kearney. 'Mention my name and Con will look after you.'

As a regular purchaser of dress suits and shirts and accessories, Con was a valued client of suppliers who were anxious to retain his custom. In time, when I had begun to favour a slightly dishevelled bohemian dress, I was occasionally dragooned into these wholesale tailors to try on tweed jackets, one or two of which we took away, to be settled up for at a later date and in a manner that did not concern me. Of more interest to me, several of Con's old colleagues from his cinema days were now themselves managers and Con arranged that I would only have to ask for them and identify myself to be admitted free.

ANOTHER MARKER along the road of self-improvement was the Lambretta scooter: allowing for social or cultural inflation, today's equivalent of that scooter would be an expensive car. For Con (and the rest of us) it was much more than a step up from the bicycle; it was what he himself would have termed 'a cut above buttermilk', a crucial degree above the common-or-garden. So proud was he when he picked it up that, five minutes before I was expected from school—he had obviously taken the afternoon off—he began driving down the road to meet me. I immediately noticed the man on the scooter but thought no more about him until I got the impression that he was looking at me from behind the windshield. It crossed my mind … but no, that couldn't be. And yet …. Please god let it be true, let it be Daddy on a new scooter.

'Self-improvement' was not in my vocabulary. If I had some vague comprehension of a rising standard of living, I assumed this was in the nature of things, at least as far as we were concerned. By the time I was ten I had deduced that, while not badly off by the standards of Cappagh Road, we were significantly less well-off than those, most notably the Bourkes, who lived in private houses. I envied them those luxuries that were beyond my family—private motor cars, holidays away from home etc.—but not for long and never, not for half a second, would I have changed my family circumstances for theirs. We had been brought up (especially but not only by Con) to believe that, far from being inferior to others, including the more affluent, we were in many ways superior to them: we had inherited the Kearney name and the heroic legacy—military and musical—of Peadar Kearney whose fame would last as long as the people of Ireland stood to attention for their national anthem.

My submerged anxiety about the next life did not weaken my assumption that I would have a successful (if unspecified) career in this. Con and

Maisie could not afford such vague optimism and were forced to conclude that my only chance of transcending the limitations of working-class life was further education, which meant secondary school. In the mid-Fifties, when the costs—fees and expenses plus lost income—excluded most working-class boys, university must have seemed a very remote possibility; but a boy with a Leaving Certificate could expect the kind of white collar job (such as Junior Ex. in the Civil Service, a clerkship in a bank or an office job with prospects) that would in time enable him to buy a house of his own and maybe even a motor car.

If Con or Maisie ever mentioned anything along these lines, I would have nodded in agreement and returned to the matter in hand: playing football on the new green, swimming in the Cabra baths during the summer holidays, collecting stamps, serving mass as an altar boy, following my stars in the cinema, hoping Dublin would win the All-Ireland, listening to the radio—*Hospitals' Requests*, sport, serialisations of novels, plays on Sunday evenings—and reading, which generally meant the newspaper and English comics.

My appetite for reading was as material as my appetite for food. I read everything I could lay my hands on, settling for useless information when adventure was unavailable. For example, on the left centre page of the *Evening Herald* (which we got until the arrival of the Fianna Fáil-supporting *Evening Press* in 1954) there were every night two long columns listing the films being shown in the numerous suburban cinemas of Dublin. Every week there were three programme of two films, 'the big picture' and a support: Sunday, Monday to Wednesday, Thursday to Saturday. At any time during those years I could have told you what was showing in any of those cinemas any day of the week, even though the information was of no practical use to me.

In October 1955 Con brought home the first edition of the *Guinness Book of Records*, given to him by his friend Dessie Clarke, a traveller for Guinness (who later supplied us with various Guinness accessories, most notably the toucan lamps). By Christmas at the latest I would have been able to answer any question based on the information in the book, even though in most cases my understanding of the issues would have been slight to nil.

There were no books in the house and we were not members of the public library, the nearest branch of which was in Phibsborough. I recall being given three books by Uncle Kevin. The first was probably Booth Tarkington's *Penrod*, which must have proved too difficult because I recall nothing of it except the cover. The second was Mark Twain's *The Adventures of Tom Sawyer*, which I inscribed in pencil as 'A Christmas Gift 1955'. His most influential present was given on 2 June 1959, Wodehouse's *Carry On, Jeeves*, my introduction to a writer who remains a favourite.

It may seem odd that there were so few books in a house where reading was held in such high regard, odder still that Con's reading was almost entirely limited to the newspaper; but it must be borne in mind that books were expensive and that Con's constant activity—especially his night work on the Abbey pantomime—left little time for reading. The bright summer evenings he spent growing vegetables in the back garden, his free winter nights in the front room, the only room on the ground floor apart from the kitchen, which was, literally, the living room, where all family life was lived. When not listening to the radio, which was in those days almost as social an activity as watching television would become, he was involved with his children, playing games or helping with homework, mostly reading and writing.

There is no doubt that he enjoyed a good read. In the late Fifties I gave him a book I had picked up in a second-hand shop: *Tramp Royal* by Michael Bruce, about as 'English' a volume as could be imagined, in which the imperialist veteran of two world wars and a stint in the Rhodesian police recalled his mad-cap adventures as a tramp trader in Africa and South America. Con relished every page. Less surprising was the pleasure he derived from a book I gave him as a birthday present, *The Ragged Trousered Philanthropist* by Robert Tressell, the *nom de plume* of Irish-born Robert Noonan, an equally colourful traveller whose socialist account of the painting trade was a favourite of all literate house-painters, including Peadar Kearney and Brendan Behan.

Recalling these two episodes recently led me to wonder if there was another reason for Con's failure or refusal to indulge the pleasure of reading that went back to his own childhood. His father had been a great reader and collector of books. Is it possible that in the years of disappointment after the Civil War he was more inclined to escape into the privacy of his own reading than to take a more active part in the rearing and education of his sons? If Con's ideas of parenting were the opposite rather than an imitation of his father's, it would explain why he preferred to involve himself in the lives of his children instead of indulging his delight in isolated reading.

MANY YEARS later I asked Maisie if I could read before I went to school. She scowled incredulously, turning away as if unable to believe I had asked such a stupid question, then wheeling and proclaiming with characteristic emphasis that I could read *long before that*. She was old by then but still as bright as a button, especially in relation to the past. If anything was clouding her judgement, it was her loving pride in her only son but, allowing for a slight exaggeration, her claim was in line with my own misty memories and with family tradition. It was said, for example, that long before I went to school I insisted on having—as a kind of comforter—a sheet of paper and a pencil with which to scribble on it. (Even more prodigiously, my baby name for pencil was 'Homer', although not necessarily with a capital letter.) There was also the 1952 *Radio Fun Annual*, which would not have made much sense unless the recipient had some ability to read.

My aptitude for reading was encouraged. Most of my 'education' in O'Donoghue Street was distinctly oral—patriotic ballads and exemplary incidents from Irish history—but, all unknown to me, Con was imbuing me with his fervent belief that education was no burden to carry.

Con's interest in my homework was above that of the average Finglas father. I was as eager for his attention and approval as he was to stimulate my application, especially when I established myself as top of the class. He remained a private tutor: parent-teacher meetings had yet to be imagined in working-class Dublin and so he never met any of my teachers in Ballygall.

Which makes all the more unforgettable the nearest Maisie ever came to the school. It was during the brief 11.00 break and I was playing in the yard behind the school when one of the boys shouted that my mother was looking for me out at the gate. I tried to reassure myself that he had to be joking because such a thing had never happened before and now seemed highly improbable. But, try as I could, I failed to disregard what he had said and within the fissure of doubt there began to grow a terrifying fear that Maisie *was* at the gate, which could only mean that some terrible calamity had occurred, most likely the death—or at least the maiming—of Daddy or one of my sisters. I turned the corner of the school building hoping against hope to be the butt of a joke, my heart popping up into my mouth when I saw Maisie standing there. She was smiling, which I could only interpret as an attempt to disguise the appalling purpose of her presence until she could take me into her protective arms. 'What's wrong, Mammy?' 'There's nothing wrong, son.' Mammy still unable to break the bad news; me loath to go within hugging distance. And yet she was still smiling, taking her hand from behind her back and holding up a brown paper bag. 'I brought you something. Here.' Still wary, I reached out and she allowed me take the bag. 'Open it.'

It was a cream doughnut.

If I was offered such a confection today—even by a grandchild at a party—I would find it difficult not to recoil visibly from the saccharine bomb with its sugared sponge casing and payload splurge of squirted cream. Back in the frugal Fifties, my hands trembled as I held this sensory feast and even now my mouth waters at the memory of the whiff of the icing sugar and the taste of the egg-yellow cake moistened by the sweet white syrup of the cream. I never have and never will experience such gastronomic ecstasy, the delights of the confection multiplied by the dreadful imaginings that preceded it.

Nor did the pleasure cease when I wolfed down the doughnut and allowed Mammy to wipe the cream from the tip of my nose, thanking her, so grateful that I surprised myself and her by allowing her to hug me, not caring who was there behind my back to see it. No: the image of Mammy holding up the brown paper became and remains an emblem of her extravagant love.

I cannot imagine what a modern equivalent might be. Not even a box of the most expensive chocolates could provide such an eye-widening surprise, generate an equally thrilling aura of extravagance. Money was very scarce in those days: some of my friends came to school with miserable lunches, some with nothing at all. We were always well fed at home and Maisie treated us with her own confections—enormous fruit trifles, apple and blackberry tarts, stacks of pancakes—but nothing, not even at Christmas or birthdays, to stand the test of time like the cream doughnut.

I knew every penny counted because I was often sent to the shop for 'a pennyworth of thyme and parsley' and once or twice for 'a pennyworth of envelopes and notepaper'. One was grateful for the gift of a penny because it could buy a toffee bar or an ice-pop or a portion of sweets, twice as much as a halfpenny. We all knew that the closer you got to payday on Friday, the less money Maisie would have in her purse. Nor could we fail to note the welcome for the gas company man who came (once a month?) to empty the box in the meter which held the shillings. Rather than wait for the supply to cease before inserting another shilling, even frugal housewives like Maisie tended to remain in a little credit, partly to avoid the panic of running out of gas while cooking, partly as a form of saving because the man rebated the difference between the cost of the gas used and the amount in the box. Three or four shillings felt like manna from heaven—especially on a Thursday or a Friday—but Maisie's first task was to identify her 'lucky shilling', a kind of charm given to her on her wedding day and now marked with chalk before being conscripted to keep the gas flowing.

The 'lucky shilling' was always in the coin box, which suggests that Maisie was frequently down to her last bob but, strictly speaking, this was not the case: as already mentioned, some few pence had to kept to rescue *The Other* Mrs O'Neill till Friday.

NOBODY ON the Cappagh Road had a bank account. The only popular form of savings were the 'clubs' run by local shops in which people could build up credit in the weeks before Christmas. If major items had to be bought—furniture, say, or a radio—they were paid for by instalments, on what we called the Kathleen Mavourneen, a song that contained the line *It may be for years and it may be for ever.*

All sorts of families for all sorts of reasons must often have found themselves literally penniless—with no sign of the gasman—and we were there or thereabouts one afternoon in early summer waiting for Con to come home from work. There had been a first communion that day and several girls with their mothers had called to be admired and accept a hansel or gift of money. Some arcane process had decided which mothers should call on us with their little angels and, more important, which should not. The mothers who called were those who would expect to be visited by Maisie when one my sisters made her first communion. Such arrangements were crucial in such a community; how else could Maisie have been at her ease knowing that all the callers had called and all the money expended on them?

'Agh, Colbert, will you look at the cut of Imelda Murphy. She's like the wreck of the Hesperus.'

I went over to the window and saw a group of girls playing Beds across the road outside Murphy's. Imelda, who had made her first communion that morning, was back from her visiting and had obviously splurged her money on every kind of sweet, chocolate and toffee. The hair that been in glistening tubular ringlets at the altar was all over the place except where it was bound by toffee. The dress had lost its virginal gleam to sticky fingers and chocolate stains, and the white patent leather shoes were well scuffed from nudging the weighted polish tin along the path. And she was bored, now that the excitement and power of affluence had passed and she could anticipate the return from riches to raggedy normality.

Suddenly Maisie half-stood up. She had obviously got the wind of something and I followed her anxious stare across the road: Imelda and her fallen angel pals were in council, lifting their heads occasionally, always to look across in our direction. Maisie stood fully up and pulled back from the window. Making rudimentary attempts to tidy her hair and clean her nose, Imelda Murphy was marching across the green to 'visit' us, looking more brazen with every bedraggled step.

'Jesus, the little rip is coming up to our door and not a penny in the house.'

Rock-of-Sense me reminded Maisie that as Imelda was not accompanied by an adult, she should send her flying with a warning that she would tell her mother. Or, better still, not answer the door. But Maisie could not leave a child on the step, not even the little rip who, when Maisie opened the door, ensured her place in the Kearney family history with the immortal line: 'Me Mammy says am I nice.'

Maisie said she was only gorgeous and apologised for having so little to give her, it being Friday afternoon and so on. Having closed the door, she muttered something about the little bitch who had taken her last sixpence, but no regrets. When I asked her why she had given in to the little liar, she admitted she could not take it out on a child.

Con's attitude to money was more complex and was, like so much else about him, derived from his father, however obliquely. Peadar Kearney had—for a variety of reasons including illness and unemployment—failed to maintain his family in any kind of secure comfort, often depending on the dole, falling into debt and obliging his wife to work outside the home. As if driven to prevent a repetition, Con had an obvious dread of debt and worked as much as he could to ensure that his Maisie would never have to neglect her children in order to supplement his income. Money for him was a means to ends: food, shelter, modest creature comforts and, ultimately, education. He frequently warned his teenage children of the corruptive power of a commodity that could 'burn a hole in your pockets'. He worked overtime to provide for his family but he was never keen for us to take up summer jobs lest the little we earned would 'give us a taste for money' and undermine our determination to continue our education.

Economy rather than health led both Con and Maisie to give up smoking around the time we moved to Finglas. Not long afterwards, the Saturday nights with 'the boys' ceased, although I am not sure if there was a general dissolution or if Con's withdrawal was unilateral. He loved to chat over a pint but he never made any real friends in Finglas and would no more have gone into a pub alone than he would have considered drinking at home except with Christmas visitors.

Con's perspective was not the inevitable result of his early years; his brother Pearse emerged from their shared childhood with an attitude that appeared much more relaxed, seeming to epitomise the scriptural adage that sufficient unto the day were the evils thereof. I loved my happy-go-lucky uncle and he doted on his nephew. As if I had no maternal uncles, Pearse was simply Uncle: nonchalant, generous, amusing, as indulgent of others as he was of himself. In Inchicore we formed a bond that developed over the years: we both smiled at the sight of the other and, until I began working myself, I don't think we ever met without him 'slipping me a few bob'.

It was a fairly widespread custom in those days (when family gatherings were not as easily arranged as today) for close relations to give children small amounts of money. As a result, some relations were more warmly appreciated than others, in my case Pearse and my godfather Kevin Bourke.

I am reminded of a particular summer Sunday when we are all over in Pearse's house in Raheny. It is time to get the buses home and as the first goodbyes are heard, Pearse is heard from the living room: 'Hold on a minute till I see if I have anything for you.' I can still see him coming into the hall, changing his cigarette to his left hand in order to pull out from his right trousers pocket a pile of change that he distributes proportionately among me and my three sisters, me getting most.

Maisie and Con are on the garden path and when she sees what Pearse is doing, she whispers to Con: 'Have you got anything to give to the children?' Con checks his pocket, estimating what remains after the bus fares. 'Give them something anyway, Con, anything at all.' Which he duly did but not with his brother's spontaneous facility.

He lacked Maisie's instinctive largesse. It may be more accurate to say that he resisted such temptations on the grounds that he needed all he earned for his family. He admired Maisie's and Pearse's open-handedness but felt that working-class people would do better to spend their money on their own family. (When grandchildren came along, he relished the ability to spoil them.)

THE NEAREST they came to a row had money at its core. Afterwards, Maisie was willing to go along with my efforts to transform it into a funny incident but Con, more protective of his dignity when it came to money, was unable to see the joke. When I tried again, Maisie threw her eyes up to heaven in melodramatic contrition, while Con stared at both of us in only slightly exaggerated disbelief at our 'lack of pride'.

As far as I can recall, we were still living on Cappagh Road. It was coming up to Christmas and Maisie would have been looking forward to the Christmas box in his wage packet from Bourke's. It was Con's practice to hand over his wage packet 'unbaptised'—that is, not opened to buy a payday drink—and so he was in no position to answer with any certainty when, early the following week, Maisie asked if the extra money had been in the previous week's packet. He reminded her that she should know because she had opened it and presumably counted the contents. Which put poor Maisie in a pickle because, though an experienced penny-pincher, she could not say for sure whether she had or had not counted the money; all she knew was that the money had gone very quickly, so quickly that she found it hard to believe the Christmas box had been included. Which left Con in a very awkward position: though loath to question Maisie's management of money, he was appalled at the prospect of seeming to question Peggy Bourke's efficiency as a wages clerk. But as Maisie remained perplexed, there was nothing else for Con to do but find a moment alone with Peggy when he could broach the delicate matter. She double-checked: the Christmas box had been included. Mortified, Con apologised profusely. Peggy told him not to worry, that anybody could make a mistake.

It was a lunchtime Maisie never forgot. There was not a lot of conversation after Con's report of his meeting with Peggy. Maisie shuddered as she recalled: 'I can still hear the door banging as he went back to work.' Banging the door was as far as Con would ever go and well Maisie knew it. 'Oh, he was raging at me.'

I only saw them at odds twice. On both occasions it was in a pub after a funeral. Maisie, unused to such occasions and obviously merry on very little drink, was having too good a time to accept Con's signal that we should leave. When eventually she waved us away, telling us we could go if we wanted to, Con was almost undone with embarrassed concern for Maisie, turning to me and asking, 'What can I do?' 'Take it easy: let her finish her drink and then she'll come home with us.' Which is what happened. There was a flash of bewilderment from Maisie but no crisis, no exchange of words, and then we were on the way home in the car, pretending nothing had happened, knowing that all would be forgotten the following day. I felt sorry for both of them—for Maisie who only wanted to get away from it all for a few hours, for Con because he had been brought up to see as shameful the least loss of polite self-control by a woman with a glass in her hand.

But generally life was good and getting better. Among the many advantages of Bourke's were two weeks' paid summer holidays, which Con took in early August. There was no question of going anywhere on holidays; the nearest we came to that was when Maisie took us for a long day on the beach at Portmarnock.

I recall a bright summer morning, most likely a Monday, the first day of those paid holidays. Con was sitting on the front doorstep. As I edged past him to go in search of my pals, he gave me a coin that felt odd in my hand because it was obviously not the penny I had anticipated. To my delighted surprise it turned out to be a thrupenny bit, a fortune. Con smiled at my surprise, clearly delighted to be flush.

I can still see him on the doorstep, like a child on the first day of summer holidays, caught between relishing the sudden freedom and wondering how he will pass the vast interval before returning to school.

I HAD been lucky in my teachers in Ballygall. For the first few years there was Mick Feeney, who was relatively gentle and who, despite seeming ancient to us, had been on the panel of the Waterford hurling team that won the 1948 All Ireland; we were all sorry when he left to return to Waterford around 1955. Almost all teachers were from outside Dublin and some were inclined to see Dublin working-class boys as tenement low life; but by pure chance I escaped the worst of them and my love of school developed.

In September 1956, when the rest of our year proceeded as normal into sixth class, Terry Cooney and I were moved up into Mr Devlin's seventh class. He was the principal and he wanted to see what he could do with two boys rumoured to be very bright. To be promoted in such a way was pleasing for two reasons: it was a reward for exceptional ability, and it also meant avoiding Mr Watters, who had a reputation for eccentricity and who was subject to occasional rages in which he fulfilled his threat to rampage through the class 'like a roaring lion seeking whom he may devour'.

Mr Devlin was more temperate, more conventional, a gentle man. He took a great interest in the school teams, devoting most of his Saturday mornings to managing us over in the Phoenix Park. What I most enjoyed in his class was reading and writing English. I can still recall the pleasure of encountering 'The Village Schoolmaster', marvelling at Goldsmith's ability to compress brilliant scenes into memorable couplets. Mr Devlin also introduced us to Shakespeare, writing excerpts from Mark Antony's funeral oration on the board so that we could copy them down and learn them by heart. Shakespeare did not go in for snappy rhymes but I could pick up enough in the speech to be drawn into the drama. I was astonished at his brilliant use of irony, starting with a polite acknowledgment of Brutus as 'an honourable man' and repeating 'honourable' over the murdered body until it meant the opposite. Despite the touches of old-fashioned language, it was as good as anything I had seen in the cinema. And there was a bonus.

Whenever—to wash me or get me ready for bed—Con was about to remove my vest and reveal my puny white frame, he would pause and, altering his voice as if on a stage, declaim: 'If you have tears, prepare to shed them now'. I had no idea where this remark had come from until with widening eyes I watched Mr Devlin write the words on the board and could not wait for him to give the context, which was Mark Antony warning the people of the terrible sight that awaited them when he removed Caesar's mantle and revealed his mutilated body.

(Years later I would wonder what productive flourish embedded this quotation in Con's mind more than others he had heard while touring with Anew McMaster. Another favourite was Lear's 'how sharper than a serpent's tooth it is to have a thankless child'. This was never delivered as a reprimand to any of us, but always with a benevolent irony and invariably followed with a hug: it was impossible to be ungrateful to such a father.)

Between lessons Mr Devlin sought to prepare his pupils for the outside world. The very fortunate might have tradesmen fathers who could get them an apprenticeship; the more physically advanced might hope for a menial job in a local factory; several aspired no higher than a messenger boy's bike. The least advantaged were doomed to hang around for a couple of years before taking the boat to England. They spent the interval at prominent points in the village mastering the arts of the corner-boy: how to lean for long periods against a wall or a window, hands deep in pockets, spitting endless little fleck-balls of saliva, pausing only to jeer at those passing by and to laugh at their own wit. One or two morsels of Mr Devlin's advice lodged in my memory, most likely because they seemed so incongruously irrelevant to my situation. He emphasised the importance of a clean collar when applying for a job: the assumption was that where a good suit or a clean shirt were out of the question, a clean collar symbolised the aspiration to decent appearance and respect for one's betters. The other item of good counsel applied especially to those with red hair and warned against getting soaked. This taboo was to guard against rheumatic fever. If he mentioned the great plague of the age, TB, I have no memory of it, although there was a folk belief that, as with rheumatic fever, redheads were more at risk than others.

If there was a plan for me after Mr Devlin's class, it was never discussed in my presence. It was somehow assumed that I would not become an apprentice house painter or a messenger boy or depend on the magic of a clean collar to make my way in the world; that I was bright enough to pass the entrance exams for secondary schools and would, at the end of the year, try for the Dublin Corporation Scholarship, which would help pay the fees and extra costs. If I didn't get it, Con and Maisie would move heaven and earth to come up with the money. The nearest secondary school was St Vincent's, the Christian Brothers School in Glasnevin on the Finglas bus route. Terry Cooney was hoping to go there and I was attracted by its reputation for games and athletics; less appealing were stories of severe punishments meted out by the Brothers, sometimes—though this was hard to believe, even in that age of tough love—with the legs of chairs. Maybe this was the kind of exaggeration older boys used to frighten you; firm as ever in my belief that all manner of thing would be well, I decided to wait and see.

AND THEN there was something afoot, something that involved me but was being kept from me.

At a time when my sisters and I were known to be elsewhere, Mr Watters called to the house, introduced himself to Maisie and arranged to call again when Con was present so that he might discuss a proposal concerning me. As he drove away, a hundred eyes would have recognised the teacher and wondered what sort of trouble Colbert was in.

A few days later, at night when my sisters and I had been sent to bed, I recognised Mr Watters' voice at the hall door and then an indecipherable mumble from the front room. Convinced they were talking about me, I went out on the landing, not so much in the hope of hearing anything as to make Con come out and send me back into my bedroom with a promise to talk to me tomorrow.

Mr Watters was suggesting that I stay on for another year at primary school so that he could prepare me for various scholarship exams, one of them at the boarding school he himself had attended in Ballinasloe, St Joseph's College, Garbally Park.

No. That would mean reversing my 'promotion' by 'going back' for another year. It would also mean having Mr Watters as my teacher. Yes, my pals enjoyed the little plays he put on in the classroom but they were also terrified of his sudden furies. I had seen him in the yard barking at his boys, something Mr Feeney and Mr Devlin would never have done. He had no interest in hurling or football: once a year he turned up the day before the school sports and we all thought he made an awful fool of himself, doing the high jump as if he was in the Olympic Games. Then there were his eyes, which stuck out so much you thought they might pop at any moment. No, not for me. I'll settle for Vincent's, with or without the legs of chairs.

To my amazement, Con did not see things as clearly as I did. He was not exactly jumping over moons but neither did he dismiss the idea out of hand. He looked at me and shrugged. It was not a matter of life and death. It was only a year and I was in no hurry: I was younger than most others in the class. If I stayed on another year, I'd be back with my old class again, with Eamonn Russell and all the others. And in the brand-new school just down the road, a two-storey school with its own theatre and everything. And Mr Watters was no ordinary teacher: as well as writing Irish pantomimes, he had an M.A. from University College Dublin.

'So you think it's a good idea, Daddy?'

'I don't see what harm it would do to try it. But it's up to you, son. How would you feel about boarding school?'

That was the one aspect of the plan I couldn't easily dismiss. What I knew about boarding schools was derived from English stories and comics where the school was always a kind of castle, called something like Belchester, in which a group of chums had a wizard time solving problems and confounding cads and bullies. They always did the decent thing, which is why they never gave up and always won the race or the game in the dying seconds and celebrated with a midnight feast. I had read so much about them I could speak the language and would have no difficulty blending in with the other chaps.

It never crossed my mind that a boarding school in Galway might differ

significantly from those in English comics; nor, to my lasting embarrassment, can I remember wondering how I would manage without Con and
Maisie and my sisters while I was resting between adventures. Nor how they
would manage without me. I would be missed as any other member of such
a close family. They would all notice my absence about the house. Maisie
would miss her eldest, her only son. What would Croke Park be like for
Con when I was away? It would be many years before I began to imagine
how much it cost them—emotionally as well as financially—to gamble
immediate contentment on the chance of future achievement.

Or to appreciate the extraordinarily unlikely coincidence of purpose
that caused the dress wear assistant and the graduate teacher-author to make
common cause. I was only twelve at the time and never pressed Con on
his susceptibility to the proposed plan of campaign; but there is no doubt
that Con, with characteristic diplomacy, questioned Mr Watters as to why
a boarding school in Galway would serve me better than the Christian
Brothers in Glasnevin.

It was Mr Watters' firm conviction that not only would my prospects be
improved by boarding school, they would be seriously hampered by going
to a local Christian Brothers School. There was no tradition of secondary
education in Finglas and it would be asking a lot of a boy to concentrate on
his studies surrounded by primary school pals who were now earning enough
money to take girls to dances and the cinema. It is unlikely he compared the
types of education available in either institution, other than to suggest that
a boarding school boy had a better chance of getting to university.

Con was a realist and knew there were no guarantees. Yes, a Corporation
scholarship plus an entrance scholarship would open the door; but without
them there would be no boarding school. Mr Watters had been in the army
during the Emergency and knew that even the most likely plan needed a
back-up: I would sit for other secondary schools in Dublin. He also understood that money might be a problem and he was willing to help financially.
The son of Peadar Kearney declined the offer, politely but firmly: 'there is
no question of that.'

When I understood that Con favoured the extra year, I dropped my
objections and decided to live with my reservations.

There must have been further meetings with Mr Watters because more
details of the plan emerged, the most striking of which was the fortnight I

would spend in Spiddal in the Connemara Gaeltacht to improve my Irish and acquire a *blas* or native speaker accent.

Mr Watters' thinking was almost entirely pedagogical—an improvement in my Irish would mean higher marks in the exams to come—but had his intention been to copper-fasten Con's support, he could not have made a shrewder move. As a dyed-in-the-wool Dubliner, Con had an instinctive sense of superiority to 'country people', but an exception was made—if only in the abstract—for the noble inhabitants of those parts of the west coast who had preserved the ancient native language that had inspired the fight for Irish freedom. His own father had spent months on Tory Island off Donegal perfecting his Irish. Con regretted his own very limited command of the language and was ambitious that one or more of his children would achieve what had been denied him.

I was my father's son and had absorbed his reverence for the language. I knew from my copybooks that Connemara was far away on the west coast and, from what I had gathered from various pictorial sources, that it could be a very wild west indeed, more Indian than cowboy. There were enormous blue mountains beneath which black-shawled, scarlet-skirted women worked spinning wheels while ginger-haired boys drove turf-laden donkeys and men with gnarled faces rode the waves in flimsy canoes called 'currachs'.

I HAVE no clear memory of parting from my family nor the drive to Ballinasloe. I presume Mr Watters and his wife took me there in their car, the black Anglia ZH 6103. Una was a less forceful presence, gentler and more solicitous, a painter who had been a librarian in Phibsborough. The house in Ballinasloe, on the bank of the Royal Canal, was bigger and grander than it looked and the family could not have been more openly welcoming. Nor could they have seemed less like Mr Watters.

His father, known as Grandpop, had been wounded while fighting with the Connaught Rangers during World War I. Later he had been driver for a Free State deputy during the Civil War. At the time I believed that Peadar had taken the republican side but I was magnanimous enough to forgive Grandpop his political mistakes, presuming he had been subjected to the same false propaganda that had led Maisie's father to enlist. Of more immediate interest was his aviary in which I saw close-up for the first time roller canaries, goldfinches, bullfinches and assorted crossbreeds. His wife, Granny, was an elegant old lady who was a famous reader of cards.

Mr Watters' brother Tom was his opposite: always loosely cheerful and making no effort to conceal his country accent or his lack of interest in the 'higher' forms of literature, painting or music. His wife Bridie was the life and soul of the house, always laughing, always setting the table with wonderful meats and cakes which she, a former pastry cook, had made herself. There were two daughters, much younger than me and noticeably well-behaved, as seemed to befit their posh names, Georgina and Linda.

As soon as I had announced the following morning that I was going up to the village to send some postcards, I realised I had said more than I had intended. The faces around me expressed a range of emotions from amazement to amusement. Hooting with friendly laughter, Bridie explained that while Ballinasloe was not quite as big as Dublin, it was a town and definitely not a village, the distinction being of importance to the people who lived in it.

The few days in Ballinasloe were filled with new experiences, notably fishing the Suck for trout and pike. This was very different from trying to catch gudgeon in the canal. The men were expert anglers, although Una was considered the best of all. They had a range of rods and lures and the use of a boat.

But Ballinasloe was only halfway. I remember flashes of the second stage in Mr Watters' car as merrily boisterous, mostly because he was acting the fool to entertain Georgina and Linda. I kept looking out the windows, too much an outsider to partake in the family fun.

Even I had noticed the difference between the large billiard-table grasslands of Leinster and the increasingly rock-strewn fields west of the Shannon but I was unprepared for the vista beyond Galway city. On our left was the expanse of Galway Bay with the hills of Clare to the south and off to the west—intermittently—the legendary Aran Islands, which I was seeing with my own two eyes. The land either side of the road looked like the aftermath of a volcanic eruption: behind the trees and thorn bushes— gnarled and cringing before the Atlantic gales—was a chaotic patchwork of tiny garden-sized fields enclosed by stone walls, so small you wondered if the walls were made not to define the fields but as a means of stacking the stones that had been cleared from them.

In those days Connemara—overwhelmingly poor, remote, sparsely populated and underdeveloped—began after Bearna, between which and Spiddal there were hardly two dozen roadside dwellings, mostly thatched cottages. About half a mile before Spiddal we turned right and bounced up a *boreen*—narrower and twistier and rockier than anything I had ever experienced—until we stopped at a surprisingly fine two-storey house. Standing at the door was a woman with a tea-towel who had heard the sounds of the car in low gear and now welcomed us enthusiastically. I would get to know her as Peig Ní Dhomhnaill, the *bean a' tí*. From the moment she opened her mouth I could not help admiring her Irish; I didn't always understand her but the language she spoke was exotically rich and musical and, especially when she spoke to me, crystal clear.

As Peig and Mr Watters chatted away, I became more and more impatient and had I not been mindful 'to behave myself and watch my manners' I would have opened my suitcase, pulled out my swimming togs and towel, excused myself and run down towards the sea; but being a good boy I waited until Peig got her younger sister Cáit to show me to my bedroom and then I pulled out my togs and towel, ran down the stairs, said *go raibh maith agaibh agus slán* to the Watters and trotted off in the general direction of Galway Bay.

My two weeks in Spiddal were everything I had hoped for and more. Living within walking distance of the sea meant I could at my whim indulge a pleasure which, at home, I was lucky to experience once or twice a year and which involved long bus journeys to Dollymount or Portmarnock. The morning lessons at the *coláiste* were more fun than anything else: I was surprised to find that my Irish was as good as anybody's in the class and wild horses would not have held me back from the strange pleasure of sharing a classroom with girls. I welcomed the chance to improve my Irish and—if only unconsciously—was grateful that my attendance changed the classification of these two weeks from 'pure holiday' to 'educational'.

(Working-class families did not 'go on holidays'. I could not have blamed my sister Maura, a mere two years younger than me, if she felt short-changed; had the situations been reversed, I would have resented her gallivanting in foreign parts while I was stuck at home.)

We learned Irish songs and Irish dancing and I surprised myself by being among the first up at *céilí* dancing, although I would not have been quite so quick if any of my Finglas pals had been watching.

As well as picking up some vernacular Irish and learning to mimic the local accent, I also had my first opportunity to study boys and girls of my own age who were not working class. Most of them were from towns in the west of Ireland, the sons and daughters of shopkeepers and farmers, civil servants, doctors, solicitors, teachers—in other words, people I had

111

been conditioned to see as different from me, rich people with purchase houses and cars who went away on holidays. I had never considered them better than us—if anything, the reverse—but I could not deny the social advantages their economic superiority gave them.

I was therefore surprised, relieved and delighted to discover that I made friends among the boys exactly as I would have done at home. Told I was from Dublin, most responded with an unintelligible phrase including the word *Doooblin*. I thought it odd that country boys should even raise the question of accents—not to mind their hopeless attempts to imitate mine—but I quickly learned that this was merely by way of greeting and, after all, this was Irish college and not Croke Park. For reasons I had hardly begun even to suspect, I enjoyed the novelty of palling around with girls. It was not because they were girls—I was the only brother of three younger sisters—but because they were my own age and because nobody called you a sissy for talking to them about most of the things you'd talk to boys about.

My introduction to the middle classes would have been a picnic had it not been for the minefield that was mealtime. We were about eight *scoláirí* in the house and we took breakfast, dinner and tea at a large table in the dining room. I have no memory of the food but can still see the looks and gestures of three convent school girls who, like theologians of the Holy Office, handed down detailed judgments on the morality of eating and drinking, anathematising the slightest infractions. So ignorant was I of the existence of this chapter in the encyclopedia of good manners—how to sit down on a chair, which knife to use for what, how to spoon soup, apply condiments, take butter from the dish, drink tea—that for the first week I lived in terror of being exposed as 'ignorant', which for them was a technical term suggesting 'untouchable in polite society'. My life in the dining room was lived at a lag of one anxious second behind the others, my eyes darting left and right to ensure I did nothing that might attract the ire of the Daughters of St Louis.

I was happy to get home. The otherworld had been full of fun and new pleasures but it was not home. It was difficult to find words for what I had missed when away from Con and Maisie and my sisters; but there was no doubting the inner warmth I felt to be back with them again. In those days absence was absence: there were no phone calls of any kind, least of all the constant mobile communication between today's parents and children. The postal service was much better, guaranteeing the delivery of cards and letters within a couple of days, but texts still meant books prescribed by educational authorities.

I imagine Con and Maisie missed me more than I missed them, being more anxious for my wellbeing than I was myself. For them the two weeks in Spiddal were the first stage of a crusade to fulfil their hopes for me; the fact that I had so obviously enjoyed myself was a bonus, the best possible beginning to the campaign. And, unknown to them, my attitude to the Ballinasloe boarding school had changed.

Jimmy, the boy I was sharing the bedroom with, was everything I wished to be myself: older, taller, with blond hair and film-star looks and the kind of gentleness that comes from physical confidence and is especially attractive to girls. He was from Mayo; why had he gone to Garbally? Friends of his had gone before him and liked it. Did he? Yes: it was a good school for sports, especially for rugby and athletics. What about Gaelic football? Of course they played Gaelic, and hurling too, but rugby was his favourite.

I lay there in bed and thought this Garbally did not sound too bad at all. I got the impression that neither Jimmy nor any of his friends had needed scholarships, that their parents could afford to send them there and not worry about the costs; but the fact that they had rich parents was not their fault: if half the guys there were like Jimmy, Garbally would be fine.

AUGUST PASSED and the year in Mr Watters' class loomed. There was general agreement—between me and Con and Maisie and Mr Watters—that this would be no ordinary year, that if I was to have any chance of succeeding as we all hoped, I would have to concentrate on studying to the exclusion of almost everything else. The rest of the family could not be expected to walk on eggshells and so, in order that I might be able to study undisturbed, Con and Maisie installed a gas fire in their bedroom beside which I would spend most of the time between school and sleep. It was a severe regime for a twelve-year-old but, far from resenting or kicking against it, I embraced my monastic solitude.

The period between September 1957 and June 1958 was a chain reaction of mental explosions the likes of which my brain would never experience again. It was like being conducted by a wizard through the evolution of western civilisation at the speed of light.

(Many years later, in 1974, I decided to pass a wet afternoon by going to see the film *Zardoz*. Knowing next to nothing about science fiction, I was more interested in the musical motif—from Beethoven's *Seventh Symphony*—than in the plot until, at the very end, a baby is being programmed with all human wisdom, all the poetry of all languages, including Rafteri's 'Cill Aodáin', and I was immediately reminded of that year in Mr Watters' class when I only had to hear something once—a word, a title, a theorem, a list of towns in a county—to absorb it effortlessly.)

I still played with my pals in the yard, still headed over on Saturday mornings to the Fifteen Acres, still went with Con to Croke Park and to the Abbey panto. The only change my sisters would have seen in me was that instead of going out after school, I made my way upstairs to my desk beside the gas fire.

Or maybe they could see that I was a boy possessed by a new spirit for which none of us had a name. Maybe they could almost hear the turmoil in my head as it struggled to control the storm generated by the new teacher who lived up beyond Cappagh Hospital.

THERE WAS no subject he could not present as fascinating, or that's the way it seemed to me, whatever about the other boys at the back of the class. An Irish poem—'Fáilte don Éan' is the one that springs to mind—was not an account of an occasion from the distant past in a language that was frequently obscure; it was a drama that happened just outside the classroom, featuring a lead actor with an intriguing story to tell, a setting such as we had often seen, a supporting cast of recognisable characters, all produced by a verse that quickly made clear sense and resounded in the memory. None of this had occurred to you before he had begun his analysis; afterwards you were convinced that not only was he perfectly right but also that you could learn this method and use it to increase the pleasure of other poems.

He could make the most unlikely subjects irresistible, subjects that have tortured students since schooling began: geometry, for example, and grammar. One minute he was explaining that geometry (from the Greek for 'land measurement') had been developed to measure portions of land in order to establish precisely who owned what; before you knew it, triangles were your favourite toys. Grammar (from the Greek meaning 'the art of writing') was a system of rules to help us write in a clear, unambiguous and conventional manner so as to be instantly understood by others. Few ever delighted in grammar as I did, and fewer still ever admitted the degree of pleasure they took in what, in the bitter experience of millions of healthy youngsters through the ages, was the dullest exercise imposed on them in the course of their education.

It was as if Mr Watters had inducted me into a priestly caste that had its own arcane language and wielded enormous power over those who could not tell the difference between a main and a subordinate clause or who, even as they spoke the phrase 'I will have eaten' were totally unaware that they had used the first person singular of the auxiliary verb 'to be' followed by the infinitive of the verb 'to have' followed by the past participle of the verb 'to eat' in order to form the future perfect of the verb 'to eat'.

I had always liked writing compositions but Mr Watters—himself a prize-winning writer—brought a new technical awareness to what had been spontaneous expression. As somebody who had taken sums down wrong from the board in Mr Feeney's class, I appreciated Mr Watters' three rules when faced with an examination answer. *Read the question. Read the question. Read the question.* I also liked his reasoning: as nobody is absolutely calm in the exam hall, we need a technique to help us avoid silly errors; after all, nobody asked to write about a cold winter deserves any credit for writing about a hot summer.

Not that his classroom had anything of the crammer about it. He volunteered our class to sing *Missa de Angelis* in Latin at the opening ceremony of our new school. It was an outrageous undertaking for a teacher, who had a rudimentary knowledge of music and no vocal abilities of his own, to attempt with a group of youngsters unable to read music and whose knowledge of Latin consisted of what they might recognise from Sunday mass.

(Why did he offer to undertake such a task? Probably because he relished the challenge, and the opportunity to show that he, alone of all the teachers, could rise to the occasion. He would also have believed that the effort to learn the words and music would benefit the boys, boost their confidence and, not least, add variety to the curriculum. It was not an act of religious piety as commonly understood. He was anything but a conventional Catholic, not even bothering to attend mass regularly, as his wife Una did. This was a dangerous indulgence for a primary school teacher and he was well aware that were he to express his own thoughts during the Christian Doctrine class, he would leave the parish priest no alternative but to fire him. Probably with this in mind, he behaved differently while teaching the Catechism, was obviously more violent and less interesting as he pretended to toe a line not his own. Our performance of the *Missa de Angelis* would safeguard his standing, not only with the local clergy but also with Archbishop John Charles McQuaid, who performed the opening ceremony.)

Equally ambitious was his introduction of Shakespeare. One day he arrived in with a huge pile of books, which he distributed, explaining that he was renting them to us for threepence a year and would be grateful if we could bring in the money as soon as our parents could manage it. The book was *The Merchant of Venice*. I had seen several plays on the stage and was not impressed with the way this opened; but in next to no time I was engrossed. I remember the mental gear-change as I heard him describe Bassanio and his pals as inexperienced young men-about-town, who had never done a day's work in their lives but wanted people to think they knew everything. Not like Portia, who somehow had acquired more sense than all the men put together: maybe she had to grow up very fast when she learned the terms of her father's will. As for poor Shylock, you could never decide whether you were for or against him, but neither were you meant to: at the best plays you're never absolutely sure how you feel because the best characters, like human beings, are neither absolutely good nor absolutely bad. Even the Prince of Morocco became more interesting if you thought about him as the heavyweight champion of the world, big, black, beautiful and well-intentioned, but hardly equipped mentally to be the husband of a bright spark like Portia.

He also introduced us to Latin, using *Scalae Primae*, a first Latin reader, copies of which he bought himself and rented out to us for a few pence a year. I was spellbound as he resolved the mysteries of Latin sentences. *Polyphemus unum oculum in media fronte habebat.* Polyphemus one eye in the middle of his forehead had. I could even detect a mathematical lucidity in the strange syntax. *Bellum semper Britannis gratum fuit.* War always to the British pleasing was. Maybe so; but it did not prevent the Romans from trouncing them. Somebody—possibly me—must have smiled to learn that there was somebody who managed to beat the old enemy because Mr Watters held up his hand, told us to hold on a minute, to remember that at this stage the English had not even arrived in what they would call England, that the British were Celts, like the Welsh and the Scots and ourselves.

It was not that he was anti-Irish; a man who wrote poetry in Irish could hardly be. There was much about Ireland he admired, especially the poets and the monks who produced the illuminated manuscripts. But he seemed to enjoy picking holes in our belief that Ireland was a good Catholic country whose misfortune it was to be oppressed for hundreds of years by the wicked English who, though always in the wrong, were always lucky. You got the impression from him that Ireland and the Irish were not as perfectly virtuous as many of the Irish were inclined to believe, 'believe' being the operative word, because these people preferred not to use whatever critical faculties they had but to operate on the principle that what was good enough for my father is good enough for me. That was nothing but tribalism and 'left us as much in the dark as the fuzzy-wuzzies in Africa.'

On the other hand, there was the pageant he wrote in English for our Christmas concert in which the dying Cuchulain foresaw the future history of Ireland culminating in the proclamation of the republic outside the GPO on Easter Monday 1916.

I played Cuchulain and before the performance I overheard Mr Watters telling somebody that I was the only one he could rely on to learn by heart the hundred or so lines of blank verse the part demanded. I understood this slight denigration of my acting talents as an attempt to counter the general sense that I was his 'favourite' and took no offence.

Aware of his theatrical experience, Mr Watters invited Con to stage-manage and light the show and one afternoon Con arrived in the new hall just as we were about to rehearse. As soon as Con appeared, Mr Watters assumed his military manner and barked as us to stand silently in line while he discussed some business with Mr Kearney. We had all witnessed his rages at any sign of indiscipline—especially in the presence of outsiders—and resigned ourselves to at least five minutes of stationary boredom. But there are some boys who are impervious to sustained regulation—no matter if the sanction was public execution—and in that regard the star of our class was Dermo Harvey. Within a couple of minutes Dermo had fidgeted enough to provoke his neighbour into half-whispering a reply. At far as Mr Watters was concerned, this was nothing short of mutiny. Instantly excusing himself to Con, he turned on his heel and strode towards us. We all flinched, especially those who like me were standing near Dermo. But to our relief he was not bearing down on us. Instead, the spin of his heel had pointed him in the direction of Enda Birmingham, possibly the quietest boy in the class, certainly the least boisterous, a chubby young fellow with a big white face and roundy glasses behind which lurked his drowsy eyes as if in retreat from the rough and tumble of life. Those drowsy eyes had not awoken to the threat before Mr Watters clattered him full force across the jaw, the reverberation of the smack echoing off the walls followed by the sound of Enda's glasses sliding a good ten yards across the polished wooden floor.

The rest of us counted our blessings, feeling sorry for poor Enda but simultaneously grateful that we had not drawn the short straw, that our cheeks were not stinging, our lips quivering in shock. Eight years of national school had inured us to corporal punishment.

No, the only person in the hall who was shocked was Con. I can still see him flinch as he gauged the menace in Mr Watters' quick march towards a row of children, his unconcealable horror as, eyes averted, he heard the impact of the wallop, then watched Enda knocked sideways by the blow.

Nor did he ever fully get over the shock. The mere mention of the incident in later years was enough to make him recoil with a loud intake of breath and shake his head slowly, as if still incapable of believing a grown man could strike a child so savagely.

Which is why I let a year or two go by before telling him that I too had felt the heavy hand of an angry Mr Watters. Again the explosion was probably aggravated by the presence of 'an outsider'.

One afternoon a knock came to the classroom door. Mr Watters answered it and, before stepping outside, commanded silence. Mine was the front desk of the row farthest from the corridor and I leaned out to see who had knocked. I was so absorbed by curiosity that I did not notice Eddie Barry—in the front desk of the row beside me—take his water pistol from his school bag and drench me. So intent was I on revenge as I rooted in my bag for my water pistol that neither did I notice that Mr Watters had re-entered the classroom and could see me squirting at Eddie. The same horror. The same rasp of shoe leather on floor. The same explosion, this time sending me on a journey into space where stars and planets sparkled and spun in front of a purple cyclorama. Worse than the pain was the fear that I would be unable to hold back the tears and reveal myself as a cry-baby in front of my pals.

By the following day I had convinced myself that, though I would not have welcomed a repeat, the clatter—and my ability to endure it with quivering lip and merely moistened eyes—had preserved my status as 'one of the boys' by proving, however painfully, that there were limits to the privileges that went with being 'top of the class'. I cannot recall ever nursing a resentment and soon I was happy to be enthralled again by the miracle of his teaching.

Not that I was always amenable to his wishes. I still have the copy of *The Coral Island* by R. M. Ballantyne, my award for coming first in the class in the Christmas exams. It would be slightly inaccurate to say 'which he awarded me'. Displayed on his desk were at least half a dozen books he had bought with his own money. I was called up to take first pick but, even as I scanned the titles, I was aware that he was directing my attention to one particular book, *Vanity Fair* by William Makepeace Thackeray. I had heard of it as a classic of English literature, which is to say, one of those books I wanted to admire so that I could congratulate myself on having 'excellent taste'. And there is no doubt I would have accepted his direction had my eye not fallen on *The Coral Island*. This adventure story had been serialised weekly on Radio Éireann and I had been glued to the set, imagining myself the companion of Ralph and Jack and Peterkin as we were shipwrecked and forced to survive on a tropical island, with the crashing of waves forever in the background and one adventure following another. The happiness and success of the conclusion was little consolation for the loss of my imaginary existence among the warring natives and dastardly pirates.

It may be that such radio serials as *The Coral Island* marked the end of the period in which I preferred to listen to enactments of novels rather than bring them to life in the theatre of my mind. Whatever the reason, my hand went out beyond *Vanity Fair* towards *The Coral Island* ... only to be arrested by an advisory clearing of Mr Watters' throat. I glanced up to receive ocular direction back to *Vanity Fair*, but on this occasion not even the wizard could bend my will to his. I made my own choice and though he could not completely conceal his disappointment as he inscribed it, I had no regrets.

Irrespective of any misgivings I might have had about Mr Watters and the rather eccentric impression he gave to the outside world, I never faltered in my wonder at his omniscience, my admiration of his skills as a teacher or my commitment to his strategy. As well as guiding me through the gates to an endless vista of knowledge, he stressed the importance of order in a way that appealed to my fondness of neatness and control. We planned for the scholarship examinations as if for a military assault: clear understanding of objective and means, constant rehearsal until all phases of the action became second nature, surprise openings to impress the examiners, fall-back positions in case of unexpected reversals.

THE CLOSER we got to D-Day, the more my world shrank into subjects, questions and answers. Maisie could fuss over me and Con could encourage me by letting me know how proud he was of my efforts; but neither could

119

actually partake in the process, as Con had once done with my sums and my spellings and, inevitably, I began to spend more time in that sphere of influence dominated by Mr Watters. I never felt that my commitment to Mr Watters was in conflict with my absolute loyalty to Con and Maisie, knowing that they understood it to be a necessary part of a campaign that they supported. But, given my immersion in study, I was perhaps not the most sensitive observer of others. If I never stopped talking about Mr Watters, it would have been easier for Maisie to bear because this new man in my life was no threat to her status as undisputed mother; but it is hard to imagine that Con did not feel an occasional twinge of resentment.

It is true that increasingly I came to look upon Mr Watters as the authority in matters of high culture; but I would never have sought his advice on my domestic or social life. I held his mind in the highest regard but never felt—or could imagine myself feeling—affection for him, certainly nothing like the suffusions of warm love that frequently overwhelmed me in the presence—or sometimes even at the thought—of Maisie and Con.

Some years ago a colleague spoke of him as a kind of father-figure to me. That he was a major influence on my life is indisputable. Who knows what direction it would have taken had I gone to St Vincent's with Terry Cooney and made a career in commerce? Some relations could not understand why I chose to do Arts at university when I could have chosen the more lucrative paths of Law or Medicine. To Mr Watters goes most of the credit or the blame for my decision to become a Modern English academic. He was the best teacher I have ever come across at any level and his brilliantly individual reading of English literature gave me an advantage over fellow-students whose opinions had been formed along more conventional lines. In time we became friends; it may even be that during my university student days I was the closest he had to a male friend and that he shared more of his private life with me—especially after the death of his wife in 1965—than with the few fellow-writers he occasionally associated with. I certainly championed his work against what I believed was the shortsightedness of popular opinion. (In 2014, fifty years after its first publication, I felt *faoi geasa* to accept an invitation to translate his 'Aifreann na Marbh', a long verse requiem for the victims of the Hiroshima bomb, into English.)

But much as I admired, respected and was grateful to him, he was never a father figure. Con was my father and the emotional bond between us left no scope for parallel or symbolic figures. Had I ever suspected a conflict within myself or unhappiness in Con, I would have done whatever it took to re-stabilise our primal relationship. Had I not been assured of Con's full support for the Garbally campaign, I would not have undertaken it.

Did Mr Watters, childless himself, ever see me as a son-figure? While I was still a student at UCD he inscribed one of his books for me beneath the printed dedication: *Is fós le dán dhá líne / Do Cholbert mac m'ealaíne* [And also with a two-line poem / To Colbert the son of my art]. To a casual reader this may seem a simple answer to the question, but not to those who knew him well.

He was not an impulsive man. *Read the question. Read the question. Read the question.* Nor was he emotional. *Sentiment clouds the understanding.* He was obsessed with precision—*the facts, sonny, just give me the facts*—and reserved his deepest contempt for careless writing: *there's nothing worse than a fool with a pen.* The inscription was no spur-of-the-moment scribble and it said exactly what he intended. Which was that as well as being the *mac léinn* (the Irish for 'student', literally 'son of learning') in whose progress he took a special interest, I was also his apprentice in the art of literary composition. (I wrote short stories and verse at the time, which he always encouraged and read with extraordinarily close attention. Looking back, I conclude that his highest hope was that I, having graduated, would emerge as a poet.) We became close, much closer than the average student/apprentice and teacher/craftsman; but there was, at least to my way of thinking, such a focus on educational and cultural matters and such an absence of emotional entanglement as to rule out what could be termed a father-son relationship.

He admired Con and Maisie, often remarking how lucky I was with my unselfishly devoted parents. I think he would have liked to establish a casual friendship with them but if he tried, he never came close to succeeding. He was too dedicated to the life of the mind ever to manage an equal social relationship with Con who, for his part, was a working-class family man shrewd enough to see that all he would ever have in common with Mr Watters was me.

It strikes me now that Con always had reservations about him, some of which may even have preceded his attack on Enda Birmingham, vague reservations based on his unconventional manner. His decision to bite his tongue—after the attack on Enda and more especially as he watched the increasing influence of Mr Watters on my life—cannot have been easy; but his overriding objective was that I would receive the best education possible and if that meant a close relationship with Mr Watters, that was a cost he would bear.

The relationship with Maisie was easier. She accepted her situation more readily than Con, had been relieved to leave school at fourteen with no regrets or thwarted ambitions. She was a working-class woman of her time, happy to run the family home and leave the public sphere to her husband. Mr Watters was like nobody she had ever known in her life and must have struck her as not quite normal, especially later on. But none of that mattered: he was exerting himself on her son's behalf and she reciprocated with large-hearted gratitude and hospitality.

It was different with Mr Watters' wife Una. Though a gifted painter and illustrator, there was nothing eccentric or 'arty' about her: she could present herself to Con and Maisie as a housewife, albeit middle class, so that they were both much more at ease in her company and both were fond of Una in a way they never were of her husband.

I think of him as a great spirit, a master of many arts from poetry to chess to carpentry, who, by the early Sixties seemed to have established a perfect studio up at Cappagh Cross with Una. His novel *Murder in Three Moves* had been published in 1960 and he had retired from teaching the following year to write full-time. Success followed success: his Irish novel *L'Attaque* in 1962, his long poem *The Week-End of Dermot and Grace* and his Irish collection *Lux Aeterna* (which included the Hiroshima mass) in 1964. Early in 1965 Una won the Arts Council Award for her design, the sword of light, which was used as the national emblem of the 50th anniversary of the 1916 Rising.

Unfortunately, as the award arrived at Cappagh Cross, Una was being buried in Ballinasloe. He never fully recovered from the sudden blow of her early death. No matter how hard he tried to disguise it, the latter part of his life must have been a bitter disappointment. Like the poor scholar in the poem he loved to quote, he escaped into an otherworld of signs and symbols, living in strange habitations. Few months have passed without his ghost flitting across my path.

> *And once, in winter, on the causeway chill*
> *Where home through flooded fields foot-travellers go,*
> *Have I not pass'd thee on the wooden bridge,*
> *Wrapt in thy cloak and battling with the snow,*

Thy face tow'rd Hinksey and its wintry ridge?
And thou has climb'd the hill,
And gain'd the white brow of the Cumner range;
Turn'd once to watch, while thick the snowflakes fall,
The line of festal light in Christ-Church hall—
Then sought thy straw in some sequester'd grange.

He saw himself primarily as a poet which, because it took up so much of his time, led him to resent the hours in the classroom at which he excelled. From the time I encountered him until 1961, he taught from half-nine until three and then, often exhausted, he returned to Cappagh Cross where he might unwind by gardening or DIY: then, after a brief post-prandial snooze, he was down to work, reading and writing, until the early hours of the morning; which meant that he began most teaching days exhausted. By the time I began to visit him he had stopped listening to classical music and would soon stop composing chess problems for the same reason: they took up too much of the time and energy he needed for writing. He had also to a great extent given up socialising with friends he had made in the training college and in literary Dublin. He was driven by a necessity—he would always use the Greek word ἀνάγκη—to fulfil himself as a writer, which involved coming home from school, and writing and reading and editing and submitting for publication and competition novels, plays and poems in English and Irish, forfeiting a decent night's sleep before driving down the road for another day in the classroom. There was not enough time for what he wanted to do, never mind for recreational socialising.

What saved him from running himself into the ground were the holidays he spent in his parents' house in Ballinasloe and fishing on the Suck. Not that there was any break from writing: when the others had gone to bed tired and happy after a day on the river and one of Bridie's substantial meals, he was at the table with his cigarettes, his paper and his pen.

It is hardly surprising that a man living such a life had lost the art of casual conversation. Though he was expert at putting colloquialisms into the mouths of fictional characters, there was often something slightly false about the way he used them himself. Apart from the time he spent in the staff room, where some of the other teachers found him arrogant and unsympathetic, he did not mix much with other men or women. It hardly mattered that he was so abstemious that two bottles of stout made him giddy; had he enjoyed drinking (and a capacity closer to the national average) he would have abandoned it as too demanding of his time. (He was a chain-smoker but that could be done alone and was widely valued as an aid to reflection and composition.) His language and his structures of thought were formed by day in the classroom teaching children and by night in the remoteness of his bungalow in Cappagh where he mingled with the greats of English literature and with some continentals, notably Dante.

AT THIRTEEN I was too young to realise just how much depended on the exams I sat at the end of the year for the Dublin Corporation Scholarship and for three schools, O'Connell's of North Richmond Street, Sandymount High School and Garbally. Consequently, although pleased with my achievements, I could not fully appreciate the joy that Con and Maisie demonstrated (and Mr Watters expressed in his more controlled way) when it became clear that with the Corporation Scholarship and the Garbally scholarship I would be leaving home and heading for Ballinasloe that September. Mr Watters' carefully planned campaign had succeeded and Con and Maisie were immensely proud that their son was, as Brendan Behan was later to declare, 'the first of his seed, breed or generation to attend a secondary school other than a Borstal institution'.

Despite the scholarships, the practical preparations of equipping me for life away from home with everything from blankets to football boots put a strain on their resources, even if it was one Con and Maisie were happy to bear. It also strained the equanimity of my sisters as they watched Maisie coming back from town with more and more of the items specified by the school, including new clothes of every description. I noted all of this but hardly showed enough concern for them. For me going away to school was, above all, a new adventure that included the prospect of living with new friends after my year of hermetical study.

There was an interval of some weeks between the beginnings of the primary and secondary school years and on his return from holidays in Ballinasloe, Mr Watters had a final surprise gift before I headed in the opposite direction: he opened the door into the secret world of Greek literature. On the first night he taught me (and I instantly learned) the Greek alphabet and then we proceeded to look at the first page of an old textbook, *Selections from Herodotus*. It was as if I had been admitted into a paradise he had been advertising for the previous year, a cultural treasury that contained the best that had been thought, done and written by the most gifted people who had ever walked the earth.

The first extract he read and translated and analysed was the story of how Arion—the greatest musician in the world who was returning from a financially successful Italian tour—had been kidnapped by pirates and escaped death with the help of a dolphin. Even to think of the text today is to remember every tiny detail, physical and emotional, of that night at the table before the fire in the front room of the bungalow at Cappagh Cross. So much so that when, on a visit to Athens many years later, I bought a packet of underpants on the label of which was written ΗΛΛ. ΚΑΤΑΣΚΕΥΗΣ (Greek under*clothes*), my mind instantly went back not to the ten years I spent studying Greek at school or university but to that night in the bungalow when, spellbound as I watched him decipher the exotic characters, I heard how the Corinthian sailors set out to rob Arion of his money, offering him the choice between drowning himself or being killed by them. Arion had one last request before he hurled himself into the sea: that they would allow him to perform a song in all his *clothes*—ἐν τῇ σκευῇ πάσῃ—presumably a reference to the special apparel the celebrated artist wore while performing. It was precisely the kind of detail Mr Watters, like Herodotus before him, would use to fix the scene in our memories. And how they succeeded! Almost sixty years later the label of my humble underpants recalled Mr Watters conjuring up the figure of Arion in his best bib and tucker.

WE MADE a mistake and, like a couple of other first years, arrived in Garbally a day early, driven down by Peadar Bourke. We were directed to the Junior Dormitory, a newish arrangement of four lines of beds each of which backed onto a partition, the inner two facing each other, the outer facing windows. Maisie flew into action, her last chance to mother me for some time, choosing the brightest section of the dormitory, checking all the nearby beds and mattresses to 'nab' the best for me: nothing but the best for her son. Con looked on, more pensive than proud, pondering my chances of survival in this strange and distant environment, constantly trying to banish such thoughts by asking me if I was alright, if I had everything I needed, reminding me to write as soon as I found my feet.

As arranged, when they got to the white gate they looked up, I waved to them from a dormitory window and they waved back. Maisie told me afterwards that she was crying and Con not far off.

A Garbally priest once told me that the boys who were least secure in their own homes were the most likely to moan and groan about conditions at school but I was in no position to know how accurate this was. A small minority were physically and temperamentally too delicate ever to relish a regime that was in some ways closer to a military academy than a secondary school. The majority, I imagine, tolerated it because they had been ordered by their parents to do so and this was a time when teenagers did as they were told. I was among the minority who actually enjoyed boarding school. I had that security the priest considered crucial and I also possessed two characteristics that were at least as important: I had recently been imbued with a genuine love of learning and I was passionately interested in sport. Of course I missed the warmth of family life, especially perhaps at mealtimes, but even then I was making and developing new friendships and it never occurred to me to want to leave.

As winter took a grip we tried to ward of the gloom by counting down the days—and eventually the hours and even minutes—to the Christmas 'vac'. But, oddly enough, there were moments when the dream of going home was clouded by fears that I would never again be at one with my family as I had been. As the Dublin train roared past Cabra there was a burst of panics. Would Con be there as he had promised in his letter? Would I recognise him? Or he me?

Imagine what Con felt when he saw his little thirteen-year-old struggle down onto the platform with his suitcase and then turn around and seem not to see him at all. I know exactly how I felt as I squinted up the platform and could not distinguish Con amid the alighting passengers. Unknown to him, I had recently discovered I was short-sighted but, controlling my rising anxiety, I walked on until suddenly there he was in front of me, dressed in his big black overcoat, his arms outstretched to greet me. I tried to run towards him but it was difficult with the suitcase and so I dropped it and crash-tackled him, burying my face in the thick black overcoat, wanting never to let him go again, not bothering to hold back the tears of joyful relief.

The house was smaller and—bright with a Christmas tree and decorations, the table set for dinner in front of a blazing fire—warmer in every way than the one I had left four months earlier in balmy September. The girls were dumb with curiosity as Maisie kept hugging me, only letting me go in order to rescue something in the kitchen. Then the questions came. What's it like? But what could I say? How could I possibly begin to give them any idea of life in that other world? A supplementary question was more easily answered.

'Would you like something to eat, son? Are you hungry?'

Faced with the tepid, tasteless school fare, I had often dreamt of such succulent steak, such mushy peas, such crisp dry chips and now I was tucking in vigorously until I noticed the wide-eyed amazement around me: they all stared at me as if witnessing a stage performance of 'the boy who can eat his weight in food in less than fifteen minutes'. When Maisie asked me if I would like some more and I, without looking up, simply nodded yes please, there were gasps from the girls and I could detect Con signalling to them not to express any surprise. I was back in heaven and would be for what would seem like all eternity because that night I would sleep in my own little bed in my own little room and there would be no prefect to keep an eye on me and, joy of joys, no bell to shatter my sleep the following morning and order me out onto a cold wintry floor.

The festive season over, I still had three weeks of freedom to enjoy. I was happy to do 'messages' for Con and Maisie in town because I was going there anyway to pore over the holdings in the many second-hand shops where I picked up books for a few pence. Most of them were novels or vaguely related to my studies but I was also willing to lay out a penny or two for books of no real interest to me apart from their beautiful late eighteenth-century binding, one of them in French, which I assumed I would read one day. I also went to the cinema several times a week, generally with a pass Con had got from old colleagues. I still had one or two friends from national school, but they were working now. As the weeks went by and my social life was largely with my own family, I began to contemplate the return to Garbally with growing equanimity.

Con was working days in Bourke's and nights in the Queen's on the Abbey pantomime where I sometimes went to keep him company. My tiny pocket diary suggests he spent a good deal of his free time with me, even playing table tennis on the front room table. That first vacation he took me over to show me off to his brother Pearse and to his Aunt Maggie, matriarch of the Bourkes.

In the fortnight between the re-opening of the primary schools and my return I spent a lot of the mornings at home with Maisie. I generally had a book or was listening to records or the radio while she got on with the housework, but somehow we always had a laugh.

The same interval meant that Mr Watters was back from Ballinasloe and inevitably, or so it seemed, I cycled up to the bungalow in Cappagh Cross, initially to report on my progress but gradually these visits developed into tutorials in which the topics included not merely my school reading but classics of English literature (most of which he had lent me), his own writing and, in time, my own efforts in verse and prose in which he always found more to praise than to question.

I can still picture the living room lit by a big fire, the walls illuminated by Una's paintings. She has cleared the dinner things away and he is stretched out in an armchair in a postprandial torpor, the lids down on his protruding eyes, the perpetual cigarette in hand, muttering an apology, something about needing to let the gastric juices digest the meal. On the table there is evidence of his own reading—Eliot's 1920 *Poems*, Dante, *Finnegans Wake*—or his chess problems, which were so much admired in *The Tablet*. Then suddenly he comes to and the air is filled with talk of writers and writing that I swallow whole without pausing to digest it. I cannot wait to make personal acquaintance with the infinite library he has in his mind.

And so a pattern was set for the next five years at least. During those interval periods between shorter primary school breaks and the longer secondary school vacations, I was a regular visitor to Cappagh Cross and this relationship was sustained during term times by correspondence in which I reported on my studies and he replied at length with long letters of instruction and encouragement in an English leavened with tags from Irish, Latin and Greek.

On a couple of occasions over the following years I accompanied him and Una to Ballinasloe and, though my stays were brief, I could not help noticing that it was as if he was the in-law and the universally popular Una the returning child. He was made welcome of course and regarded with the respect due to a man of his achievements; but I never detected any easy warmth between him, his parents, his siblings and their children. If anything there was a hint of repressed trepidation and I wondered if he had ever exploded with one of those rages I had witnessed in the classroom.

(After his death I learned that his brother's children had dreaded his arrival, knowing they would have to be on their best behaviour until he left. The fact that their parents and grandparents allowed this situation develop implies a kind of fear that any intervention of their part was likely to produce a situation worse than that in which they found themselves. I must add that all the Watters—from that first visit on my way to Spiddal, through my five years at Garbally and many afterwards—always greeted me and Con and Maisie with the warmest of welcomes.)

IN THE notes at the back of my 1959 diary are autographed, under the heading 'My Pals at Garbally', the names of nine boys from my class, Junior A. Such is the enforced intimacy of a small boarding school that bonds are formed that become frayed in time without ever snapping completely. Ours was considered 'a good year' and, unlike most other years, we have continued to organise reunions at which those who were close more than half a century ago can chat away as if resuming an earlier conversation.

IT MAY seem odd in the case of a teenage boy and his father, but to a great extent Con was in many ways my best friend. This was possible because, at home in Finglas during the vacations, I had only one friend from primary school, Eamonn Russell, who had also come under the influence of Mr Watters and was an avid reader and who, while working in the Post Office, still nurtured hopes of continuing his education.

I recall one occasion when we were riding into town on the scooter and Con took advantage of the fact that we were not face to face to express a hope that we would have more than the usual father-son relationship: he had no desire to be the distant, 'heavy' parent and hoped I would never be afraid to raise anything with him. (Did I, even then, detect a desire not to repeat his own relationship with his 'poor father'?) He must have known that there were inevitable developments in the life of a teenage boy that, if not fear, then embarrassment would prevent him sharing with his father; but if I did not share such feelings with him, nor did I with anybody else, not even with my school pals. His brief tutorial on sex also took place on the scooter when, again his back to my face, he asked me if there was anything I wanted to ask him and I replied, more innocently than untruthfully, that there was not.

My vacations improved beyond my wildest dreams when Eamonn Russell introduced me to the record 'hops' held in the Glasnevin Tennis Club. Once I had grasped the rudiments of dancing and the more daunting semaphore of asking a girl up, the Nevin was my pulsating paradise. There were three types of dance: a slow foxtrot (known as a 'lurch'), a fast 'jive' and, in between, a 'semi-demi'. Few later experiences have surpassed the bliss of jiving with a competent partner to Chuck Berry's 'Sweet Little Sixteen', even that of being wrapped around a compliant girl as we lurched to Del Shannon's 'The Answer to Everything'. During the breaks between records I performed feats of equivocation in order to avoid confessing that I was away at a boarding school in Galway: to do so would have been to encourage the girls to believe I was studying to be a priest. I was not surprised I did not acquire a real girlfriend, not like Eamonn, who had a 'steady' and who set me up with girls with whom we could make a foursome at the Casino cinema. What girl, I asked myself, even if convinced I was not a clerical student, would settle for somebody who was away in the bogs of Galway for half the year? But what could not be cured had to be endured and, lying in bed, having walked the couple of miles back to Finglas with Eamonn and others from Finglas West, I could not think of a better way of spending a night nor imagine how I would survive until the next 'hop'.

Oddly enough, on one occasion the doubts of my dancing partners were raised at home.

IT WAS almost certainly on a Thursday—Con's half-day from Bourke's—during the Easter Vacation of my third year when I still short of sixteen. The school retreat the previous term had been conducted by a priest of the Passionist order, a burly man who had made a big impression with his no-nonsense direct sermons and his anecdotes of jet flights all over the world doing God's work. When he mentioned that his order had been founded by St Paul of the Cross, I decided to go to confession with him, assuming (wrongly) that a fellow-Passionist must have been St John of the Cross, the great Spanish poet of whom I had read. As was the wont of retreat priests (who often doubled as recruiting sergeants for their orders) he took my name and address and promised to send me on some literature. When this arrived in a big brown envelope at 262 Cappagh Road—where such packets were a great rarity—I found a quarto booklet in which, to my dis-appointment, there was no mention of John of the Cross or of Teresa of Ávila, merely news of missionary work throughout the world, and so I put it back in its envelope on the front room table. Which is where Con found it, picked it up and asked me what it was. I told him it was just something a priest had sent me and indicated that he was welcome to have a look. I will never forget the shock on his face as he looked across at me. Nor the exact phrasing of his question: 'You're not thinking of becoming a priest on me, are you?' The full meaning of this is available only to native speakers or students of Hiberno-English. It is not be confused with 'you're not thinking of becoming a priest, are you?', which is a relatively simple question, anticipating (or pretending to anticipate) the answer 'no'. The crucial addition 'on me' is what is generally known as a dative of disadvantage but in this case could be more accurately labelled a dative of devastation. Con's question might be paraphrased: *after all we have achieved together, don't tell me you are about to dash my hopes and break my heart by throwing it all away by becoming a bloody priest?* It was the only time he was ever so blunt and direct regarding my future. When I assured him I had no intention of becoming a priest, he gave a great sigh of relief: 'Thank God for that.'

He need never have worried that I would waste my talent in the priesthood. I had a brief period of piety during my first year at Garbally—probably in the aftermath of the retreat—but I could never seriously consider a life of celibacy. An average of half a dozen boys went from Garbally to various seminaries. Some went to Maynooth with a view to coming back and working in the diocese of Clonfert. The most admired went to Dalgan where they trained to be missionaries in the Far East, living—as priests had in Ireland during the Penal Laws—in perpetual fear of capture and torture, if not martyrdom. By my final year, it was known among my friends that literature was my religion, Stephen Dedalus my patron saint, *A Portrait of the Artist as a Young Man* my New Testament.

During my early vacations from Garbally, having discovered that we had few books at home, Mr Watters began dropping in a dozen or so before heading off to Ballinasloe on his holidays. They were mostly classics of English fiction such as *Emma* or interesting oddities such as *Father and Son*, *The Way of All Flesh* and *Erewhon*. Before either Christmas 1959 or Easter 1960—when I was in my second year at school—his selection included a dark blue Penguin paperback, *Dubliners* by James Joyce.

The name tinkled a tiny bell. I had somehow got wind of the word that this Joyce was anti-Irish and had spent a self-imposed exile writing dirty books and attacking the Catholic Church. None of which made him sound like my kind of writer. But, then again, Mr Watters was suggesting I give him a go. I began reading the first story, following on the shoulder of a young boy as he listens to elderly people in a gloomy room discuss the recent death of a priest who had had to give up his clerical duties as a consequence of some vaguely improper behaviour.

131

No other work, not *The Coral Island* beforehand or anything—even *Ulysses*—afterwards, produced anything remotely like the effect this shadowy sketch had on me. Somehow or other, this was my world in print: characters who were sitting before me as I turned the pages, conversations I could hear as if taking place beside me, the streets of Dublin I had walked myself, faces and gestures I recognised. This was not the fine wine of the classics from sunlit Athens nor the ale of Elizabethan London. This was literature as heroin: one fix and I was instantly and helplessly hooked. I wanted to read everything by this James Joyce, know everything about him.

It never occurred to me to hide this book from Con. When he asked and I told him what I was reading, he muttered something about Joyce being very bitter against the Catholic Church. Not in this one, I replied: these were brilliant stories set in Dublin, many of them hilariously funny, none of them particularly anti-Irish, that he would enjoy them himself.

He never to my knowledge tried them himself but neither did he suggest that I should give them up in favour of something more wholesome. This example of his tolerance should be seen in the context of 1960 Ireland when Joyce—now one of Dublin's favourite sons and a tourism magnet—was generally considered a renegade.

During the Easter vacation of 1960 I bought the Penguin edition of *A Portrait* in Easons of O'Connell Street. As soon as I started it on the bus home I felt I was reading about myself. Despite blatant differences of time and place and personal circumstances, it was as if I had heard that Christmas Day row, as if I had sinned, cowered at that terrifying sermon, then confessed and breathed the beatific air of purity. I had never had the courage to have sex with a prostitute, nor had I ever known either the luxuries of the house in Bray or the squalor of that in Drumcondra—or the cruelty of a drunken father—but there was something in the book more powerful than these differences.

The Dublin of 1960, still untouched by the prosperity that came with Ireland's membership of the Common Market, was still close to the city Joyce had described. The Finglas bus took me from Eden Quay—close to where the Cabman's Shelter had been—up Gardiner Street, on the western edge of what had been Nighttown, past Mountjoy Square and the Jesuit house in which Stephen imagined himself S.J., into Dorset Street where Bloom's odyssey began. I had spent my first months in Eccles Street when

Bloom's house still stood down the street on the far side. Having started to read Joyce, I was proud to boast of such connections.

As the years passed I realised there had been several Joycean contacts about which the family did not boast. Among Peadar's longest and closest friendships was that with Tom Pugh, who had been born in Talbot Street and whom he met when they were boys in Marino CBS. They had both been 'out' in Easter Week and a chance meeting in later years led to a weekly session in Sean Farrelly's. Of Peadar Kearney, Pugh said: 'I can safely say I never met a man in my life I was so akin to. There was complete affinity between us. We talked books all the time.'

In his 1959 biography of Joyce, Richard Ellmann acknowledged the assistance of Pugh who had maintained his friendship with Joyce, whom he visited in Paris: 'In recovering Joyce's Dublin background I had the help of T. W. Pugh, with his extraordinary recollection of the details of life sixty years ago, and his minute knowledge of *Ulysses*.' In his biography of Peadar Kearney, dedicated to Tom Pugh, de Burca writes that Pugh gave Kearney *Ulysses* to read and that Kearney had later remarked to de Burca that 'it would be an excellent book for a theological student in a seminary, because every possible mortal sin is mentioned in it'. It is a disappointing comment from a close friend of Tom Pugh: perhaps it was made in specific circumstances and was not what Kearney would have offered had he been asked for his overall opinion of Joyce's novel.

NOR WAS Joyce the only writer of dubious reputation in my life. On Stephen's Day 1960, aged fifteen (and a half), I knocked at the door of 5 Anglesea Road, Ballsbridge, the home of Brendan Behan and his wife Beatrice. The arrangement had been made when Brendan called into Bourke's and learned from Con that I was at secondary school and mad about literature.

I had been about four or five when I first encountered him in 70 Kildare Road but had never forgotten his singing of 'My Lagan Love' or his claim that his luggage for Paris consisted of a toothbrush. A couple of years later he was back in Dublin, pausing on a sunny Grafton Street to chat with Maisie before disappearing. Maisie encountered him again, this time in Moore Street where the now famous Brendan Behan had been chosen to turn on the Christmas 1959 lights. When Brendan had accidentally bumped into my sister Eileen, Maisie had abused him, causing him to turn around to confront this cantankerous person, then laugh when he recognised her. He later made reparation in his Sunday newspaper column with the headline I'M SORRY, EILEEN.

I notice that each of these early encounters was with Maisie. There was something about the Behans in general—I suspect it was what he took to be their lack of interest in bettering themselves—that did not appeal to Con, who preferred to socialise with his Bourke cousins. Although he was fond of Brendan, it would never have occurred to him to take us over to visit Brendan's parents, as Maisie had done; on the other hand, he felt duty-bound to visit his aunts Maggie, mother of the Bourkes, and Maura, widow of his father's old comrade Mick Slater, which makes one wonder what went through his mind when agreeing to Brendan's suggestion that I should call out to see him and Beatrice on St Stephen's Day 1960.

Brendan had underlined his success as a writer by paying cash for 5 Anglesea Road. He gave the job of painting the new house—including the wooden sign on the front railings that read *a cúig* [five]—to Con's brother Pearse, who had an interesting tale to tell about it. When the painting was finished, Brendan took him into the front room, opened a suitcase stuffed with cash, and told him to take what he wanted. Brendan loved the money success brought, but not in order to save or invest it: he saw money as a means of indulging hitherto unaffordable habits, among them treating his old working-class friends. It was typical of the Kearneys that, as much as Pearse would have liked to have earned or won a wodge of money, pride prevented him from accepting it as a gift from a friend.

Brendan frequently dropped into Bourke's to chat with Con and Jimmy and 'the girls' upstairs, and to advertise his success in the nicest possible way by inviting them out for a drink. It was not necessity that led to Con turning down such invitations—Jimmy, his nominal boss, would have had no objections—but, again, some form of the Kearney pride left Con thanking Brendan but explaining that he had a job to do. To which Brendan would reply like a true philosophical bohemian: 'Come on, it'll be there after you.'

In 1960—in late August or early September—Brendan had a kind of victory when he managed to get Con and Maisie to join him and Beatrice for a meal in the rather posh Bailey restaurant. They must have been singing my praises every bit as much as Brendan was advertising his own emergence as an international celebrity: he signed a menu for Con and Maisie to bring home for me: *Slán a Choilbeard ó Bhreandán ar a thuras go Nua Eabhrach 1960*

[Farewell Colbert from Brendan on his trip to New York 1960].

It is likely Brendan was in top form. He had always been a heavy drinker and, to make matters worse, had been diagnosed as diabetic in 1956. More mindful of the publicity value of his drinking than of his diet, he was now more likely to end up in hospital rather than suffer a mere hangover and in April 1960 he decided his only hope was to give up alcohol entirely and follow a healthy regimen, which he did (with a couple of minor blips) for the best part of a year during which he rediscovered his social genius and charmed all who met him, including me. (I doubt if Con would have sanctioned our meeting if Brendan had not been on the dry.)

Those in the Bailey that evening must have been surprised (and relieved) that, fuelled with nothing stronger than soda water, he was the most winning and entertaining of hosts; but their admiration of an old friend's conversation was not to be compared to the adulation that was showered on him in New York where he went to attend (and enliven) the American premiere of *The Hostage*. The man I met that Christmas had just returned from America in sober triumph.

As almost anybody who met him during this period will testify, he was irresistible company: warm, witty, carrying his learning lightly, endlessly entertaining. For a boy of fifteen who had been rather 'properly' brought up but had fallen under the spell of James Joyce, this was like having Rabelais for an uncle, a Rabelais who was interested in me, in my studies, in my life at the mercy of 'the druids' at a Catholic boarding school (compared *passim* with his warders in Borstal), my extra-curricular reading, my budding ambitions to write. He was extravagant in his praise for Con and Maisie, hoping I realised how lucky I was to have such a father and mother. (This from a man who in other circumstances had declared that expecting a child to be grateful to a parent was like expecting a car rolling off the assembly line in Cork to be grateful to Henry Ford.) Con and Maisie were at the front window when I emerged from the taxi with a signed copy of *Borstal Boy*, money in my pocket, dying to tell them of the wonderful day I'd had.

I went out to see him again a few days before returning to Garbally: he gave me a couple of books of short articles by an American Jewish journalist named Harry Golden. I could not deny their appeal, although I remember wishing he had given me something more 'highbrow'. There was a flurry of communication in the next few months. He spoke to me by phone in Garbally before he went to America, wrote a letter (enclosing a $5 bill) as soon as he disembarked from the *Queen Elizabeth*, sent postcards from New York and Mexico, and a programme from Sea World in San Diego. We met maybe half a dozen times afterwards but he had resumed drinking and the atmosphere was never as perfect as during that Christmas vacation. There were moments when he found his old form but they tended to be early in the morning and short-lived. One brandy was enough to send him into a daze in which he was haunted by a cavalcade of ghosts. He was in and out of hospitals. If ever a man welcomed death, it was Brendan. It broke Con's heart to see the old joker in such obvious distress. (The old joker was five years his junior but looked at least twenty years older.) I had only known him for three years when he died and for most of that time he was making miraculous recoveries from collapses that would have finished lesser men, with the result that (like many others) I assumed he would somehow survive and re-emerge as the man who had phoned me at Garbally.

(When news of his death broke on 20 March 1964, I was stunned. I can still see myself sitting in the Taidhbhearc Theatre in Galway, totally at a loss, glad that I was not alone, that my girlfriend, Sheila Killeen, was with me. We were both part of the UCD team—she as Ismene, me as translator—putting on *Oedipus the King* in the Irish-language Universities Drama Festival. I had recently visited Brendan in the Meath Hospital: he had not been in particularly good form but it never occurred to me that I was talking to him for the last time. I made it back to Dublin for the funeral on the 22nd.)

IT IS now possible to see him as a harbinger of the social revolution we call the Sixties. I could hardly have chosen a better time to emerge from the quasi-monasticism of Garbally (where I had been very happy) into the big, bright world. A new optimistic era opened up in Ireland in the early 1960s, prompted by the economic programmes of Sean Lemass and T.K. Whitaker and sealed in June 1963 by the visit of John F. Kennedy, the ultimate incarnation of the Irish emigrant made good. The Kearneys shared this sense of a rising tide. In 1962 we moved to 112 Cappagh Avenue, about a ten-minute walk from Cappagh Road. Once again we were on the edge of the city with fields across the road from us but this house offered the possibility—once Con had added on a commodious kitchen—of having a 'good room' to the front of the house. A more significant symbol of our social progress was the second-hand car Con bought in 1963 and nothing better illustrated our *nouvelle richesse* than the family visit down to see me in Garbally.

Given the Spartan fare supplied by the college, great importance was attached to 'calls', Sunday visits by parents who arrived by car bearing all sorts of food and soft drinks. I assumed from the very beginning that Con and Maisie could never make such visits simply because they lived so far away and did not have a car. I accepted the situation without the least sense of grievance; but when Con and Maisie learned about these 'calls', they were aggrieved, on my behalf, that I was deprived of treats enjoyed by some of my friends, most notably meals in the dining room of Hayden's Hotel in Ballinasloe. The few visits they managed to make were in cars owned by Con's cousins, Kevin or Peadar.

But all that changed when Con graduated from two wheels to four and I would guess that the first trip he planned was to Garbally, thanking his stars that the car had arrived before I had left. It was a fine Sunday when the Morris Minor made its way up to the main house and out got Con and Maisie and my younger sisters in all their finery, the girls getting their first glimpse of the strange place in which their brother went to school.

My recollection of the day is generally hazy. I presume I showed them around the elegant house, formerly the seat of the Earl of Clancarty, with its lordly chambers now adapted to more crowded and less luxurious uses; but I have no record of acting the tour guide, either inside or outside. It may be that Con was conscious of the long return journey and was at least as keen as anybody else to get on to what was the main event of the visit, Hayden's Hotel.

Working-class people did not eat out in those days. The extent to which the meal in Hayden's was a gesture may be gauged from the fact that the hotel was not much more than a minute's walk from the Watters house, where Bridie would have been happy to feed us. Pride would have prevented Con and Maisie from calling on anybody at mealtime, but that was beside the point on this occasion. The meal in Hayden's was to compensate for those Sundays when I had been left in the college while my better-off friends had been feasting 'out town'. It was to mark a change in circumstances: the Kearneys were now in a position to arrange and afford such treats. Without its symbolic dividend, Con would most likely have considered it a waste of money that could be better spent on less evanescent pleasures. But today was a day to push out the boat.

I had been in restaurants before but not very often and always in the charge of adults, Brendan Behan on a couple of occasions, the parents of a Garbally friend on a couple of others. Brendan had taken my lack of experience for granted, summoning the waiter (*garçon!*), reading out the entire menu, asking my opinion on every item, then ordering the waiter to bring me everything I had said I liked. With my friend Philip Pettit and his parents I simply had the same as everybody else, a mixed grill. My limited experience had not seriously dented my lack of confidence until we picked up the menus and I noticed there was no sign of a mixed grill. At which point, relieved that most of the patrons had finished and gone, I went back to the beginning.

We all looked at our menus with varying degrees of disingenuousness. The girls knew they were not expected to make decisions on their own and were comfortably bemused by exotic terms. Ever willing to disguise my feelings in the interest of the greater good, I studied the menu as if it were a Latin text that would, given time and effort, yield up its meaning in plain English. Out of the corner of my eye I caught the look that came over Con's face when perplexed by an unexpected problem; but this time there was no sign of the enlightenment that normally beamed when, say, he examined a jumble of wires.

As ever it was Maisie who spoke her mind—'There's nothing here I like'—and licensed the girls to confess their inability to make head nor tail of the menu. Honest confusion spread around the table and threatened to degenerate into catastrophe when it dawned on me that the others (including perhaps even Con) were looking to me take charge, explain matters and restore order—that it was my fault if this long-awaited treat turned out to be a disappointment.

Nobody, not even Maisie, would have dreamt of saying out loud what everybody, even little Eva, knew: that though I was the nominal cause, this was Con's day. I would have done anything to make the occasion a success for him (and everybody else including myself), anything but sacrifice a seventeen-year-old classical scholar's sense of status by admitting that I was as much at a loss as anybody else about what to order and suggesting we ask the waitress for assistance. Instead I stared at the menu until my eye lit on the word 'chicken'.

'We all like chicken. Why don't we order chicken?'

'Where's the chicken?'

'There. Curried chicken.'

'What does that mean? That could be anything.'

'But the main thing is it's chicken and we all like chicken.'

None of us had ever heard of curry, which is why we all thought the waitress had made a mistake when, instead of the beautifully roasted and aromatically stuffed bird Maisie served, she put in front of each of us a yellowy-brown gruel that looked and smelled dangerously like scraps you'd give to the dog.

The meal was such a disaster that details of its conduct were (at least in my case) quickly shrouded in embarrassment. In all likelihood Maisie saved the day (at least for the others) by going into the nearest shop and buying ice creams. It would have taken more than a choc-ice on a stick to sweeten my imagination or to prevent the creation of a memory that has to this day preserved its power to generate a shiver of mortification. I have long since come to terms with my pretence to know what a curry was; what still grieves is my failure to have saved Con whatever disappointment he felt at his failure to organise for me the kind of social occasion a middle-class father would manage effortlessly.

I had probably enjoyed my five years at Garbally as much as any well-balanced boy could be expected to, so much so that I was happy to return the following year for the reunion and have to this day never missed the opportunity to meet up again with my classmates. But even as we drove home to Dublin—Con and Maisie and I—I could feel my universe expanding.

I was due to go abroad for the first time, having arranged jobs in Butlin's Holiday Camp in Bognor Regis with half a dozen guys from Garbally. I used what I saved there to fund a trip to Hamburg to visit a pen-pal, then returned to London to work until it was time to go home.

Did it ever occur to me that Con and Maisie might be concerned for my welfare during this summer of international adventure? Probably, but I reckoned that if they could keep their anxieties to themselves, I did not need to worry. Had they been utterly opposed to me going abroad, I would have argued and sulked before surrendering; but Con had never laid down any laws for me and was not going to begin now when I was almost eighteen years of age and about to crown his hopes by going to university.

University College Dublin was as exotic as Hamburg. None of us had a clue what it would be like. Mr Watters was probably the only graduate we knew—and he had attended by night while working as a teacher. Graduates were few in those days. I was in town with Con once when he nodded to a passer-by who, he later informed me, had a B.A. Con had long been convinced that university was the highest form of education, the surest guarantee of culture and professional employment. I had no thoughts of employment: I was hoping to discover the ferment of intellectual debate described in Joyce's *Portrait* sixty years earlier and had no idea of the changes that were blowing in the wind.

WHEN I arrived in Earlsfort Terrace in 1963, Irish students were still perceived as a tiny elite of exceptionally intelligent and responsible people who behaved and dressed as befitted those who, as top civil servants, economists, lawyers and doctors, would assume the leadership of Irish society. During my five years there UCD remained a predominantly conservative institution where the vast majority of students were practising Catholics and which included a large cohort of nuns and clerical students in traditional black attire. It was perhaps this predominance that allowed it to tolerate heterodoxy, especially among students and particularly those, like myself, whose literary interest gave them a degree of quasi-bohemian licence. Like my closest male friend, Mick Lillis, I made no secret of my Joycean attitude to religion and never felt disadvantaged as a result. Sheila Killeen and I were mildly annoyed when the Catholic chaplain—with whom I got on well and shared an interest in short stories—asked her to pray for me. Little did he or I or anybody else know that the political radicalism that was sweeping America—civil disobedience and rioting, burning of flags and bras, recreational drugs, casual sex and long hair—would soon reach Europe and disturb the tranquillity of Earlsfort Terrace. But it would come too late for my friends and me: most of us were politically apathetic, but some of us would have welcomed the casual sex.

Initially I was uneasily aware of being working class in an overwhelmingly middle-class community and did not really find my feet until asked to translate the choral odes for an Irish-language production of *Oedipus the King*. The invitation could only have come through Eugene Watters, who had been too busy to take on the task and suggested me. From then on I was part of a group with an interest in literature and drama, English and Irish, including Mick and Sheila. Suddenly I was involved in a life that underlined in retrospect how monastic Garbally had been. At UCD the only discipline was self-imposed. Nobody cared if you attended lectures or not. (I attended every one in first year.) Most of your day was free: you could either study in the library or drink coffee in mixed company. In the evenings there were meetings of various societies, which for me and my friends meant the English Lit, the Cumann Gaelach and the Cumann Liteartha. Most exotic of all were the improvised gatherings and parties held in the flats of students from outside Dublin.

My arrival at UCD coincided with the so-called ballad revival, kick-started by the success of the Clancy Brothers in the US. Soon folk groups were springing up all over the country—most notably, as far as I was concerned, The Dubliners—and matching the showbands in popularity. People haunted pubs such as O'Donoghue's in Merrion Row, where singers and musicians gave extempore concerts in the back room, and after-pub parties such as those I attended in student flats were dominated by the singing of ballads, generally by those who had learned them from recordings.

Initially I could not believe my luck. As far as the Kearneys were concerned the ballad revival was a meaningless term: for us the ballads had never died. Nor were we dependent on recordings: in the normal course of growing up I had acquired at least a hundred ballads, including such Peadar Kearney favourites as 'Down by the Liffeyside' and 'Whack-fol-the-Diddle'. (The campaign for civil rights in Northern Ireland was growing and anti-British songs were welcomed with enthusiasm.) My first offering at a student party was 'The Zoological Gardens' and it was obvious even to anxious me that what had been a minority family practice was now a social passport.

It took Maisie even longer than me to get used to the freedom of university life. She and Con must have worried that the enforced order of Garbally had not prepared an eighteen-year-old male for the temptations of co-education. They found it hard to believe that there were mornings and afternoons when I did not have to be in UCD and were anxious lest I squander the opportunity of a lifetime. In the course of that first year she several times asked me—with a show of nonchalance but probably prompted by Con—if I could provide her with a timetable, just so she'd know when I had to go to the university and when I'd be studying at home. I fobbed her off as kindly as I could, explaining that it was not like school, that the schedule changed all the time, assuring her that I had everything under control and that neither she nor Con had anything to worry about. The timetable did not change all that much but I was enjoying the new freedom and loath to surrender any part of it. There was never any friction between us. They knew I was asserting a greater degree of independence but they also knew that, for all my delight in my new social life, I was a competitive, hardworking student and whatever doubts she or Con had were dispelled by my success in the First Arts exams.

AS THE oldest child and only boy I was culturally bound to form child-hood bonds with Con that did not apply to my sisters. Sport, work and politics, for example, were almost exclusively male and so I was the one to accompany Con to Croke Park and the Manhattan Bar afterwards, the one most likely to lend him a hand with gardening or home decorating, the one at his shoulder watching him take down election counts from the radio. For whatever reason or combination of reasons—arising from her gender or personality—Maura did not develop my early passion for study or for seeking applause by singing nationalist songs or reciting Irish poetry. It may even be that while Con loved Maura as much as any of his children, he felt that responsibility for her formation was more Maisie's than his and/or that he considered unladylike the passions he wanted to inspire in me, such as football, gardening, political fervour, higher education.

On the other hand, secondary school vacations had meant I was at home almost half the year and, with Con at work five and a half days a week, I probably spent more time with Maisie. This was even more the case while at UCD.

Which may explain why I am in some ways temperamentally closer to Maisie, why to this day I tend to quote her more often than Con. We were both early morning people, both allergic to silence in company, instinctively filling the empty space with a stream of light-hearted banter, singing and joking. I recall those Sunday mornings when I came down and attempted to strike up a lively conversation with Con as he read his paper after breakfast. He would close his eyes and shake his head and sigh: 'Talk to your mother.'

I cannot imagine Maisie ever waving me away, even in jest. She was always willing to show an interest in anything I was up to. It still raises an uneasy smile to recall her coming from the kitchen into the front room to listen to me wax lyrical about a piece of classical music I had just discovered. Only slightly less embarrassing is the image of her standing in that front room, a tea towel in her hand, nodding her head in time as I try to accompany Barney McKenna on my tin whistle.

The more I studied the history of the English language, the more appre-ciative I became of the 'ould sayings' that salted and peppered her conversa-tion. She was amused that I, the student of high-falutin books, should be fascinated by phrases she had acquired and retained unconsciously. Or maybe not so unconsciously: none of her siblings spoke in such a colourful manner.

She had several verbal runs that were like orphaned quotations (or Homeric similes) that had lost their context. Any reference to red would produce what sounded like a mother lauding the virtues, temperamental and physical, of her son, Alex. *'O, my Alex loves red! The more glarin' the more darin'. Six foot two and I own to God he wouldn't come through that door!'* The final word was pronounced to rhyme with 'poor', which suggests that the lines came from an older Dublin rather than from the stage of the Queen's or some silver screen, and one could only speculate what had inspired them in whom, where and when.

Even then I guessed that Maisie had inherited her linguistic brio from her mother, to whom she had always been very close, never more so than when, as her apprentice between leaving school and working in the Queen's, she would have spent a lot of time alone with her, as I did with Maisie during my breaks from studying.

It helped that she doted on her white-headed boy as much as he adored his large-hearted mother. I had no sooner acquired a taste for 'real' coffee than she arrived home with a Russell Hobbs percolator and a bag of Bewley's beans. When I took up the pipe, she presented me with a tobacco jar with a fancy leather sleeve. As she would say herself, not caring who heard her: 'Nothing but the best for my Colbert.'

I am quite sure that Maisie would not have swapped her lot with anybody, equally sure that had the culture in which she lived permitted, she would, for example, on our visits to Raheny, have preferred if she and Bridie could have accompanied Con and Pearse to the Manhattan rather than staying at home, minding the children and preparing a tea for the men when they returned. (Actually, they could not have gone to the Manhattan, which was, by a custom stronger than any law, men only, but there were lounges nearby that welcomed women.)

This culture, seen by all of us as the natural order, was memorably questioned by Dominic Behan's wife, Josephine, who demanded to know why the fuck she should have to sit at home with the women while the men went off to enjoy themselves in the pub. Dominic must somehow have placated her because she ended up sitting at home while the men went to the Manhattan. Maisie and Bridie tried to convince her that they were better off without the men, but with a glaring lack of success. Josephine's revolutionary ideas were beyond the Kearneys and most likely considered as odd as the woman herself who, apart from wanting to go to the pub with the men, smoked a pipe and swore like a trooper. Besides, being Scottish and divorced, she was probably a Protestant. Neither Maisie nor Bridie could have believed that when—within a few short years—their own daughters came of age, they would echo many of Josephine's arguments.

Maisie had much to be thankful for. She found fulfilment in making and keeping a home for her husband and family. She was married to the love of her life, who worked all the hours god sent and always handed over his pay packet unopened. In the governing of the home, she was the minister for finance who had no desire to be Taoiseach. In extra-mural matters she deferred to Con without the least resentment, acknowledging the superiority of his intellect in analysing politics and other 'important' matters in which she had not the slightest interest, just as he acknowledged her more instinctive and emotional intelligence.

Imagined scene. The children gone to bed, Con and Maisie sit beside the fire: partners mulling over the day's events, the latest trials and triumphs, she respecting his judgment, he modifying it in the light of her apparently tentative observations.

THOUGH I might occasionally envy the romantic aura that (at least for me) surrounded living in student flats, I knew I had the best of both worlds, with all the comforts of home and, simultaneously, a full social and cultural life at UCD. Finglas was on the far side of the city from college but I could get a lift in with Con in the mornings and home at tea-time whenever I wished. I also had the use of his scooter, which he had held on to for my sake. And I had the privacy of the front room where I could read and write and listen to my records. Besides I was a star in my own home, guaranteed the approval no fellow-student could provide. Maisie glowed in the belief that her only son, thanks (as she would have put it) to his own brains and his own hard work, was well on his way to making for himself a more secure and comfortable life than she and Con had ever known. Con was equally thrilled at the increased opportunities a graduate would enjoy; but he had other reasons to be pleased.

I am not sure when he first told me—a broad smile of contentment on his face—that he was happy to live 'in the reflected glory' of my success. Possibly when I got a first in the B.A., but it could have been earlier, and it was a statement he made at every stage of my progress in academia. I hated to hear him say it. It made me squirm to think he saw himself as in any way secondary to me, or anybody else. Yes, I had done well in exams but, had it not been for his inspiration and support, I would never have sat them. He had a great deal to be proud of besides rearing me. He was more intelligent than I was, liked and respected by almost all who came into contact with him, inferior to nobody.

I am less irked now: now that I have given it some thought, I think I have a better understanding of what he meant. The revision began as I recalled him sitting beside me as I do my *ekker* on the table in the front room on Cappagh Road.

I am in a hurry to impress; he slows me down, so gently as not to be noticed, inviting me to watch as he writes out the alphabet or the numerals from zero to nine. I am lost in admiration as the symbols appear in perfect order, level, consistent and clear.

That memory fades into another of the relative gloom of the house in O'Donoghue Street where he must have done his *ekker*. The room is empty and my mind hurries out into Ring Street and down to the schoolroom where he sits—sharp-eyed, skinny, well-worn tweeds and hobnailed boots—as the teacher praises him as one of the brightest boys he has ever encountered. But he knows that, for all the teacher's praise, his education is coming to an end and he will have to choose a life very different from that for which he is obviously qualified.

What were his thoughts when I began to come top of the class in St Canice's? If he recalled his own childhood successes, he kept such memories to himself rather than take from my triumphs. It was probably inevitable that mine should remind him of his own early promise but I was too young even to suspect the degree of his determination to ensure that I would be given the opportunities he had been denied.

Thanks to his and Maisie's support and sacrifices, I made it to secondary school and university. Even when he could no longer sit beside me and help me with my *ekker*, I knew he was there in spirit. It would be many years before I realised that part of his reward for his dedication to my advancement was the possibility of redeeming time past by fulfilling his childhood dreams through me.

He knew better than I did that there were no certainties in the turmoil of adolescence, least of all success in competitive exams, which is why he was more relieved than I was whenever I cleared a hurdle, why he suffered more than I did during the examination season, why he cheered much more than I did when I won a scholarship. That's what he meant by 'reflected glory'.

Such patterns were buried in deep silence. The casual drama of our relationship is better illustrated by an episode that took place when I was at UCD.

IT IS early on a Saturday afternoon. Con has come home from work, eaten his dinner and is relaxing with a mug of tea before changing his clothes and finding something to do in the back garden. I have joined him in the living room with my coffee and he is telling me how in town that morning he had bumped into an old friend he hadn't seen in years, not since he'd been in the cinema business. Even before he'd recognised his friend, he had noticed the dog he was leading: 'the most beautiful Red Setter you've ever seen in your life'.

Knowing I liked dogs as much as he did, he details the perfect proportions, the noble outline, the richness of the coat, the lustre of his eyes. 'That's a real beauty you have there,' he had commented as he ruffled the dog's ear, then stood open-mouthed as his friend told him he was just then taking him to the Dog's Home to have him put down. Shocked, I ask: 'Was the dog mad?' Con looks away, purses his lips thoughtfully, then turns to face me. 'Well, he wasn't too pleased.'

It took me a couple of seconds to realise I had walked into a well-laid trap. Me, of all people? If anybody should have detected some activity behind the casually straight face, it was me. I knew that face better than I knew my own.

It took me longer to get over my gullibility and appreciate the outrageous skill that enabled him to gull me.

Everything hinged on me interrupting his narrative at exactly that point with exactly that question and using exactly that word. What if I had asked if the dog had bitten once too often? Had some fatal disease? What if I had kept my mouth shut?

But I hadn't. He had somehow seen to that.

It sounded like a gag he had heard in Jurys Hotel Summer Cabaret where he operated the spotlight from the mid-Sixties until the hotel relocated from Dame Street to Ballsbridge in 1972. I can imagine the star comedian Hal Roach—whose humour involved lots of puns and misunderstandings of the mad dog variety—getting a laugh with it during his stand-up. To present it as Con did, as an encounter that had actually happened, took not only skill but an outrageous confidence: he had to use every ruse at his disposal so that, without giving the game away by arousing my suspicion, he sowed in my mind the seed of the idea that the only reason such a dog would be put down was madness.

The joke was on me, but it was not at my expense. He would never have risked hurting my feelings for anything. Far from thinking me a fool, he had a high opinion of my mental capacities (even if he considered them better adapted to the examination hall than to the world outside) and that was an important part of the game. More than once I asked him what he would have done had I said nothing. His reaction was always the same: a shrug and an apparently helpless smile. If he knew the answer, which I am inclined to doubt, he was keeping it to himself.

(What would he have done? Probably told the story as Hal had told it, relegating himself to the role of 'feed' and surrendering the wonderful punch-line to his fictional friend. The electric shock would have been diminished but it would have kept the show on the road.)

Though he could obviously tell a good story, I never saw him as a performer in the sense of a man who put himself forward in company, who set out to amuse others with jokes or 'funny incidents'. Nor was he 'theatrical', never craving attention, preferring to provide the limelight rather than bask in it. He liked the company of players before and after the show but, like so many who work behind the scenes, he was protective of his privacy, as he demonstrated one night in Jurys.

I often took a lift into town with Con, leaving him at Jurys as I went up to meet friends in McDaid's, coming back down to Dame Street in time to get a lift home. If I was early I simply sat beside him on the balcony from where he directed his spot over the audience below and onto the stage. We would usually have a whispered conversation about who had been in McDaid's and so on, but this particular night he hardly acknowledged my arrival. Assuming there was a problem, I checked the stage where the vocalist, Des Smith, was thanking various people: there was no hint of a hitch of any kind, which made Con's distraction hard to fathom. He was sitting forward on the edge of his seat, muttering to himself, repeating: 'You were warned not to try it.' Who warned whom not to try what? I looked down at the stage where Des Smith, now glancing at the band like a naughty schoolboy, was asking the audience to put their hands together and give a big round of applause to the man without whose guiding light the show could not go on: the one and only Chilli Con Kearney!

Bang!

Before Des had finished his light-hearted tribute, the place was thrown into darkness, as if a sudden power failure had left the stage blacked out and the audience depending on the candles on their dining tables. But there had not been a power failure, not as commonly understood. Con had disconnected the spot and was now sitting back on his chair, apparently unconcerned what effect the darkness would have on the nerves of the audience and resolutely deaf to the apologetic entreaties of Des Smith. I sensed the audience becoming anxious and looked at Con as if to say he had made his point and it was time to turn the light back on. A long five seconds later he plugged the spot in and stared down at Des Smith as if daring him to try it again. He didn't, and the show ended. As we stood up to make our way down to the dressing rooms, I glanced at him as if to suggest he'd overreacted. He shrugged: 'I warned him not to try it.'

It wasn't the pun on his name that had provoked him but the invasion of his privacy, the removal of his anonymity. He had obviously got wind of it during the interval and made his feelings known. He was the man who put others in the spotlight; if he wanted to be in the spotlight, which he didn't, he would be on the stage, which he wasn't. Meanwhile, each to his own.

Nor was he furious with Des, or with the others in the band with whom Des would have concocted his little prank. He was very fond of them, as they were of him: there were smiles all round when we got together for a drink after the show. Everybody was happy: the boys had had their bit of fun and Con had ensured they'd never try it again.

Nor would any of them have been surprised that the quiet-spoken Con had taken such radical action. They knew he had been around show business most of his life and had learned when and how to draw the line. And, after all, he was the son of Peadar Kearney.

HAD SUCH knowledge been available some years earlier to a parking attendant on the Clonliffe Road near Croke Park, he might have been spared a moment of unsettling bewilderment.

The problem was Con's new Lambretta scooter. He wanted to park it in such a way as to give it the best chance of surviving the inevitable chaos when, just before the game, country people left their cars anywhere they liked, as if they were in some quiet village. His chosen method was to angle the scooter in at forty-five degrees to the pavement but this was quickly corrected by the attendant—a tough-looking customer—to an angle of ninety degrees and right up against the boot of a parked car. *His* intention was to pack as many cars into his available space and for him the scooter was a nuisance, especially as parked. But as far as Con was concerned, the Lambretta was no mere two-wheeled vehicle to be manhandled by anybody: it was his pride and joy, for which he had saved long and hard, and, as a payer of road tax, he questioned the right of anybody else to lay hands on it for whatever reason.

All the attendant saw was Con's gentle demeanour, reckoned him a pushover and brusquely explained why he had moved the scooter. He was a little surprised that the quiet man showed no sign of accepting his ruling and so, raising himself up to his full height and pulling down his peaked cap over his eyes, he was about to lay down the law more forcefully when the quiet man spoke: 'My father fought for this city.'

The craggy-faced attendant came to a sudden stop, stared into Con's eyes and realised that, yes, the calm-faced man had indeed said what he thought he had heard him say. *My father fought for this city.* The attendant raised his hands, palms outward, gesturing complete surrender. 'You're right. It's grand as it is.' And off he went to bully and hector those who, after all, were merely citizens of the Irish Republic, and not the son of a gun-toting founding father.

(As with the priest on Berkeley Road, Con had played his hand perfectly. Such a success was only possible in an Ireland that today seems ancient: a contemporary lockhard, far from being stunned into surrender, would probably reply that he couldn't give a flying fuck if Con's father had fought Muhammad Ali.)

THERE WERE few things Con enjoyed more than a good chat with his favourite customers, show business people and politicians. With the former he could recall the past and keep up with the latest inside information; with the latter he could enjoy a friendly argument. He did not conceal his support for Fianna Fáil, but to a great extent he took people as he found them, irrespective of party. What he liked was a gentle three-minute round in which he used his poker face and gentle bearing to conceal a devastating irony from all but the most alert. His objective (fortunately for Bourke's) was not to leave an opponent out cold on the floor: he would settle for an inner victory, even if the customer was convinced *he* had won.

His strangest gambit involved a malapropism he had heard and which had struck a strange chord. I can still see him out near the front door of Bourke's jousting with a Fine Gael deputy who had listed off the achievements of his party and is about to march off in triumph over this shop assistant, when Con smiles his gentle smile and interjects: 'There's nothing like a bit of humbility.' The deputy is momentarily knocked off his high horse, trying his polite best to hide his surprise that such a well-spoken man would be guilty of such a gaffe. Con cannot help him: the picture of innocence, unable to imagine why the deputy has lost his tongue.

My favourite story was of Garret FitzGerald's first day as Taoiseach in 1981. Formal wear was required for his visit to the President to receive his seal of office and a secretary phoned Con to alert him to Dr FitzGerald's requirements. The secretary was all excitement and Con sought to set her mind at ease by assuring her he was familiar with the situation: he had dressed several Fianna Fáil *taoisigh* for the ceremony and would doubtless dress another after the next election. At this point the secretary must have realised she was not dealing with a Fine Gael supporter but, nevertheless, she could hardly have believed her ears when asked to inform Dr FitzGerald that he could come down to Dame Street for a fitting at any time convenient to himself, even—given the exceptional nature and national importance of the transaction—during Con's lunch break. The exasperated secretary: 'But, Mr Kearney, Dr FitzGerald is a very busy man.' Con, hardly able to believe his luck in being 'fed' such a gift: 'Are you suggesting I'm not?' Soon they were both laughing and making arrangements for Con to call on and facilitate Dr FitzGerald.

Bourke's of Dame Street was a theatrical institution which few old troupers could pass without dropping in to say hello to 'the girls' up in women's costumes or to Peadar Bourke and Sean Parnell on the floor beneath in men's costumes or to recall times past with Jimmy in his office and/or indulge in a spot of ball-hopping with Con on the ground floor. Con always mentioned it when Donal McCann stuck his head in. He was very fond of Donal, not so much because he was the greatest acting talent of his generation, more because he was young and had a drink problem. Besides, he came of good stock, the son of John McCann, Abbey playwright and Fianna Fáil TD and

Lord Mayor of Dublin, and had a nice line in the dry humour Con enjoyed.

Even I, maybe Con's biggest fan, was often surprised by the range and number of people who were obviously fond of him and eager to help in any way they could. Serious help was needed when Con acquired a car. He could park the scooter in the narrow lane beside Bourke's but parking the car legally in the centre of the city would be very expensive. Somehow or other, through the influence of a friend, he managed to park across the road in the Castle Yard. The legality of this was never confirmed in writing and was never accepted by the warden on the gate; but Con (whose father had after all 'fought for this city') was not one to be frightened by petty bureaucracy and in time his entitlement to park there was established by custom and practice.

A mild-mannered man, I never knew him to show any aggression other than in the theatre of Croke Park. He was characteristically courteous and charming with people he met on an equal footing but if confronted by ill-treatment or condescension, he displayed a resolve that took no account of the status of the offender.

Back in the early days in Finglas, a nun decided to 'cure' Maura of her left-handedness by rapping the errant fingers with a ruler. Few if any parents in Finglas would have dared question the behaviour of a nun in her classroom but Con was down the following morning. Nobody knows what he said but the nun never attempted to 'correct' Maura again.

While working on the lights of a religious pageant in the same school, he got on well with the Reverend Mother and this may have encouraged one of the sisters to suggest that Mrs Kearney might like to offer her services in the cleaning of the parish church. Con thanked her with a show of politeness and pointed out that Mrs Kearney had more than enough to do at home, adding that the nun might consider asking wives who had more time on their hands, helpfully listing the wives of prominent shopkeepers and professionals.

I was actually present when he displayed what would have been considered a lack of customary working-class respect for 'God's holy anointed'.

One sunny evening in the early Sixties—by now we had moved to Cappagh Avenue and I was at UCD—one of my sisters ran into the house to say that there was a priest at our gate. Con frowned at this disturbance of his leisure by somebody he had no desire to meet and, before retreating into the kitchen, signalled to me to 'look after him', presumably reckoning that my years at Garbally had made me more comfortable with priests than he was. I opened the door and exchanged greetings with the priest, who asked me if he could come in. I took him into the front room—the 'good' room—where, naturally enough, he asked if my father was at home. What else could I do but go out into the kitchen and tell Con he'd have to come in?

Having watched him say mass, Con knew this priest was one of new type, licensed by the Second Vatican Council to adopt a more democratic, not to say folksy, manner with parishioners. Ironically, however much Con disliked the superiority complexes of the old guard, he was contemptuous of the younger trendies who tried to be 'one of us'.

'How are you, Mr Kearney?'

'How are you, father?'

Did the priest feel (as I certainly did) that Con's manner was more casual and less deferential than that of other men he had encountered in other houses on Cappagh Avenue? If he did, he decided not to be discouraged.

As he must have done a thousand times since his arrival in Finglas, the priest launched into a routine designed to reveal his charm, wit and humility. (To understand what follows, one needs to know that there was at the time a prominent Fianna Fáil politician, Jack Lynch.)

'O please don't call me "father", Mr Kearney. I hate when people call me that. The name is Jack Lynch, but in order not to be confused with the man who's always on the telly, I ask people to call me Jackie.'

'Jack Jackie?'

There was a sudden silence. The unfortunate priest did not know what to do or think. I think his first resort was to smile, as if acknowledging that Con had made a joke, however weird and unfunny he found it. But Con remained straight-faced and, to the bemusement of the priest, looking like a man who had asked a simple question and would wait for an answer, for all eternity if necessary.

Eventually the priest decided to make the best of a bad lot. He let the question (and the possible joke) pass, inquired as to the general welfare of the family, then checked his watch, mentioned something about the number of houses he still had to call on, and made his escape.

Although I felt a teeny-bit sorry for the priest, I could not help laughing. I had only recently come out as an agnostic and could hardly berate my father for failing to defer to a Catholic priest; but I did warn him out that if Maisie got to hear about it, she would be mortified, not on any theological grounds but because a visitor to the house had not been shown basic civility and hospitality, not even been offered a cup of tea. Con was unmoved.

'What did he want anyway?'

'I don't know. Maybe you should have asked him.'

GROWING UP on the Cappagh Road I knew several houses that regularly resounded with the shouts and screams of violent argument, frequently followed by the smashing of crockery and the slamming of doors. Little or nothing was ever said about these brawls, not even by the children who had witnessed drunken fathers pummel their mothers and threaten them with worse. This did not surprise me: I assumed the existence of a natural law preventing children, no matter how deprived or abused, from speaking ill of their parents.

Just as Garbally had been socially superior to the national school in Ballygall, UCD, which attracted not only the children of Dublin's professional classes but also many of their ambitious country cousins, was a step up from Garbally. I was pleasantly surprised to find myself adapting so quickly, thanks largely to the innately anti-elitist atmosphere of literary societies, especially the Irish-language variety, as distinct from, say, the L & H debating society. Another surprise awaited me as I got to know an ever-widening circle of friends and discovered that it was common, if not the norm, for many of them—all from apparently comfortable and respectable families—to refer to their parents in highly unfavourable terms, dismissing them as irrelevant nuisances or castigating them as mad, malign or worse. I was shocked, unable to imagine myself ever talking of Con and Maisie in such a way; but this filial treachery (as I saw it) was so widespread that I soon took it for granted.

Even at the time I could recognise its evolutionary function: young adults on the edge of maturity and independence, their minds being opened to new possibilities by higher education, flexing their freedom muscles and indulging in Oedipal gymnastics. But where did that leave me? Why was I deficient in whatever it was that drove the others? Was I deluded? Still imprisoned by some working-class taboo? Perhaps, but before I could chip in with a catalogue of Con and Maisie's failings, I would first have to discover them. And what fault could I find with parents who were loving and infinitely generous in word and deed, interested in everything I did without ever becoming dictatorial or heavy-handed, giving all they had and wanting nothing in return except that I should be successful and happy?

This disparagement of parents was probably the most discernible form of rebellion in a very conservative atmosphere. There was not a lot of drinking during our first year at UCD, partly because we did not have the money and partly because it was not considered good behaviour to get drunk. Many male students were registered abstainers in the Pioneers, and female drinking in pubs was generally deemed unladylike. A considerable proportion of those who drank kept it secret from their parents. Those of us who had literary pretensions felt almost obliged to drink and were probably seen by our more demure fellow-students (and by ourselves) as daring and Bohemian, although by modern student standards we were very small beer indeed.

During most of first year my friends and I tended to take our breaks in Kirwan's at the Leeson Street corner of Stephen's Green where, more often than not, we talked endlessly over cups of coffee. Literary types, like myself and Mick Lillis, graduated to McDaids in Harry Street where the post-war tradition of

Brendan Behan and J. P. Donleavy was continued by the likes of Paddy Kavanagh, Tony Cronin, John Jordan and others. As Tony Cronin noted, such pubs then provided a stage on which the private life of extroverts could be acted out in public. Those who sought to keep themselves to themselves were the oddballs. It still attracted a colourful clientele, still provided people like Mick and myself with a rich floorshow, all overseen by head barman Paddy O'Brien with a shrewd blend of toleration and control.

Had I not been interested in the legendary exploits of Behan and Donleavy, I would still have been drawn to McDaids, where I was flattered to be recognised as 'one of the Kearneys' and thus related to the Behans. Pearse was a sufficiently regular client for me to drop in on my way down Grafton Street just in case he was there. Con too was known well enough for Paddy always to call me Con. Such a passport brought more than a word of recognition: it entitled me to join the select few infrequently allowed to remain while the pub was closed during the Holy Hour from half-two till half-three and, on at least two occasions, when Paddy had copped that I had no more money, free drinks were put in front of me with a gruff instruction to drink up and not come the poor fucking student.

Con's theatrical connections put him in the way of getting complimentary tickets for the Olympia and the Gaiety and often used them to make a foursome with Pearse and Bridie, adjourning after the Gaiety to McDaids, where I might join them for a drink and a lift home.

There was also a period when the four of them met on Saturday nights in Peter's Pub, just around the corner from the Gaiety, where they joined up with Frank and Kathleen Behan, Brendan's parents. I found these sessions very enjoyable and loved to sit and chat with Uncle Frank, a little man full of wit and fun. More often than not I brought Sheila Killeen. Con and Maisie were discretely charmed by her youthful attractions and her ability to hold her own in a company very different from anything she had previously experienced. Con used to recall that she was the first woman he had ever seen with a pint in her hand. The times they were a-changing but Con and Maisie were happy to change with them. Sheila also came along with us when we attended Dubliners' concerts in the Royal Hotel in Howth.

I knew nobody my age who socialised and went drinking with their parents, as I had done from childhood lemonades in the Manhattan after Croke Park and as I would continue to do over pints for as long as possible; but however natural it seemed to me, my friends took a while first to accept, then to welcome their presence.

On several occasions Con joined me and my friends in McDaids. This generally happened on Friday or Saturday evenings when he was at a loose end at home and Maisie suggested I ask him for a lift into town. (I now presume she had cleared it with him beforehand.) Outside McDaids I would ask him if he felt like a pint and he would shrug why-not and agree to come in for just-the-one. As his principles forbade him to accept a drink without buying a round, more often than not he had three or four before heading home.

Such drinking and driving seems scandalous today but back then it was normal for a temperate man to know his limits and act accordingly. Cars were fewer then, becoming more common as the country emerged from recession. For Maisie, I suspect, this economic relaxation was a happy relief; but for Con, with his permanent consciousness of history, it was much more than financial: at last, half a century later, it seemed as if we were reaping the benefits of the fight for freedom in which his father had played so important a part.

Con relished the company of my friends whom he recognised as representative of his new country: young, independent-minded, optimistic. He would have liked them to acknowledge the past sacrifices that had eventually released these creative energies; but it was more important that they took advantage of the new circumstances to make better lives for themselves.

Though essentially congenial, Con was initially reserved in his relationships and so it was striking that while he would have been slow to relax in the company of their parents, he was almost immediately open and easy with my friends. (I say 'would have been' because, to the best of my recollection, he only ever met the parents of one of my friends, coincidentally the only one who lived in a corporation house, and that was briefly on the steps of Earlsfort Terrace at our graduation in 1966.)

Even back in McDaids I could admire the way he conducted himself, never trying to pass himself off as 'one of the lads' nor assuming the easier role of the widely experienced, condescendingly tolerant older man. He was happy to take them as they were and they reciprocated: I seldom meet any of them without hearing an affectionate tribute to him.

I never met Mick Lillis' parents. I knew them only through his stoically resigned accounts in which they were distant and censorious. His father was from Clare, a fluent Irish speaker with IRA sympathies and the puritanical outlook that often went with them; his mother, from west Cork, outdid her husband in the extremeness of her republicanism and of her opposition to those signs of moral compromise she saw as characteristic of the new 'modern' Ireland. Mick enjoyed the more relaxed atmosphere of our house and long afterwards recalled with relish the platefuls of food Maisie put in front of him. Though he and I were seen by some of our fellow-students as 'wild', we both worked hard at subjects we loved and both got firsts in our finals. The English Department was happy to award me a scholarship with which to fund a master's. Despite his degree and his academic potential, Celtic Studies made no such attempt to hold on to Mick. It was commonly believed they had held his attendance record against him. In a large department like English nobody bothered with attendance, provided you handed in the work. In the much smaller classes in Celtic Studies, every absence was noticed and, it seems, resented; nobody seemed to have argued that a student who attended sporadically but still got a first deserved a special award rather than a cold shoulder. Maybe it was all for the better: he went on to become one of the most successful diplomats of his generation.

Con and Maisie formed a mutual admiration society with Mick. Con came to his rescue when the luggage—including the tuxedos—of an American delegation had gone astray and he had (outside normal hours) brought them all into Bourke's and fitted them there and then. In 1976, in his capacity as Consul General in New York, Mick was in a position to reciprocate. On their first visit to my sister Maura and her husband in Montreal, Con and Maisie had driven down to New York to see Maisie's youngest brother, Bennie. All was well until a neighbour called from Montreal with the news that Maura and Michael's apartment had been gutted by fire. Deciding there was no point going back to Montreal, Con contacted Mick to see if the return tickets could be changed to an earlier date; this proved impossible but the resources of the Irish Consulate were made available to them with a magnanimity they never forgot.

SUCH WAS my contentment with student life that I was never tempted to seek gainful employment out in the real world. I accepted my tutorial scholarship with a view to taking two years to prepare for the Travelling Studentship that would, if I was successful, enable me to study abroad for a doctorate.

The Studentship did not stipulate any particular university but my passion for English literature inclined me towards Oxford or Cambridge and I was happy to accept the suggestion of the Head of English that I should choose Cambridge. But first I had to beat whatever opposition came from the other constituent colleges and attain a sufficiently high standard. And I would have to do it by myself: there were no classes or courses and, it was somehow understood (at least in UCD), no tradition of preparatory supervision.

But all that seemed far in the future and meanwhile the academic year 1966/67 was sweet. I felt I was well paid for teaching small groups of undergraduates in tutorials that demanded no great effort. I did not see the need to begin what would be an arduous programme of study, not just yet. I was due a break.

Four of my closest friends were qualifying as teachers, doing their 'hours' in secondary schools and attending evening lectures for the Higher Diploma in Education, which was generally regarded as a cinch. Mick's work in Foreign Affairs was more demanding but it was better paid and left most evenings and weekends free for long walks and literary discussions that were continued in pubs. Besides, there were lots of parties and even, weather permitting, tennis on Saturday mornings in Herbert Park.

I continued to see Eugene Watters. His grief at Una's death took many forms, including a decision to break down and rebuild the bungalow. I lent a hand, swinging a sledge and reducing to rubble and dust those delightful little rooms where Una had painted and where he had opened my eyes to the cinemascope of civilisation.

Meanwhile I was enjoying all the comforts of a happy home. Con still did a lot of overtime, working as stage electrician on school shows directed by Tomás Mac Anna (who knew him from the Abbey pantomimes) and this culminated in the Croke Park pageant to mark the fiftieth anniversary of the Easter Rising. It was probably on Mac Anna's recommendation that he began working for Gael Linn, the Irish language organisation that produced plays in the Damer Hall, most notably the original version of *The Hostage* (before Con's time) and including several by Eugene in his Irish guise, Eoghan Ó Tuairisc.

I sometimes helped Con putting up or taking down the lights. I remember arriving into the theatre for the first time and assuming that the chaotic jumble of lamps and leads and connections at the back of the stage was the legacy of some *gunterer* (sloppy worker): Con was compulsively tidy. When we returned at the end of the run, I decided to make life easier for him the next time by rationalising the situation: as he stripped the batten and handed the lamps down to me, I wrapped each in its own lead and lined them up neatly at the back of the stage. But when he noticed what I was doing, he told me not to bother, to go easy with the lamps but throw the leads anywhere. I was surprised to hear this, flabbergasted when, having come down off the ladder, he picked up the leads I had carefully coiled and threw them on top of the heap. Noticing my amazement, he smiled and explained. If everything was left neat and tidy, somebody might decide that there was no need to get Con Kearney in at all, that they could save the company money by doing it themselves. But faced with that chaos of equipment ....

His attitude to the Damer company was ambivalent. His inability to converse casually in Irish placed him at a disadvantage and while he got on well with most of the cast, there were others he accused of a sin he despised, that of being secretly opposed to the revival of Irish, preferring to keep it to themselves for their own selfish advantage. Though he was innately suspicious of those, almost all of whom had come from 'down the country' to make good lives for themselves by working in the civil service in Dublin, his favourite among the actors was Barry Houlihan, a roguishly jovial senior civil servant from Cork who, on entering the theatre for a rehearsal and seeing the others chatting in Irish would shout out in a broad Cork city accent: 'Jesus, Con, how do you stick it among all these culchies?'

I SPENT the summer in London, working for the Baltic Timber Company and staying in nearby Acton with Maisie's sister Annie and her husband John McManus. John introduced me to his friends, a swashbuckling group of Irish building workers who were up to every *divilment* and onto every fiddle from petty theft to benefit fraud. We seemed to get on very well together. Never having encountered a university student before, they were intrigued by my presence (and by my inability to calculate dart scores as instantly as they could) and took good care of their very own 'Brainbox'. I could have listened forever to their tales of outwitting all forms of authority, from the police to welfare inspectors to site foremen.

Just before I was due to go home, my girlfriend of several months ended our relationship. If this had happened the previous year, the effect would not have been so painful or have lasted so long. As one of small group of close friends who had been together for more than four years, I would have had less time to nurse my wound and ample opportunities for distraction. I would have accepted that such break-ups were the norm of student life, that the sensible reaction was to continue going to pubs and parties on the look-out for a new girlfriend.

But I was going back to an empty city, with nothing but study on the horizon. Employment had taken the others away from Dublin. The old round table was dissolved and I, the last, returned companionless.

I did my best at home to give the impression all was well, but to little or no avail. Con and Maisie tried to hide their anxiety on my behalf, but with a similar lack of success. It may seem odd that in such a family neither they nor I ever gave any expression to our feelings; but back then it was as unbecoming for a male to admit to a broken heart as it was to cry or show fear.

The person to whom I revealed most was Eugene for whose opinion I submitted a long poem of loss. He instantly recognised what was clear in every line but our conversation was conducted under the partial anaesthetic of literary criticism.

He himself was still in such a bad way that Mammy got me to invite him to the house so that she could feed him. He groaned like a starving man as he worked his way through the food, savouring every drop of her hot milk coffees, so much so he began to come down on a regular basis.

At least once a month he was convinced he had found a new way to re-establish his life and so start writing again. The remodelling of his house was one such plan that, once the destruction had satisfied his need to express his rage at fate, revealed itself as impractical. Wanting to show his gratitude to Mammy for her generosity, he proposed to sell the house to Con and Maisie for a nominal amount they could afford. Even he can hardly have imagined the appeal for them of a house of their own. And no ordinary house: a bungalow perfectly positioned out in the rich farmland of north-west Dublin but with a city bus terminus just outside the door to take us into town. And less than a five-minute drive from where we were living. It would need some work, but who better than Con to turn a mess into a dream come true?

They were devastated when, once again, he changed his mind: he needed to make an absolute break with the past, which ruled out the idea of installing his friends in a house he wanted to banish from his life. It was the end of his friendship with Con and Maisie. I remained faithful: I knew his treatment of them had been disgraceful but I also knew—much better than they could even imagine—just how unhinged he was, how different from the man who, with Una, had entertained them and enthralled me in the bungalow at Cappagh Cross.

(We all lived to see the silver lining appear in that dark cloud of disappointment. Shortly afterwards Eugene told me he had given the house to a homeless family he had found living on the side of the road in north County Dublin. They moved in and turned the place into a junkyard, prompting Con to guess that Eugene had done this to spite his brother-in-law who lived adjacently and against whom he bore a grudge. Within a few years the pastoral calm was shattered by the building of the M50 circular motorway little more than a hundred yards away.)

I had to find something to keep my mind off my own loneliness and chose to immerse myself in preparation for the Travelling Studentship exams. When not tutoring in UCD I was poring over books in the National Library, in Trinity or in the front room at home. I became, literally, a full-time student, hell-bent on acquainting myself with everything of value in English literature from Old English to the mid-nineteenth century, measuring out my life in cigarettes and cups of coffee.

And rugby. In an inspired moment it struck me that I needed to take regular breaks, to do something completely different, get out in the air, preferably with other people, and so for a season I was scrum half for the minors of Clontarf RFC. Though I had not played since Garbally, I rediscovered my old affection for the contest, the muck and the sweat, the relief of physical and mental exhaustion.

Eugene was the only one with whom I could share my literary explorations but he had his own cross to carry and on one occasion his support was uncharacteristically tentative. In a gloomy moment I must have mentioned (or written) that I was less than sanguine regarding my chances of success in the studentship exam. Shortly afterwards a letter arrived in which he claimed to understand my anxiety, adding that he had felt for some time that I was 'riding for a fall'. This shocked me to such an extent that I told Con about it. He thought it was a shameful remark by a former teacher who should have known better in the run up to a crucial exam. I could not but acknowledge its unhelpfulness but attributed it to Eugene's disturbed state of mind. Con was less inclined to forgive what he put down to the envy of an embittered man.

I sat the exams in late summer in the National University of Ireland building in Merrion Square. Had I entertained thoughts of failure I would probably have handicapped myself, if not broken down altogether; but I was a seasoned sitter of scholarship examinations—thanks more to Eugene than to any other teacher—and, like a fearful soldier, I assumed an aggressive pose to suppress any anxieties, constantly reminding myself that there was no question the examiners could set that I could not answer.

At the end of a week of exams I was in a state of anticlimactic collapse with no battle to get my adrenalin running; the orals were not for another three weeks. One evening Con came in from work and tried in vain to liven me up. Minutes later—presumably after a confab with Maisie—he came out of the kitchen, found me at the foot of the stairs outside the front room and suggested I go over to London for a couple of weeks. When I shrugged, he dropped his casual manner, as if surprised by a sudden thought.

'Is it money? If you had the money, would you go to London? Don't move. Stay where you are.'

At which point he actually ran up the stairs to his bedroom and came running back down the stairs with notes in his hand. The following day I was on my way to London to play cards and darts, drink pints and talk petty crime with the hard men of Acton.

My only other oral examination before the studentship had been for Leaving Cert Irish in which, instead of testing my fluency, the examiner had detailed his pleasure in encountering a grandson of Peadar Kearney at

Garbally and urged me never to forget what an honour it was to be related to the man who wrote the national anthem. This was not ideal preparation for a grilling by some ten professors on the canon of English literature from *Beowulf* to Byron but, yet again, I managed to cloak whatever anxieties lurked behind my politely aggressive demeanour and to convince the bench of inquisitors to give me the studentship.

I rang Con in Bourke's with the news; he stayed long enough on the phone to say he was on his way to meet me in Lincoln's Inn. I don't think I have ever seen him so happy, so relieved, so triumphant. *We* had won. *We* had overcome all obstacles and trounced the opposition. And *his son* was into the next round, in the illustrious University of Cambridge, for the ultimate educational prize, the Ph.D.

When we met in Lincoln's Inn there was no question of ordering pints. It was glasses of brandy and Tuborg lager. And feelings too strong for words. The release of tension had left me exhausted but alert enough to gauge the significance when he announced that he had told Jimmy he would not be coming back to work. We were pushing out the boat. Another drink and then home to Maisie.

SUCH A triumph demanded a party. Occasionally in the past we had had small get-togethers thrust upon us by Christmas or an overseas visitor, but nothing as organised or as large-scale as this. Invitations were issued, food prepared and, as Maisie would say, enough drink laid in to float a battle-ship. I was only slightly disappointed that none of my close college friends were around because I realised that while I was, so to speak, the guest of honour, the night really belonged to Con and Maisie: it was their chance to glow with pride and pleasure as another of their dreams came true and I encouraged them to invite their friends.

On the appointed night a fleet of cars arrived such as Cappagh Avenue had never witnessed and I was duly congratulated by a gathering of Kearneys, Bourkes and Bradys who set about enjoying themselves. The last to arrive were Pearse and Bridie who came by bus. Seeing the cars outside and hearing the jovial tumult within provoked a characteristic eruption of disgruntlement in Pearse, his hair soaked by rain, his family pride ruffled that none of the Bourkes had thought to offer them a lift. But he was, as he had always been, my favourite relation and I knew that if I took him into the kitchen and made him a stiff drink and mocked his crabbiness, he would instantly shake the rain out of his hair, break into a broad grin and assure me that this was fucking great.

And so it was, a night of story and laughter and song. Top of the bill was Lorcan. Peadar Kearney had been well represented when somebody gave Lorcan their noble call. The front room was crowded but he instinctively positioned himself in the corner between the door and the window so that he was in the spotlight and the rest of us became his audience. There was a barrage of requests but this old trouper knew what the occasion demanded and, lowering his voice to whisper-level to get maximum attention, he began 'Lily of Laguna', interspersing the lines with stage directions and lecherous glances at the imagined Moonbeams behind him. By the time he got to the chorus they were all at least thirty years younger and back in the Queen's, eyes glistening and bodies swaying, Con maybe holding the spot on the singer, Maisie looking up from the stalls trying to catch his eye.

> *She's my lady love,*
> *She is my dove, my baby love,*
> *She's no gal for sitting down to dream,*
> *She's the only queen Laguna knows;*
> *I know she likes me. I know she likes me*
> *Because she says so;*
> *She is my Lily of Laguna.*
> *She is my Lily and my Rose.*

Before the applause began to subside, Lorcan was into his encore, 'On Mother Kelly's Doorstep', showing off his soft shoe shuffle.

> *She's got a little hole in her frock,*
> *A hole in her shoe,*
> *A hole in her sock*
> *Where her toe peeps through,*
> *But Nellie was the smartest down our alley.*

Maybe the soft shoe shuffle was a polite distraction but I cannot have been the only one to notice that tonight Nellie's sock was as good as new; her problem was 'the hole in her knickers where her fanny peeped through'. Had I been quick enough to catch Con's reaction I might have been able to confirm my suspicion that this variation was an old routine from days that were by now distant but happy memories.

I ARRIVED in Cambridge expecting a life of high seriousness and monastic assiduity; to my great relief I quickly discovered that King's College was more Hell Fire Club than Tintern Abbey.

Structurally the college was a collection of architectural gems, including the world-famous chapel. Meals were taken in an opulently high-ceilinged hall: there was a menu to cater for various tastes and pockets and whenever, very occasionally, somebody criticised the food I smiled and wondered what they would have made of Garbally fare. My room, in the new Keynes Building, had its own bathroom and a shared kitchen across the corridor, all kept clean and tidy by a friendly Glaswegian woman, who was my 'bedder'. Downstairs was a spacious bar and a basement discotheque.

There were the usual rules but no evidence of enforcement, and one got the impression that the Fellows who ran King's were more inclined to accommodate the students' wishes than obey the university authorities. There were gate hours, outside which no students could enter or exit. The Porter's Lodge displayed these ordinances, but made no mention of what they surely knew, that 'somebody' had removed a bar from the front railing, thus enabling even a portly student or guest to come and go whenever they wished and that 'somebody'—perhaps the same skilled metallurgist—had added a ledge to one side of the back gate so that even a young lady in high heels could climb around it on a wet or windy night.

The Sixties, rumoured to be about to arrive in UCD, were firmly established here. Every morning at breakfast there were girls who made no effort to conceal the fact that they had spent the night with a student. Every evening in the bar I heard talk of the pleasures of marijuana. I was shocked and could not wait to surrender to all these temptations.

Some people managed to be unhappy at Cambridge—mainly undergraduates who had been top of their classes all their lives and who now found themselves closer to the bottom—but my three years were the time of my life.

The subject of my research was a genuinely fascinating painter, Benjamin Robert Haydon (1786-1846), who had dedicated his life to the establishment of public 'historical' painting in Britain and who had known many famous writers and encouraged the young Keats. His campaign for 'high art' had failed and he had ended his own life but he had detailed his efforts in a wonderful diary that had recently been published in full. While I found the writing of a doctoral dissertation rather limited and dull, social life was anything but, thanks mainly to the friends I made, almost all of whom were undergraduate mathematicians and natural scientists. I had initially associated with research students but most of these were in long-term relationships, which meant that they were of little help to me in getting into any kind of relationship, no matter how short-term. I did not consciously seek undergraduate company: finding it was a consequence of playing regularly on the rugby and occasionally on the football team.

Although the Troubles were well under way in Northern Ireland, I never felt the need to disguise my Irishness. My friends were characteristically broadminded, tolerant and liberal, vehemently English (they were almost all English) when supporting England teams but otherwise, by Irish standards, devoid of 'national feeling'. They would have given short shrift to anybody of any nationality who picked on me: I was their friend.

EARLY IN 1969, Con arrived in London on some business. I met him in London and brought him up to Cambridge by train and showed him to his college room. It must have been February or March because I remembering him wincing in the cold outdoors, never having experienced anything like the icy blasts that whipped in from the fens (and were reputed to have originated in Russia). I distinctly recall one morning as we emerged from the warmth of the bar into the frosty air of the front court on our way to see some of the sights. Con braced himself and then, seeing me coatless and with the top button of my shirt open, implored me to do myself up. I should of course have done what he asked but I callowly replied that I wasn't cold. With characteristic dexterity he told me that looking at me was making him cold. And so I did as he asked.

We concentrated on libraries, chapels and pubs, nipping smartly from one to the next, merely glancing at the river. We must have visited all the usual places of interest—the various colleges, King's Chapel, the Wren Library and, our own favourite, the Eagle bar—but neither of us had a camera and so, with one or two exceptions, I only have a general memory.

The first is set in my second-floor room, which contained a low bed that doubled as a sofa, a desk and work chair, a coffee table and armchair; length-of-the wall windows looked down into Chetwynd Court. As one entered the room there was a wardrobe on the left and a bathroom on the right.

It is about half past eight in the morning and early rising Con has come from his guest room to get me to take him down to breakfast. I leap out of bed and head for the shower, telling him I won't delay. A couple of minutes later I wrap myself in a towel and head into the room. I see him through the door, standing over by the window. He looks ill at ease, relieved at my return. Perplexed, I enter the room and, directed by his glance, turn around to find a girlfriend, Emelie, sitting on the bed. The three of us smile uneasily, none of us sure what our next move is.

Emelie was a nurse in nearby Addenbrooke's whom I had met towards the end of first term. She was an extremely attractive blonde in her early twenties, had just come off a night shift and had dropped in to see if I was back from London. She was wearing a skirt so mini that, when she sat on my low sofa-bed, it ceased to fulfil its traditional role of concealing her underwear.

Finding the door open and hearing me in the shower, she had not bothered to knock and was dumbfounded to find an older man in my room. If he was equally taken aback by the unannounced arrival of a mini-skirted blonde, he had concealed it well. With some aplomb, he introduced himself as my father and refused to hear of her leaving before I came in from the shower. All I could think of doing was asking if she would like to join Con and me for breakfast but (with equal aplomb) she explained that she had to get back to her flat to admit a tradesman who was due to fix some fault. At which point she and Con shook hands and exchanged the usual compliments, I promised to phone her, she left and I got dressed.

Hardly a word was said about her visit. For all our closeness we were still father and son. He was an unusually understanding father who, despite the narrowness of his upbringing, was sufficiently open-minded to accept the ways of a changing world. And what was there to say that would generate more light than embarrassment?

(Later on Maisie told me he had noticed Emelie's charms but was more concerned with the large windows that opened fully up and out. During my mid-teens I had several bouts of sleepwalking. In the course of one I climbed out my bedroom window on Cappagh Avenue, settling on the little canopy over the front door until it got too cold and I went back to my warm bed. For the rest of my year in the Keynes Building Con had been haunted by the thought of me climbing out through the second-floor window.)

The other clear picture of the visit is a longer silent shot. Con and four or five of my friends are seated around one of the low white tables in the college bar. I see them as I return from the toilet and pause. Despite remembering similar scenes in McDaids, I am still taken aback to see how comfortable an Irishman of Con's educational and political background is with these bright young things—all long hair, floral shirts, flared trousers—who are visibly caught between pleasure and surprise to be having a perfectly normal chat over a pint with a man who is not only Irish but old enough to be their father and the actual father of a fellow-student.

Our time in London—a couple of days before and after the Cambridge visit—was divided between days in the city and nights in various pubs around Acton. We did the museums and galleries, paused at the famous theatres, rambled around Soho, still residually a place of ill repute. Con was impressed by the sheer splendour of London, was mildly interested in what the British Museum and the National Gallery had to offer but what really captured his attention was the costume section of the V & A.

The other highlight of our wandering in the great city was more mundane. Though not quite as arctic as the plains of East Anglia, the temperature on the streets of London was uncomfortable for a 'cold creature' like Con and it was with some relief that, having looked around theatre land, we opened the door of a pub on Cambridge Circus and sensed the warm, welcoming air. And something else. Hot food.

It was late lunchtime and I was not sure if it was still being served. Con would have settled for a comfortable seat and a pint and a sandwich—in those days Dublin pubs seldom rose above a skimpy sandwich and a bowl of soup—but I had higher hopes for him and, from the way his eyes followed the evidence of his nose, it was clear that Con was thinking along the same lines. Up at the bar I was disappointed to learn that the only food remaining was shepherd's pie, but Con was too hungry and cold to have a second thought: he got stuck into it with relish, pausing only to express amazement that such lowly fare could be so delicious, and to congratulate me on leading him to this oasis. When the barman came to collect our plates and sensed the genuine nature of Con's compliments, he mentioned that there was a little left in the tray that we were welcome to have on the house. Offer gratefully received, the crowning glory of a pub lunch that entered the family annals.

He quickly found his feet in the Prince of Wales in Acton. The semi-criminal patrons were not the kind of people he had ever mixed with but he was every bit as won over by their feckless good humour and generous welcome as I had been.

He was all ears when a barman in the Prince told him he was from Knockcroghery, a village in Roscommon about which Con's father had written a rollicking ballad. The barman, equally fascinated to meet the son of a man who had not only composed the Irish national anthem but had immortalised a place few in Ireland had ever heard of, insisted on standing Con a couple of drinks. Which Con had reason to remember the following evening when he learned from the guv'nor that 'Knockcroghery' had had to be let go, his generosity to his friends being more than any business could bear. As his flight was called, I smiled at him: 'No need to ask if you enjoyed yourself.'

'I certainly did, every minute of it. [*Pausing, looking around to make sure his whisper would not be overheard.*] But I wouldn't go away again without your mother.'

(Years later Maisie told me he had written to her every day he was away. What did he say? And how come Maisie did not keep the letters? Maisie, who kept everything, from my first teddy to my early annuals? What had she done with Con's letters? My guess is that she kept them for a while and then destroyed them: they were a private matter and she would no more have divulged the contents, even to me.)

MY YEARS at King's were probably the most turbulent of the second half of the twentieth century. In the US the cocktail of anti-war protests and attendant race riots was aggravated by the assassination of Martin Luther King in April 1968 and guaranteed another 'long hot summer' in the cities. Watching TV coverage of *les événements* of May in Paris, it was possible to imagine a social revolution was imminent. In August 1968 the first Civil Rights march took place in Northern Ireland: paramilitary police attempts to suppress it would lead to thirty years of civil war.

King's was, at least in Cambridge, notoriously left-wing. Two of those imprisoned for their part in the 1970 Garden House riot against the Greek junta were King's men with whom I was fairly close. But the vast majority of my friends were more typical of their time and type: liberally inclined to the left, generally tolerant but more immediately concerned with self-liberation through sex and soft drugs than any grander political commitment. They were at least as dismissive of imperialism—British or American—as any Irish republican. I presume they resented IRA attacks on their innocent fellow-subjects but they never fulminated in my company; nor did they ever suggest that I, because I was Irish, was in any sense responsible, any more than I ever thought of blaming them for the excesses of the RUC or the Paras. My guess is that before the year was out me being from Ireland was no different from any of them being from London or Yorkshire or Lancashire.

I enjoyed my time in Cambridge, which I thought of as a kind of Toytown, a place or state of almost perfect happiness, protected from the real world. There were, of course, sub-ecstatic moments when a disregarding girl or an unexpected wing-forward brought me back to earth; but they passed and I regained equilibrium in the camaraderie of the college bar or on a quiet walk with a new girlfriend. Bliss was it that dawn to be alive, to be at King's was very heaven, but as my stay was coming to an end, clouds began to appear in the distance.

Back in Dublin during my final summer vacation, my UCD English professor and I had discussed my future plans and he had told me there was no reason why, with a Cambridge doctorate, I should not return to UCD as a lecturer. The following term my Cambridge supervisor had sighed with relief when he heard of this arrangement, relieved that there was at least one of his students whose future he did not have to worry about.

Shortly afterwards a letter from Con included a newspaper cutting in which the president of UCD announced an embargo on new staff due to financial constraints. I wrote to assure him it would not apply to me, but I was not as convinced as I pretended and when I checked with my UCD professor, he confirmed the embargo. He made no reference to our 'understanding' nor was there any point in complaining: he had merely made a promise he did not have the power to keep.

MY RETURN home contrasted with my triumphant departure. Given my uninterrupted ascent up the academic ladder, this was a catastrophe, the end of an enterprise that had defined me and Con and Maisie for as long as any of us could remember.

I instinctively put on a brave face. Con and Maisie did the same but even Maisie could not always contain her furious inability to understand how anybody could treat her son so unfairly. I was ignorant of the economics of higher education; but I had been a student for eight years and knew that academics looked and behaved like other mortals, more or less. As far as Con and Maisie were concerned the university was another world, with rules they did not understand, a language they did not speak, and a system of justice that took no account of fairness. How else to explain how or why, when their son had fulfilled all their requirements by passing all exams with flying colours, they had slammed the door in his face?

I felt very sorry for myself—and for Maisie—but even worse was the feeling that I had failed Con. It looked like the end of reflected glory.

I applied for jobs and was called for interviews in England but there was always a reason not to appoint me. Polytechnics were rightly suspicious of my Cambridge doctorate, knowing I would leave when a university post came up. At two universities I was pointedly informed that a local candidate for interview was currently filling the post in a temporary capacity. At one of them there was a fellow-applicant I had known at King's: when we learned of the local tenant, we collected our expenses and, over pub lunch and a pint, tried to make light of being used as extras in a charade.

I cannot recall how desperate or despondent I was when I applied to the Dublin Vocational Committee for 'hours'. This normally involved standing by until somebody went sick in one of the vocational schools; but in the first school I went to there was almost no hanging around because there was always at least one of the permanent staff out sick and it didn't take long to see why.

In such a school as this, in a large working-class estate, about a third of the boys were bright enough to see that they might pick up something useful, especially in the craft classes; another third accepted that the law demanded they stay in education until they were sixteen and decided to serve out their sentence and get it over with; the final third, seeming to consist of the smallest brains in the biggest bodies, set out to pass the time by causing as much trouble and disruption as possible and, in the process, leaving the less hardy of the staff in regular need of rest and recreation.

The Principal of this boys' school was straight out of Cloud Cuckoo Land and was later rewarded with a university appointment in Education. He had replaced old-fashioned classes in Irish history and geography with multi-media presentations on the history and geography of the Masai tribe; the interest of the boys lasted as long as the slides of bare-breasted women. So far removed was the Principal from reality that he thought my postgraduate studies would benefit both me and the school. In fact, the most useful part of my education was my time in Ballygall national school with boys not unlike those who faced me now.

I survived by convincing them that I was not as stupid as I looked, no mean feat in the circumstances. I seldom knew (or bothered finding out) what teacher or subject I was substituting for. My job, as I saw it, was to get from the beginning of the period till the end without serious trouble and I did this largely by bribery. I offered each class a choice: we could either do a quiz with each of the four rows forming a team, or solve a crossword that I would draw on the board. In either case the prize was the same: cash.

I could well afford it. I was possibly the best-paid teacher in the school. Substitute rates had been set high in order to attract people who might only get one or two hours a day; but there were days when I did not have a single hour off. Had I been told I would spend the rest of my working life there, I would have run out the door; but believing I was there for a year at most, I decided to make the best of it. If the strain of coming up with new schemes to maintain some kind of order began to get to me, I reminded myself I was being well paid for my distress.

Cheerfulness was always breaking in, if not in the classroom—or in the pub where I had lunch with three or four female teachers perpetually on the verge of nervous breakdown—then at home as I offered my daily report. One incident made its way into the family saga. Boys were playing handball on a gable wall and, as I was walking past, I stopped an out-of-bounds ball by dropkicking it back to the player, who reacted with 'Jaysus, sir, you're a fucking shark!' (To her dying day Maisie liked to refer to me as The Shark.)

A memorable moment I did not share with my family. I was outside the gate of the school as the boys came rushing out, two of them examining the page of a magazine with adolescent concentration, the holder stuffing it into his jacket pocket as soon as he saw me, although I had no intention of interfering and they knew it. Once beyond the gate and all authority, one grabbed the arm of the other and exclaimed 'Weh-heh-hey! The vagina!' (He pronounced Vag-in-ah with a hard g and the stress on the first syllable).

But I did not always have the circus of the classroom to distract me from the spectres of failure and despair that hovered above my solitary bed.

And then, as unexpectedly as they had lowered, the clouds lifted. At a UCD party I met Alan Bliss, my old professor of Old and Middle English, who had heard that University College Cork (UCC) were about to make an appointment in Modern English and suggested I make inquiries. There was indeed a job, which I applied for and got. Con and Maisie and I could breathe more easily. Suddenly the misery of the previous months seemed a bad dream. We had survived the winter of our discontent and could resume our faith in glorious summers to come.

ON 10 June 1972, a bright sunny day, Con and Maisie and I were in Cambridge for my conferring and this time there was a camera with which to record the event [*Images*, 36, 37, 38]. Maisie (55) is resplendent in her new costume and hair-do; a trim, black-haired Con (53) as happy as I have ever seen him.

One of my friends has entered into the spirit of the occasion by placing a hand on Maisie's shoulder. Like the others, he has been pleasantly surprised by the informality of the occasion and specifically by parents who are willing to relax with their son's friends. Among my favourites is one of Maisie wandering around the Senate House lawn, absorbing the atmosphere [*Image 37*]. (We have no connection with the other graduates.)

I also like the one in the Eagle yard with the three of us and my close friend Richard turning my hood up into a stove-pipe hat to general amusement [*Image 38*]. Again, what makes it endearing is Con's smile, which exudes a happiness he very seldom revealed to a camera.

Had he himself just been conferred Ph.D (Cantab.) he could not have been more pleased. In the eyes of the world he was a proud parent, but I was aware of another dimension in which his was the name on the parchment and this gives pride of place to the photo of the two of us outside the Senate House immediately after the ceremony [*Image 35*].

I am almost twenty-seven, he exactly twice my age. We are both dark-haired, mine fashionably longish, his short and neat, but strong. My academic apparel aside, we are similarly dressed, in dark suits and black shoes, and both of us have heavy black glasses. I cannot with any confidence match facial features—the conventional basis for look-alike—but nobody comparing us from the chins down could fail to notice the uncanny resemblances, the genetic *tour de force*. Had we been trying to follow a photographer's instructions, we could not have mimicked each other's stance so perfectly, from the slope of our shoulders to the clenched hands all the way down to the angle of our feet.

The following day was another summer special and I decided to punt them up to Grantchester for the ritual cream tea in the Orchard. I explained what was involved, being careful to mention the strict rule against bringing any food or drink into the Orchard, and then Maisie suggested that Con and I could have a pint in the Eagle while she had a look around the shops.

Imagine the mixture of anticipation and anxiety as we made our way down to the river and saw the bank thronged with people sunning themselves and checking the talent on the water: sun-hatted damsels gazing up at their squires as—aloft on the till, all concern and casual manliness—they drive their ten-feet-plus poles into the gravel and send the punt shooting along in intermittent bursts. Imagine Maisie's trepidation as we helped her aboard the undulating punt. How long before they managed to relax in the knowledge that I seemed to be a competent pilot capable of steering them safely through the traffic? Probably when we had pulled the punt over the rollers and proceeded into the countryside, passing from the sparkling shade of overarching branches into the perfect blue sky, then back again.

They were seated on rubber cushions and not on burnish'd thrones, in a King's punt and not a royal Egyptian barge, but they were perhaps happier than Antony and Cleopatra ever were as they shed their sense of being interlopers from a corporation scheme in Finglas and enjoyed the occasion in the knowledge that the ceremony in the Senate House the previous day had entitled them as much as anybody else.

We tied up at the Orchard, found a free table and, having ordered our cream tea, set about observing the beautiful people all around us. Maisie said nothing when the waitress put the tray down in front of us but I could see that she found the fare rather skimpy. I tried to calm her: this was not a meal but a token snack that was the price of relaxing in these idyllic surroundings before heading back to Cambridge and getting something decent to eat. She understood all that—of course—and, while pouring Con's tea and buttering his scone, agreed that everything about the place was only beautiful.

When did I notice the strange looks from neighbouring tables? Immediately before I sniffed an aroma more pungent than tea or cakes. My efforts to interpret this change of mood were interrupted by Maisie tipping my knee and using her eyes to direct my attention under the table. I reached down and felt what turned out to be a cold leg of chicken in a paper napkin. 'Here, take this and pass it to your father.' I was about to remind her of the regulations, but what would be the point? I did as I was told, then waited for the other leg. Her glance said it all: I might have picked up some strange ideas in Cambridge, but there was no way her Con was going to be fobbed off with a bun, especially after all that lovely fresh air on the river.

SHORTLY AFTER arriving back in Dublin I was offered a job in La Trobe University in Melbourne—(Maisie, muttering: 'It never rains but it pours.')—but I do not recollect ever giving it serious consideration nor, looking back over forty-plus years, can I say for sure why I was not attracted by the prospect of such an adventure. I had said yes to Cork and I had been brought up not to break my word without very good reason. Not that I envisaged spending much more than a year in Cork, it still being my ambition to return to UCD when this recession had passed and the embargo was lifted.

And I had to bear Con and Maisie and my two remaining sisters in mind. (Maura had just settled in Montreal.) Given a reasonable alternative, I would have been loath to put myself where a pint with Con or one of Maisie's enormous dinners would become annual treats, both for their sakes and my own. Even Cork must have seemed a long way, especially for people who, in much leaner times, had been unable to tear themselves away from working-class Dublin in order to enjoy a higher standard of living in Limerick.

If I was beset by any doubts during that summer, I was not aware of the them nor, my guess, was anybody else. Two of my close friends from UCD were back in town and we saw a good deal of each other. There seemed to be a lot of parties and I was flush, making good money teaching in a Ballsbridge language school. And there was my next adventure: on Monday, 4 September 1972, I took the train to Cork.

CEDARWOOD AVENUE

Most weekends during that first term in UCC I 'went home' to Dublin. Like Con and Maisie, I assumed Cork was but another stage in my career, that within a year or two I would end up 'back home' in UCD, where I would inevitably meet somebody with whom I would set up a home of my own, just as my sister Maura had recently done in Montreal and Con and Maisie themselves had done thirty years earlier.

I was probably the only one not taken aback when, before the academic year was out, I got engaged to Jean, a native of Cork city, who worked on the college switchboard. Jean's friends were stunned; my colleagues raised eyebrows; I smiled, convinced that, given the charmed nature of my life, all manner of thing would be well.

Con and Maisie had seemed taken by Jean when I had introduced them in Dublin and so I was surprised, as I entered the public phone box in St Luke's, to be chilled by a cloud of doubt as to how they would react to our announcement, but quickly dismissed the possibility that they could be less elated than we were. Until I replaced the hand-piece. They had expressed themselves delighted, congratulated us and wished us all the best; but I knew them too well not to detect a tiny nuance of reservation. At the time I attributed this to the shock of being ambushed with such life-changing news late at night in a long-distance call; almost twenty years had passed before I began to realise how callowly self-obsessed I had been not to anticipate their point of view.

Con and I were having a pint in Dublin when suddenly—or so it seemed to me—he went into himself and muttered something to the effect that as he had put down the phone that night, he had been holding back the tears. Neither of us was willing to go into the details, not there and then, but his words continued to haunt me and my mind was made up to raise the matter with him at the next suitable opportunity. The perfect moment never arrived and he was dead when my suspicion was confirmed.

I was visiting Maisie, passing the night in our usual way, going back over old times. When I recalled Con's remark in the pub, she fell suddenly silent, transfixed by the memory. Ten seconds must have passed before she spoke, in a tone totally at odds with the cheerful nostalgia of our previous conversation.

'Poor Con cried his eyes out. As soon as he put that phone down. O Jesus he did. Cried like a little boy.'

177

What made him cry?

Characteristically level-headed, he knew that such an announcement was inevitable: he was not the first or the last father to grieve as his child signalled a final farewell to the family home. Exceptionally clear-sighted, he could see that getting married to a Cork girl, while not ruling out a return to Dublin, lengthened the odds against it. Knowing me infinitely better than I knew myself, he probably anticipated what actually happened.

(While drafting these thoughts I attended a poetry reading by Robin Robertson. I was savouring his carefully carved lyrics until he read 'Donegal', which describes a man on Rossnowlagh beach, on the last day of summer, watching his twelve-year-old daughter running into the waves. She calls on him to join her but he stays on dry land, holding her clothes, and is granted a vision of himself that caught my heart off-guard.

I saw a man in the shallows
with his hands full of clothes, full of
all the years,
and his daughter going
where he knew he could not follow.

Suddenly the man at the lectern was Con and I was the girl in the sea.)

What I in my self-obsession had failed to take into account was that while my world was expanding—new city, new job, new colleagues, new fiancée—his was shrinking proportionately. Back in the days of the Lambretta, he had voiced his hope that we would be friends rather than conventional father-and-son and he had succeeded to such an extent that, although we both had wide circles of acquaintances, and despite the obstacles of time and place, he and I became 'best friends'.

JEAN AND I got married in September 1973 and moved into a new McInerney semi near Glanmire. If we were relieved to get a mortgage, Con was triumphant: his son was living in a 'purchase' house. On one of his first visits, he presented me with a Black and Decker drill, a considerable act of faith and encouragement because, thanks to his mastery of all crafts, I had never been called upon to do anything useful about the house. On another, he painted the living room walls for us.

Having tried a few test strokes, he turned to check my reaction and immediately noticed the absence of total satisfaction on my face. What was the problem? The shade was lighter than that advertised on the tin, more Burnt Sienna than the Burgundy we had chosen. No problem: he'd give it a bit more depth. Was there any brown polish in the house?

Within minutes he had blended some ground polish—plus a little ritual spittle—into the mix and the boosted paint on the wall was exactly what we had originally gone for. I was back in the bathroom on Cappagh Road, staring in admiration, never imagining that I could attempt such a task.

But his expertise must have been inspirational because I began to discover, to my own amazement, that I was far from useless about the house and garden. I tried my hand at hanging wallpaper and curtains, attaching fittings to walls, tilling the back garden to produce vegetables and herbs. I always knew I was giving expression to instincts inherited from Con, never more clearly than when I painted the walls of the utility room late in the summer of 1974.

> Ghostly, covered in white dust I stand
> In the kitchenette on Saturday afternoon;
> All movables have been removed, floor
> Covered with old newspapers, walls rubbed down;
> I hesitate, begin to count the cost, proceed.
>
> The lid comes off the can dripping
> Thick unstirred Avocado emulsion:
> The milk of sound and substance recalls
> Soft out-of-focus childhood rooms
> And the form of father the creator ...
>
> Thin men in coarse white overalls,
> Ties, hair oil, thin moustaches,
> Perched on ladders at freezing gutters
> Or singing along a length of railings;
> Red tea, cards and sandwiches in the hut
> Where the air is alive with strange language:
> Billy cans, wet time, country money.
>
> I scoop the six-inch brush and dab it,

179

Try to re-enact the steady hand
Moving unerringly along the line
Between wall and ceiling, then
Sweeping down and across and back
In a succession of smart slop-slaps.
An enlightening of the hand
Gives speed and energy and I see
Before me on the wall—as on a screen—
The old forgotten patterns re-emerge . . . .

CON AND Maisie were besotted with their grandchildren and lavished on them the generosity they had not been able to afford with their own children. Maisie was happy to become Nana, but Con did not want them to call him any form of grandfather. Perhaps this was a development of his earlier desire to deconstruct the conventional father-son bond with me; perhaps both were forms of reaction against his relationship with his own father. Sally, born in 1975, and her subsequent sisters—Clíona and Maeve—believed that 'Con' was a generic term for grandfather. Meanwhile they looked forward to Con and Nana's visits, assured of every kind of super-parental indulgence.

Life in Cork got better and better. The arrival of Clíona in 1977 coincided with my first academic monograph, *The Writings of Brendan Behan*, which turned out to be something of a passport, on the strength of which I was invited to lecture on his work in various institutions, including the Yeats International Summer School in Sligo. Thanks to the networking of an old UCD friend, I was invited to spend the first semester of 1980 teaching in the University of California at Irvine and accepted without a second's hesitation. Sally and Clíona would not grow up dreaming of California, as I had in the cinemas of my youth; they would be able to tell their school pals they had actually travelled on the freeways, window-shopped in the malls, frolicked in the warm waves of the Pacific. Maeve, born in 1981, joined her sisters for a return visit to the Irvine campus, where I taught in the summer session of 1982 (and a holiday in Boston, where I taught in the Harvard summer session of 1988).

In 1980, we had moved from Glanmire into St Luke's, within walking distance of the city centre and of St Angela's, Jean's old school, where we intended to send the girls. Our new home was a three-storey Edwardian house in need of refurbishment: Jean worried that the task of restoration was beyond us, but I had fallen in love with its scope and elegance—ample rooms, high ceilings, large windows and doors, antique fireplaces—and was happy to take it as it was until we could afford to fix it up to our satisfaction. (Con and Maisie were similarly divided: he excited by the possibilities, she daunted by the cost of realising them.)

IN DUBLIN things were not getting better. Between visits I was in phone contact at least once a week and, as the Seventies gave way to the Eighties, the tone of our conversations became more and more doom-laden. Working-class areas like Finglas should have been 'maturing', but deep recession and consequent social turmoil had broken the traditional pattern. To the petty crime always associated with high unemployment was added the villainy and gangsterism spawned by the new drug culture.

Burglary was commonplace. So many attempts had been made to steal Con's car—parked on a front garden drive-in—that he went upstairs at night not to sleep but to sit for hours at the front room window, on watch. One night a man—clearly lit by the street lamp and making no attempt to disguise himself—walked up to the car and tried to force the driver's door. Con threw open the window and threatened to call the police. The intruder hardly bothered to look up: 'Call the police, old man, and you're dead.' Then, having tried and failed the other doors, he gave up and continued on his way.

Con was a respectable man in his early sixties. The thug was probably in his twenties. Both knew the police had more pressing obligations than entering Finglas in the early hours of the morning to deal with the attempted theft of a car. For them, it was a misdemeanour; for the Kearney family it was terrorism.

Relatively safe and secure in our own homes, my sisters and I were racked with guilt at our inability to do anything to save them from what was a communal collapse of law and order. We lay awake in our beds imagining Con and Maisie in theirs.

It was Jean who first proposed what became the solution. Con and Maisie had bought their corporation house. If they were to sell that house and their children could raise enough between them, then they could buy in a safer area. And so it was that in 1984 they moved into a bungalow in Cedarwood Park in Ballymun. Though physically in sight of Finglas village, culturally it was a world away from Cappagh Avenue: a small, well-established, private estate.

On several occasions in the following years, Con suddenly paused in the middle of our conversation to thank me for making the move possible, shaking his head slowly as he dared to imagine what life would have been like had they been unable to escape from Cappagh Avenue. For him, even more than for Maisie, I suspect, the bungalow in Cedarwood was the ultimate dream come true. Maisie was content to make the best of any situation; Con was more aspirational, wanting the best possible for his family. He was not a snob, who looked down on other decent people, nor was he enamoured of any middle-class ethos. He was proud of his own background, most obviously of his father (who identified with the working class) but was in less obvious ways more influenced by his mother who had, famously, 'gone to school in a hackney' and who, despite long years of poverty, had never lost her aura of gentility. His inclination to think for himself led him to prefer the relative privacy of a middle-class lifestyle to the more communal culture that had evolved in overcrowded cottages and tenements.

Con felt at home in Cedarwood in a way he had not known since Inchicore: within a year he was on more relaxed terms with his neighbours than he had been during his thirty years in Finglas. The new house needed little refurbishment and he had all the time he needed for the gardens, front and back, which he developed as little rose-bordered lawns.

Apart from newspapers, he was not a great reader and, having worked in cinemas and theatres, had little or no interest in going to films or plays. The television was usually on in the background but only the news and sports claimed his full attention. Wine would be produced for visitors but it would never have occurred to Con or Maisie to have a drink themselves during or after their evening meal.

He loved his pint but would no more have gone into a pub by himself in the hope of finding company than he would have drunk alone. He was openly delighted when I came up, telling me out straight how much he had been looking forward to a drink and a chat together in his new local, The Willows.

We seldom touched on the profound mysteries of life or paid much attention to the state of the planet, preferring to chat away about 'the news' from Dublin and Cork. It often struck me on my way home that our chats were conducted in a private discourse, oblique and indirect, but, consciously or unconsciously, we both knew this and could not have been more transparent with each other.

We almost always stayed longer and had more pints than planned. Invariably the fourth pint was called as 'one for the road', but several entries in my diaries confirm my recollection of nights when this was followed by another couple.

Nor was the night at an end when we got back to the house. Maisie, delighted to observe that we were both 'diamond-eyes', would sit us down to a supper of spare ribs, hot for Con and cold for me. And then the three of us would go at it for another hour, *gawstering* away about time present and times past.

At one point a neighbour who had seen Con and me walking round to the pub had remarked to Maisie that it was like watching two brothers. I think I know what she meant. It was not merely that Con, twenty-seven years older than me, looked younger than his years or even that, to her eyes as to many others, we resembled each other physically; it was more a case of sensing an ease between us more often found in brothers than in father and son. Our different experiences and formal educations had given us divergent views, but nothing of vital importance had ever come between us: both of us loved to argue the toss but we never had a row, never fell out, never even raised a voice to each other.

IN LATER years we seldom went to Croke Park together, my youngest sister Eva eventually taking my place. I clearly recall one game, an All Ireland hurling semi-final between Cork and Galway in the early Eighties. There was a decent crowd but nothing like capacity, both sets of supporters probably saving themselves for the final, and for whatever reason, we found ourselves not on Hill 16 but behind the goal at the canal end.

Galway started much better, to Con's obvious satisfaction. When I attended matches in Cork, which was not often, I was surrounded by hundreds shouting for Cork and would have felt foolish opening my mouth, while just to be in Croke Park was to be reminded just how irredeemably Dublin I was. Then, much to my surprise, out it came:

'Come on, Cork!'

It was the annoyance of a hurling fan rather than the fervour of a Cork supporter. I wanted a good game and the Cork players were showing no signs of providing the required resistance. Con looked at me as if I had made a fool of myself in public.

'What are you doing that for?'

'What are you shouting for Galway for?'

'Galway was always our second county. You went to school there.'

'For five years. I've been twice that long in Cork.'

'You know what I mean.'

I had a fair idea. Galway had been Spiddal and the holy grail of the Irish language, Garbally and the highroad to university, places from which I had returned home in triumph. Cork was a high-status job, family and purchase house, but it was not Dublin. I would have left it at that but when he increased his support for Galway, I did the same for Cork.

At half-time we sat down on the terrace to enjoy the substantial sandwiches Maisie had made for us. We were untying the twine to open the greaseproof wrapping when a man leaned over us, one hand on Con's shoulder, the other on mine, speaking in a country accent that was neither Cork nor Galway:

'Isn't it great to see the pair of you sitting down together as friendly as you like, you from Galway and you from Cork and the two of you getting on like a house on fire?'

Con turned around to him, no trace of a smile on his face.

'He is *not* from Cork. He is my *son* and *we* are from Dublin.'

I felt sorry for the unfortunate stranger. If he had no ear for accents, he caught the tone of Con's voice, realised he had somehow upset him and retreated to his original position, leaving us to our sandwiches.

ON SEVERAL of his visits to Cork I took him bowling with a small group of friends who used to meet at Cloghroe on Saturday afternoon, bowl two scores up and back, ending the afternoon with games of forty-five for as long as it took us to have two drinks. He was intrigued by the more skilful bowlers as they hurled a 28 ounce steel ball along a country road, pitching it so that it stayed on course for as long as possible, but he was even more taken by the manner in which *professors* unbuttoned at the card table, voicing their jubilation and disappointment just like painters in their hut at a lunchtime game of Don.

I also inveigled him into attending a couple of rugby internationals. The first was the famous match in February 1973 when Scotland and Wales (citing the security problem) refused to travel and England (whom we had already beaten in Twickenham) agreed to play us again.

Con had grown up with a disdain for rugby that was widespread in the

IMAGE 12: Con and Maisie cut the cake in Maisie's family home on Jarlath Road, Cabra, on 7 September 1943.

IMAGE 13: Con and Eileen flanked by best man Kevin Bourke and bridesmaid Eileen, Maisie's sister.

IMAGE 14 and 15: The early years with Maisie.

IMAGE 16: Me with Con and Nana (Eva) at O'Donoghue Street in Inchicore.

IMAGE 17 (left): Con with his cousin Kevin Bourke.

IMAGE 18 (above): The wonder horse won as a prize during the first year of school.

IMAGE 19 (below): Con with Colbert, Maura, and Eileen in the back garden at Inchicore.

IMAGE 20: Me and Maura with Nana— bony arms, not soft and warm like Maisie's, but loving. And constantly singing.

IMAGE 21 (left): the treasured trike acquired by some scraping and saving on Con's part.

IMAGE 22 (below left): Con with his mother.

IMAGE 23 (below right): in town with Nana and Maura.

IMAGE 24: In town again with Nana, this time on O'Connell Bridge.

IMAGE 25 (above):Brendan and Dominic Behan at home with their parents, Kathleen and Stephen. 'The first of his seed, breed or generation to attend a secondary school other than a Borstal institution, ' Brendan said when he heard of my scholarship to Garbally.

IMAGE 26 (left): Me, Maura, and Eileen with a maternal grand-aunt who spent her life teaching in South Africa.

THOMAS ASHE
SEPTEMBER 1917

PEADAR KEARNEY
NOVEMBER 1942

PIARAS BÉASLAÍ
JUNE 1965

IMAGE 27 (above):
Pearse and Con at their
father's graveside in
the Republican Plot in
Glasnevin Cemetery.

IMAGE 28 (right): Con
and Pearse with their
mother, Eva, in St Anne's
Park, Raheny—including,
I think, my cousin Cónal,
Pearse's son.

IMAGE 29 (left): A rare smile for the camera from Con beside a portrait of his maternal grandfather. The photograph appeared in the *Evening Press's* 'Dubliner's Diary' where Terry O'Sullivan noted his contribution to two stage productions.

IMAGE 30 (below): The Queen's Theatre on Pearse Street (at one period a temporary home for the Abbey). Managed for a number of years by Con's cousin Lorcan Bourke, it was where he met Maisie, who worked there as an usherette.

IMAGE 31: Eugene Watters as painted by his wife, Una. He was the best teacher I have ever come across at any level. (*By kind permission of Eamonn Russell.*)

IMAGE 32 (left): Una Watters' sketch of me in 1959 while I was in Garbally. She was a less forceful presence, gentler and more solicitous than Eugene.

IMAGE 33 (below): In my third year at Garbally. I was among the minority who actually enjoyed boarding school.

IMAGE 34: Con (listed as Colbeard O Cearnaigh) following in the footsteps of Peadar as a theatrical properties manager. His day-time employment from the mid-1950s was at P. J. Bourke's, the leading costumier and dress hire business owned by his cousins.

IMAGE 35: Con and I in Cambridge on the day I was conferred with my doctorate—mimicking each other's stance so perfectly but unconsciously.

IMAGE 36 (above): With Con, Maisie and friends on the day of the my conferring at Cambridge.

IMAGE 37 (right): Maisie absorbing the atmosphere on Senate House lawn.

IMAGE 38: With Con, Maisie and my friend Richard. A rare smile again for the camera from Con, who could not have been more pleased if he himself had just been conferred.

IMAGE 39: An *Irish Press* photograph of Con and me taken on the occasion of a showing of a documentary on Joyce, for which I had written the script.

IMAGE 40 (above): with Con and Maisie and my sisters Maura, Eileen and Eva.

IMAGE 41 (right): with Maisie in her later years.

Ireland at the time and was essentially political. Compared to Gaelic football and hurling, rugby was a 'foreign' game, traditionally associated with pro-British elements and unionists and consequently banned by the Gaelic Athletic Association until 1971. Con resented those players from south of the border who had in his lifetime stood to attention for 'God Save the King' when internationals were played in Belfast and did not alter his stance when reminded that players from north of the border stood for 'Amhrán na bhFiann' in Dublin. He had also shared with the majority of Irish sports supporters a hostile sense that rugby was the game of the posh schools. His prejudice had been somewhat weakened by the fact that I had played rugby at Garbally and with Clontarf. Even more influential was meeting a couple of Garbally old boys who played for Ireland and came into Bourke's for dress wear. He became quite friendly with Ray McLoughlin, a great player who in his manner and bearing was anything but the toffee-nosed snob of the popular imagination.

Years later we discovered that the English players had travelled only because they had been blackmailed by their Rugby Football Union—play in Dublin or risk being dropped—but on the day a packed Lansdowne Road gave a sustained ovation to our Saxon brothers who came to our aid when our Celtic cousins had deserted us. Even Con had to admit he had never experienced anything like it, and that was before the crowd gave 'Amhrán na bhFiann' everything they had. I think he was surprised that rugby supporters knew the words so well but more than pleased that the spirit of his father was honoured with such gusto. And, to crown it all, Ireland tore into England from the kick-off and won the game 18-9.

Though impressed, he had not been converted and it was almost ten years before we found ourselves in Lansdowne Road again. This was a day both of us wished we could forget.

It was always our custom to go to Croke Park together, straight from the house to Hill 16, without even thinking of having a drink beforehand. For whatever reason—it may have been to collect tickets—we met a friend of mine in Kehoe's of South Anne Street a good hour before the game and this friend was in company and spirits were high. Con agreed to have a pint but, advised against long drinks before a game, he accepted glasses of whiskey. He was not a whiskey drinker but did not wish to seem ungrateful or rude and accepted them. More whiskey was consumed during the match. Scottish fans, equally primed, offered us their flasks when Ireland scored, the idea being that my friends would reciprocate when Scotland scored. The points did not come quickly enough and soon anything was a cue for a toast. By the time we got back into town, it was deemed mandatory that we should celebrate the great victory. In Kehoe's—for one last drink—the unaccustomed load of the unaccustomed drink hit Con and he was suddenly very drunk, the only time in my life I ever saw him helpless. He would not hear of getting a taxi: he might not have been able to stand up unaided but there was no way he would embarrass Maisie and himself by arriving home in such a state. When eventually we got home, Maisie blamed me for allowing this to happen.

A tacit decision was made to erase the day of shame from the records. Once or twice afterwards, when Con and I were alone and something was mentioned in conversation that reminded him of the episode, he would shake his head and shudder, still at a loss to understand how he could have allowed it to happen.

THE LAST game Con and I went to together was the 1992 All Ireland football final between Dublin and Donegal. We were both supremely confident and laughed when, on the way in, an old friend of Con's, the actor Niall Tóibín, warned us that Donegal would give Dublin a lesson in football. It took me a long time to realise that, whatever about anybody teaching anybody a lesson, Dublin were going to lose; it was almost as if they did not want to win, squandering many opportunities, including a penalty. I was disappointed; Con was shattered, so much so that we hardly exchanged a word as we made our way out of the stadium.

We were not going home, having arranged to meet my sister Eva in The Shakespeare, a pub at the O'Connell Street end of Parnell Street, to toast another All Ireland for Dublin. But it was more like an enormous funeral as the vast disenchanted mass trudged across Mountjoy Square on the way into the city centre.

One man tried to lift the spirits of the silent throng. He was coming against the crowd and had picked up a bamboo cane (which had presumably held the flag discarded by a Dublin supporter) and was pretending to be blind, tapping his way and repeatedly asking: 'Ah lads, come on, tell us who won?' I had to laugh at his sense of humour, but not for long: Con looked at me as if I had no soul. To hell with this, I thought: if we were going to enjoy ourselves in The Shakespeare, it was time to get him to snap out of his despondency.

'Come on, Da. We're all disappointed but there's nothing we can do about it now except get over it.'

It was as if he hadn't heard me.

'They were terrible. They threw it away.'

Ditto.

'If they had lost with the last kick of the game ....'

No reaction. Time for a change of tack, and I thought I had it. It was Donegal's first All Ireland success and, had they not beaten Dublin, Con would have welcomed it.

'If Donegal had beaten Kerry, you'd say it was good for the game.'

He had heard me this time, instantly turning to me.

'You've been down there too long.'

I knew what he meant. I was not as heartbroken as a true-blue Dublin man should be in these circumstances, as he and hundreds around us were. The purity of my loyalty had been contaminated by twenty years living in Cork.

A passing stranger might have heard his retort as caustically critical of me but I knew it was a momentary venting of bitter disappointment. In The Shakespeare, pint in hand, chatting with others who drowned their despondency in black humour, he came back to himself. I could see his spirits rise, especially when he saw Eva: face white, eyes raw, cigarette vibrating, in no condition as yet for any kind of social intercourse, her agony making Con's dismay seem minor.

By the time we left the bar, we sounded as if we had actually won the match. Even as we promised Eva we would get a taxi home, we knew we would take the bus. That was our way.

CON NEVER showed any great interest in my work as a university teacher, but my writings were a different matter, especially those concerning Dublin writers such as Joyce or O'Casey or Brendan Behan. He was understand-ably slow to accept his entertaining rapscallion of a cousin as a literary craftsman (any more than he was a craftsman with the paint brush) but he was well-disposed to my argument that what many dismissed as the coarse obscenity of a foul-mouth was the elaborate orchestration of oral speech of Dublin city and he was always keen to help with biographical and historical details when I was working on *The Writings of Brendan Behan,* which came out in 1977.

In 1982 he and I attended the first showing in Bloom's Hotel of a centenary documentary on Joyce for which I had written the script. It is only worth noting because afterwards Con arranged with the photographic editor of the *Irish Press* to have a picture taken of the both of us [*Image 39*]. It catches Con in characteristic pose, refusing to be impressed—or even look into the lens—the hint of a smile suggesting a very private joke that will always remain just between the two of us.

The only lecture of mine he attended was on the language of Brendan Behan in the Tailors' Hall during the 1992 Féile Zozimus. I remember asking him afterwards if he found the academic material on the oral tradition tedious. His response was instantaneous: no, it had all been very interesting and enjoyable.

I had always been fascinated by the old-style working-class songs and stories of a Dublin that was fading fast and I tried to put as much of them into a novel that would be published as *The Consequence* in 1993. (The title was a private pun, suggesting not only the cockiness of the narrator but also the fact that his father's name was Con.) Some of the stories within it were versions of events I had not witnessed myself, in some cases because I had not been born at the time. I never came up to Dublin without a sheaf of material and a list of questions—names of shops, prices of goods, that sort of thing—and when Con and I got back from the pub (and consumed Maisie's supper) I read extracts from the novel based on material or characters they recognised. Sometimes emendations were suggested, more felicitous phrasing found; sometimes we howled with laughter, sometimes we fell silent in memory of those who had died. They were great nights, just the three of us there in the kitchen, playing with language as we had always done, looking forward to the launch, Con urging me to get a date from the publishers as soon as I could.

CON HAD always been the picture of health, partly because he was a natty dresser, mostly because—as his friends often joked—he showed no signs of looking his age. His hair had receded a little but was still vigorous and dark and he had all his teeth. He had given up smoking around the time we moved to Finglas and, though he loved his pint, was not a heavy drinker.

He seems disturbingly thin in his wedding photograph, but Maisie's loving care soon remedied that. He enjoyed his food as only those can who have known shortage; for Maisie, feeding her family was more an expression of love than a physical necessity. Sunday breakfast was probably Con's favourite meal: back from mass, he tucked into an enormous spread of eggs, rashers, sausages, black and white pudding, a mug of tea and thickly buttered bread.

Inevitably, when he moved up from the pushbike to the scooter and then the car, he began to put on weight. He was not proud of this but neither was he particularly upset, knowing that his combination of moral strength and self-control would enable him to get back to normal. If he and Maisie were due to visit Maura and Michael in Canada that summer, he would stand up from the table, clutch and shake his stomach with both hands and announce that 'all this has to come off for Maura'. As invariably it would.

He had an operation for piles when I was about sixteen and during the nineteen-eighties seemed more susceptible to winter colds that needed no more than a bottle from the chemist shop. In retrospect I can recognise signs of a change in his demeanour that I tended to overlook at the time.

He was normally so pleased when I picked him up from work on a Friday evening, rubbing his hands and looking forward to a chat over a pint in The Willows, that I was taken aback by his grimace as he struggled into the passenger seat. I asked if everything was okay. He sighed, looked out through the windscreen and shook his head: he had 'a bit of a headache'. Things improved when we got to The Willows but while driving back to Cork on Sunday evening I could not help thinking how uncharacteristic it was of him to be so done down by a headache.

Not long after that he was in the Mater hospital. Nothing to worry about; just precautionary tests; better to be sure than sorry. Nobody looks good in a hospital bed, least of all your father or mother, but Con put on a good face. In accordance with family tradition, there was no detailed discussion as to what the problem was or might be. Most likely Con and Maisie agreed to maintain the official line—general tests to find out what was causing the headaches—in order not to make their children worry unnecessarily. (Their eldest child was in his mid-forties.) I cannot speak for my sisters but I am convinced that I colluded in this conspiracy. I knew little of medical matters, not even enough to connect headaches with the heart, and terrified (however unconsciously) by the implications, I instinctively buried my head in the sand.

Another occasion, having collected him outside Bourke's and merged into the traffic.

'Now, don't get excited; but it seems I had a little heart attack.'

I failed not to get excited. What did he mean 'it seems'? And what was 'a little heart attack'?

'If you calm down and listen, I'll explain.'

I listened as he described how even he had not been aware of his 'little heart attack'—a TIA or mini-stroke—which had been detected by doctors on their machines. No matter how much he downplayed its significance, it could not be other than a bad thing. (Did the doctors tell him that one-third of those who experience a TIA suffer a full stroke within a year?)

When I told him the date for the launch of the novel he made an instant decision: due to go into hospital for tests, he would go in sooner rather than later in order to be out in time for the celebration. (Con had no private medical insurance but, as ever, he knew somebody who could get him admitted at his convenience.) The operation was declared a success: when Eileen visited him in is post-op room, he was in good spirits, producing chocolate for the children and inviting them to inspect the scar on his neck.

But his luck had run out. He developed pneumonia and Eileen remembers overhearing doctors with x-rays remarking how quickly the lungs had deteriorated. He was returned to a ward and shortly afterwards suffered a stroke that left him paralysed on his left side, confined to a wheelchair and kept in nappies.

Eileen witnessed an incident that underlined his humiliation. She was there when 'a bitch of a nurse' came into the ward and Con told her he needed to be changed. The nurse, who could never get his name right, paid no attention to this request and within his hearing remarked to Eileen that 'a lot of them think they need changing when they don't'. Con, generally the least aggressive of men, raised his voice and commanded the immediate attention of the nurse, who realised that it was in her best interest to do as he wished.

That his speech was unimpaired was a mixed blessing: he was too bright and thoughtful not to realise what lay before him, an independently minded man who had never been inactive in his life.

Maura came over from Canada and we all began to imagine the terrible prospect of our father locked in a body that could do almost nothing for itself.

One day a nurse asked me if I would help her move him in the bed. She showed me how to join our hands from either side and lift him. When she had gone, he took my hand and said: 'You know I always thought the world of you, son?' And I replied: 'I always thought the world of you too, Da.'

I have no idea how I managed to function so well in a situation the memory of which fills my eyes more than twenty years later. I assume both of us were in our different kinds of shock.

Reviewing our lives together—from way back in the beginning when *he* was lifting *me* in and out of bed—it strikes me how much of our communication was indirect, how seldom we resorted to intellectual analysis when it came to our deepest feelings, how we tended to find objective correlatives in the world around us, in song and story, fun and games. Which is why I feel so blessed that at the very end we sealed the undying love we had for each other in such terms.

Saying 'I always loved you' would not have been nearly as effective, not between this father and son. I am not sure why. Perhaps the word 'love' had (for us) lost some of its actuality in the process of being appropriated by innumerable Christian martyrs, Irish patriots and assorted sweethearts, prayers, heroic ballads and popular songs. It's not that we were unwilling to say it; this was no time for qualms. But I think that Con hit the nail on the head, not for the first time. We both knew what we were saying and that we could not have put it more strongly or more clearly.

It was heart-breaking to see him in increasing distress, not helped by the doctors' decision not to sedate him. At some stage Eileen and I approached a doctor and made it clear that we did not want our father to endure another bad night and asked that he be sedated. Then, relieved that he would have something like a good night's sleep, we took Maisie home and went to bed ourselves. When we had left, Maura repeated the request for sedation, probably with more effect. That night, 28 October 1993, he suffered another stroke and died. In her grief Maisie railed at Eileen and me for taking her away from her rightful place by his side.

Though he had gone into hospital expecting to be home before my book launch, he knew nothing was guaranteed. He had left documents in his coat pocket at home that were meant to be discovered by Maisie if he did not make it back to Cedarwood.

Weeks earlier I had been surprised and disappointed to see him bless himself when passing a church on the way home. Now I realised how selfish my reaction had been: like everybody else in the valley of the shadow of death, he was entitled to grasp at any support or consolation.

The funeral arrangements were made in a blur of phone calls and condolences, so my memory is only of vivid patches.

One episode brought a smile to all our faces. The removal from the Mater to the church in Finglas took place around teatime and involved the cars moving out into the traffic-jammed North Circular Road and negotiating the right turn onto the Phibsborough Road at Doyle's Corner. We were anticipating being (as Mammy would say, and probably did) 'here for the duration' but, no, we proceeded as if we had a royal right of way. As indeed we had, thanks to Eva's friend Ciarán Baker, a policeman, who had parked his motorbike in the middle of the intersection and countermanded the traffic lights in order that we would not be held up. We were all delighted at the gesture, especially Maisie who smiled: 'Con would have loved this'. After all, as he had informed the lockhard outside Croke Park, his father had fought for the city, the implication being that there were certain hereditary rights. (I was also thinking that Doyle's was once Dunphy's Corner, where Sergeant William Bailey, satirical target of his father's anti-recruiting satire, had sought to entice young men into the British Army.)

For related reasons we felt it was only proper that the son of Peadar Kearney should have Irish music at his funeral mass and Eileen had engaged an uilleann piper. But—echoes of my Berkeley Road christening—the priest explained that, because the mass was being celebrated on a saint's day, non-ecclesiastical music was prohibited. We had no theological Ciarán Baker to countermand this holy ordinance; nor was Con in a position to threaten to take proceedings to where there *would* be Irish music.

I am an emotional slave to many kinds of music but none of them hits me with the visceral urgency of the pipes. I was seated in the front row, numbed by grief and cold bewilderment, when the piper inflated the bellows and allowed the first sound to shatter the muffled silence, filling every nook and confessional, piercing my heart like a hypodermic, stirring up sediments of memories that had been laid down long before I had been born. The only way I could prevent myself from sobbing was by biting into my cheek until I could taste the blood. (The piper had cleverly chosen Shaun Davey's *Brendan Voyage,* the Brendan of the voyage being a saint and therefore qualifying the piece as ecclesiastical music.)

Con was buried with his mother. He could not be buried with his father in the Republican Plot but, even if that had been possible, it seemed right that his remains should lie with his mother.

I have no idea what I said at the grave other than that I quoted a verse of Irish poetry, prefacing it with an explanation as to why I had chosen it. One night in The Willows, for a reason long forgotten, I had brought up the poem and summarised it, lingering on the extraordinary final verse in which the poet, the Kerryman Aogán Ó Rathaille, had lamented the demise of the ancient Gaelic society to which he would nevertheless remain faithful unto death, a society which he claims had been well established before the death of Christ.

> *I will stop here—death is fast approaching*
> *Now the dragons of Laune, Lough Lene and Lee are overthrown;*
> *In the grave together with my cherished chief I'll join*
> *The kings my people served before the death of Christ.*

I was about to make some further point about the closing line but Con signalled that he had somehow grasped what was in the poet's mind and asked me to say it in Irish.

> *Stadfadsa feasta—is gar dom éag gan mhoill*
> *ó treascradh dragain Leamhan, Léin is Laoi;*
> *rachad 'na bhfasc le searc na laoch don chill,*
> *na flatha fá raibh mo shean roimh éag do Chríost.*

I am still not sure I was right to quote a poem the majority of those present could not understand. It was fine for my sister Eileen and her Irish-speaking family and for my UCC friends, especially Seán Ó Tuama, who knew something of Con and who accompanied my Connemara with his Munster Irish as if joining in a decade of the Rosary; but for many others it was merely symbolic and it was not an occasion to exclude anybody.

The fact is I was addressing myself to Con's memory rather than anybody present. It had meant something to him in The Willows: he recognised the indomitable loyalty of the poet, almost certainly associating it with his father just as I was associating it with him. Like Ó Rathaille, Peadar had been born into some comfort but spent his latter days in poverty and disappointment when his former patrons had been replaced by others who had no time for his talents.

My Uncle Kevin, one of Con's oldest friends, rescued the situation with a high theatrical flourish worthy of a Bourke. I had so sooner indicated that I had finished when Kevin made his unscheduled entrance and rushed over beside me, coming so close to falling into the grave and down on top of the coffin that there was a general gasp as the audience—consciously or unconsciously—feared a re-enactment of the graveyard scene from *Hamlet*. He spoke of Con as his youthful pal and the friend of so many there who would miss him. And I am glad he did. One or two others said a few words and before we adjourned to the Botanic House for a traditional post-funeral party, Jimmy Bourke led us in 'Slán Libh'—Peadar's lament for his friend Paddy Heeney, which had been adopted as our graveside finale.

SUCH FUNERALS are designed by the bereaved not only to honour the memory of the dead but to get through the immediate aftermath of their loss. Although I was heartbroken that I would never again enjoy Con's company, I managed to rationalise some of my sadness away by imagining what life would have been like for him had he survived in a wheelchair, bereft of the independence that had been one of his characteristics.

About a month after the funeral I was at home alone and on the stairs up to the bathroom when, out of the blue, I experienced a terrifying seizure. My entire body was gripped by spasms so sudden and so strong I thought I might die. My mouth was open but I could not breathe properly, merely make choking sounds. (The attack seemed to go on for ever, though it probably lasted less than thirty seconds.) Still in panic I somehow stumbled forward and gripped the rim of the hand-basin and watched helplessly as my reflection in the mirror dissolved in childhood sobs and I heard myself whinging *I want my Daddy, I want my Daddy.*

He is never far away for long. People who knew him have said how much I remind them of him. It would be surprising if I had not imitated, however unconsciously, a man I thought the world of.

MY SISTERS and I had our own homes to go to, our own ways to make, our own children to look after. Maisie was suddenly alone in an empty house, bereft of her life-partner, her *anam-chara*.

I tried to use her love for him to subvert the absolute nature of her loss, recalling what a loving husband he had been, the most caring and the kindest of fathers, the most unselfish of providers, who had worked hard all his life so that she would have a good home and their children the best of everything, hinting at my own loss by reminding her of the great times he had shared with me, taking me to Croke Park when I was only a child and afterwards to meet Pearse in the Manhattan where, when I was old enough, we had enjoyed our pints.

'Jesus, he looked forward to you coming up; he wouldn't be in that door but he'd be saying "I'll be having a pint with the quare fella at the weekend".'

'But that's just it, Mammy. He wouldn't be able to do any of those things. Imagine Con in a wheelchair. He'd be miserable. A man who didn't have an idle bone in his body, to be sitting there helpless, having to be looked after hand and foot.'

She stared across the room at his empty chair, shaking her head slowly:

'I'd have made sure he was never miserable. I'd have nursed him twenty-four hours a day, seven days a week, for as long as I lived, twenty-four hours a day. I'd have seen to it that he wanted for nothing. I'd have been happy to take care of him.'

She never let go, never losing sight of his photographs and, as she proudly admitted, constantly talking to him when they were alone in the house.

But she was a working-class woman of her generation and never expected life to be easy. *We saw the two days*—meaning good times and bad—*but sure we never died of winter yet and, with the help of God and the aid of few policemen, we never will*. She had endured her share of hardships but never buckled. Her instinct was to put a good face on things—*you may as well sing grief as cry it*—and when the good times came, there was no better woman to enjoy them.

FOR MANY years my sisters have all agreed—with amused resignation rather than any detectable resentment—that I was Maisie's favourite. I have always tried to deny this, or at least qualify it sufficiently to absolve her from any charge of unfairness, arguing that she loved us all equally, but her treatment of us was dictated by cultural conventions so deeply embedded as to be accepted as laws of nature. What distinguished me was not any moral or social virtue but the irresistible fact that I was her only son, the more precious and cosseted because she had lost her first-born in heart-breaking circumstances.

Whether as a cause or a consequence of this mutual admiration, Maisie and I were temperamentally in tune and remained so despite differences of gender or education. We both rose in the morning in high spirits, were both playful, liking to joke and josh, instinctively filling any silence with skittish conversation, songs or, as a last resort, facetious soliloquies.

Long before I even heard of the oral tradition, I recognised and admired the way Maisie used language not merely as a neutral means of communication but also as a bravura performance in which she herself took pleasure and by means of which she gave pleasure to others, especially me. Even as I was drawn to the modish Americanisms of the cinema and Radio Luxembourg, I had begun to catalogue and repeat her treasury of words and phrases that were flamboyantly out of date.

I never heard anybody of my own generation say 'in all my born days' or 'down on my bended knees' and was (years later) delighted to find the former in Dickens and Mark Twain and the latter in several blues songs. Both adjectives would be cut by a literary editor as redundant but if the illiterate poor had little else, they were rich in words and spent them with a lordly liberality, especially when they added to the rhythm. 'Bended knees' is easier on the tongue and the ear than 'bent knees' and the same applies to 'born days' where 'born' is a disyllable, *bor-rin*. Asked if she had met anybody while out shopping, Maisie would never settle for a simple 'no', preferring the more elaborately emphatic 'I never saw the face of one'. She delighted in resurrecting old nicknames and creating new ones. A neighbour on the Cappagh Road, who leaned forward as she walked, was dubbed 'Here's-me-Head-me-A-is Coming'. I was there when Con described how a friend of his who was below average height had behaved aggressively with him. Maisie was outraged on Con's behalf: 'Jesus, he'd want to stand up on a butter box to talk to me like that'. There and then the offender was christened 'Butterbox'.

I was lucky that my literary studies led me to recognise the 'high' value of the everyday conversation of people like Maisie and my Auntie Maureen Brady, but the nearest we ever came to a literary discussion followed a performance of *Lysistrata* on BBC TV while I was at UCD. Con was working late and I tried to avoid any embarrassment by suggesting to Maisie that she have an early night while I stayed up for Con. Out of the question. What was I going to watch on the television? An old Greek play that was on the course at UCD. (It was not on the course but I would have said anything not to have her in the room as I watched the sex-striking wives of Athens prick-teasing their husbands who had arrived home after a long period of celibacy fighting the Spartans.) She said she would doze away by the fire and wake up when Con arrived. Which was good to hear because she was breathing in a very sleepy manner and the play would be over by then. As she snored away peacefully, I enjoyed the broad salaciousness with a relatively easy mind.

But no sooner had the credits begun to roll than she stood up and made her way to the kitchen to prepare a bit of supper for Con, stage-whispering en route: 'That was lovely. If that's what they're teaching you in the university, Jesus help us all.' Her use of 'lovely' was heavily ironic, meaning something like 'most improper'. But she had worked in that temple of double entendre, the variety theatre, and was neither shockable nor censorious. Children, of course, had to be protected but it was up to adults to protect themselves.

MAISIE AND Con lived for their children to such an extent that they must have watched with mixed feelings as—within a four-year period in the early Seventies—we all left to make our way in the world as they in their own time had done. Few couples can have relished less the prospect of an empty nest. Con still had Bourke's but for Maisie it was a long day in the deserted house. Relief came in the strangest guise: she went out to work in the nearby Gateaux cake factory.

We were all a bit anxious as to how she would manage at the age of fifty-eight. (I was privately amused to remember Con's indignation when her employer had expressed the hope that Maisie would return to the Queen's after her honeymoon.) But it all went better than anybody expected: Maisie was rejuvenated, loving the company and chat of her workmates and being paid for something she would probably have done for nothing. Con was delighted for her, but could not banish the old reservations. Nobody was to say anything to the Bourkes and he even went so far as to pretend to talk to Maisie on the phone while at work. But within the safety of the family he, like the rest of us, revelled in Maisie's tales of life in the world of cakes until we felt as if we knew the most colourful of her fellow-workers, many of them resplendent in Maisie's nicknames, and we all shared their fears and excitement before and during the arrival of a team of English inspectors. We were not the least surprised when she was promoted to Bluecoat and we all felt deprived when she was obliged to retire on pension in 1981.

The move to Cedarwood was another new lease of life for both of them, and for those of us who were aware of the situation on Cappagh Avenue. For the next ten years they luxuriated in the security of having a house of

197

their own in a quiet estate, surrounded by neighbours who were friendly and helpful.

MAISIE WAS at least as shocked as anybody else at the suddenness of Con's death and the one best placed to count the cost. She had compensated for the absence of her children by getting a job in Gateaux; but now she was truly alone in the empty house, with no prospect of Con arriving home in the evening. Her family and friends tried to nurse her through the aftermath, but we were visitors who would go home to our families: when Maisie closed the door after us, she was left alone in the house, surrounded by memories of sixty years with the man who had been so cruelly taken from her and with all the time in the world to measure her misfortune. Together they had survived the death of baby Peadar, the expulsion from Eccles Street, the ups and downs of family life; but here she was, aged seventy-seven, for the first time in her adult life alone without her Con and with no earthly hope of waking up and finding it was all a bad dream.

When I came up for a weekend I was greeted like the prodigal son: the best sirloin, chips fried 'with her own lily-white hands' and mushy peas. I experience a stab of guilt when I recall how I acceded to her insistence that I go out to meet some old friend on one of the nights, Friday or Saturday. I understand that she considered it 'normal' for a man to go out for a drink, but I regret I did not spend every second with her, talking of 'the olden days'.

Shortly after the break-up of my marriage, she came to Cork, more anxious about my ability to survive than her own. As I watched her make her slow way up the front steps, I realised how frail she had become; but her spirit was undimmed, as she showed in the English Market.

I had been in the habit of bringing fish up to Dublin with me and, rather like Maisie with her butcher, I would warn Pat O'Connell that his reputation as a fishmonger and the good name of the English Market were at stake. As Pat recognised my mother inching towards his stall, he shouted out in market mode: 'Well, Mrs Kearney, what did you think of that fish last night? You wouldn't get fish like that up in Dublin.' Unlike many of Pat's customers, Maisie was unfazed, snorting derisively and saying just loud enough to be heard: 'It near poisoned me.'

She was, in her way, as proud of her native Dublin as Con was. She was happy that Cork would have every modern convenience so that the girls and I could enjoy them but, like Con, she was incapable of believing that Cork could ever be the equal of Dublin.

My sister Maura recalls how when Con and Maisie visited her and Michael in Canada and socialised with their friends, Maisie listened with approving attention as Con recounted episodes from the family history that were the staple of our get-togethers; but when, after Con's death, Maisie visited Canada she carried on where he had left off, ready, willing and well able to entertain the company.

Knowing her fondness for dressing up and going out, my sister Eva used to take Maisie over to the bar in the Good Counsel GAA club where she became a favourite with young and old who were enthralled by her high spirits and obvious love of social life. Eva told me of an occasion when she had to take a phone call, leaving Maisie with a group of young girls, returning to find signs of happy surprise on their faces. They had, she discovered, been equally shocked and delighted that such an old woman would talk to them so directly and with such authority on aspects of their relationships with the opposite sex.

AFTER CON and her children, the person to whom Maisie was closest was probably her older sister Eileen who had lived with her family in London since the late Fifties and came over on two memorable visits. The first was to Cappagh Avenue and probably took place in the mid-Sixties; it was definitely during the summer because Con was working in Jurys Cabaret in Dame Street and, as often happened, I had left my friends in McDaids and taken a lift home with him.

Pulling into the driveway, he stared at the house, obviously perplexed. 'Not like your mother not to have the hall light on.'

As we got out of the car, I could see he was still expecting the light to be switched on and Maisie to appear in the hall; but still no sign and no sound as he opened the hall door, wondering aloud: 'What in the name of God are they up to?'

I thought he was being a little melodramatic, until he opened the door of the living room and the only light came from the embers of a fire on its last legs. Maybe they had gone to bed early, not something Maisie would ever have done by herself but ....

Con pressed the switch and there were the sisters in their armchairs, fast asleep.

He smiled ruefully:

'Will you look at the dirty drunks.'

By then Maisie had woken up and, while attempting to rouse her sister, launched into a defence against Con's accusation.

'Jesus, will you listen to him, Eileen! Eileen! Did you hear what Con said? The nerve of him and us sitting here all night without so much as a glass of water.'

Con was smiling broadly but showing no sign of apologising. I was pondering his attitude when Eileen woke up, then turned around to face us and ask us how we were. Grabbing her arm and her attention, Maisie repeated Con's accusation and her indignant rebuttal. Eileen confirmed her sister's every word and I was about to insist that Con retract his slander when Maisie stood up and there was the unmistakable sound of a large bottle rolling across linoleum, clinking against the fireplace and identifying itself as a container of Smirnoff vodka.

By the following morning it was something to laugh about; by the following evening the vodka had been relegated to a mere prop, and attention had settled on the story of the naughty fibbing sisters and the dramatic silence that fell on the scene as the bottle began its fateful journey to the fireplace.

Eileen was widowed in 1983, Maisie ten years later. The second of the memorable visits was in the mid-1990s. When I imagine the two of them reminiscing on all they had been through, I see them shrugging off the losses as best they can, never missing an opportunity to hoot with laughter. They were both coming to the end of the road and both had every reason to believe they had managed well and were entitled to live out the remainder of their days on their own terms.

It was their custom to shuffle around to the shops in the afternoon to do their messages and, when Eileen had bought her packet of fags, slip into The Willows for a quiet drink.

What they could not have been expected to know was that on one of those afternoons Ireland were about to play a crucial soccer match in Lansdowne Road in their efforts to qualify for the European Football Championship. There was still a degree of euphoria associated with the Irish team and any pub showing the match was guaranteed a full house, which was why The Willows had given tickets to regular customers and (because the lounge had been ticketed to capacity) put a man on the door to direct casual punters around to the bar.

Imagine Eileen and Maisie knocking on the locked door and receiving the opposite of a warm welcome; Maisie wanting to know why there was no problem yesterday and today they're barred.

'Misses, yiz can't come in here. There's a match on the telly.'

'We don't care about your match. We won't be in your way.'

'But it's ticket-only, missus. Have yiz got tickets?

'Say that we have.'

At which point the doorman loses his absolute control, just for a couple of seconds but long enough for Maisie and Eileen to get halfway past him, far enough to see the lounge laid out like a cinema, with rows of seats facing a huge screen.

(What undid the doorman was Maisie's response, which is very difficult to gloss. The phrase—meaning, very roughly, *pretend we have tickets*—is redolent of children's games where the lack of any necessary item is instantly remedied by an act of the collective imagination. For half a moment the doorman, sent by Maisie's spell back into his own childhood, half-believed that these elderly ladies actually had tickets and pointed them to a pair of spare seats farthest from the television.)

Some of the seated fans stood up and no doubt were about to ask those at the door to sit the hell down and shut the hell up, when one of them—who had been at school with me and who had got to know and like Maisie from her visits to his butcher's stall in Superquinn—recognised her.

'Hey! That's Mrs Kearney back there. Mrs Kearney, come up here. There's room here. Push in there, lads, and make room for Mrs Kearney and her sister.'

I listened open-mouthed to Maisie's account. While she claimed—with a broad smile on her face—to have been mortified with embarrassment at hearing her name shouted out like that, I was wondering what she would have felt had she known what the other punters were thinking as everything was held up while this bloody oul' wan and her sister, who had turned up late without a ticket, were ushered into the front row and a drink called for them.

I had watched some of the game at home. Ireland had played poorly and were lucky to be only a couple of goals behind with five minutes to go, at which stage they got what struck me as a consolation goal until Kevin Moran—late star for Dublin, Manchester United and Ireland and now co-commentator on the television—had pointed out that the goal might be significant if the placings came down to goal-difference.

'And what did you two soccer fans make of the game?'

'Weren't they only desperate? What was wrong with them at all? And then getting a goal when the match was over.'

'But that goal might turn out to be very important, depending on how the other teams get on.'

'Isn't that what I was telling the man beside me?'

Sweet Jesus! I could suddenly imagine what it was like for hardened football fans to have Maisie and Eileen among them, offering their expert opinions. It was bad enough to have to watch Ireland throw away a golden opportunity to qualify, but to have to listen to these two ....

IN ONE sense Maisie had never enjoyed the best of health, suffering all her life from constipation and headaches, which were probably related, but she was never down for long and when well into her eighties—she turned eighty-four in 2000—she showed few signs of weakening. When she agreed that I should take out power of attorney, it was not because she—or anybody else—felt her mental powers were fading: there were important documents to be checked and signed and she was as happy then to leave such matters to me as she had always left them to Con.

I remember sharing a bottle of wine in her kitchen one Saturday night and smiling as she pondered how we view our own age.

'I'm eighty-four years of age now and I suppose that means I'm very old; but I don't feel old, not that old anyway.'

A couple of years later she could not help seeming old. Doctors figured more and more in her life and she was on several pills a day; but her spirit remained indomitable and in my presence she never showed any of the signs of surrender or apathy. In the summer of 2004 when we were discussing birthdays—mine fell on 25 July, hers two days later—she insisted she did not want any fuss when she turned eighty-eight.

'I don't want any going out or big presents. I want you all to save it for my ninetieth.'

By then she was nearby in a brand-new nursing home, Beneavin Lodge. It had become obvious that she was no longer able to take adequate care of herself and there did not seem to be a reasonable alternative. I had come to dread driving away from the house, watching her wave from the front window. Even if coming to live with me had been practical, she would never have moved to Cork. Nor do I think she would have considered moving to Canada. We all agreed that it would be unfair on Eileen and her children if, having looked after John's mother for so long, they now took on Maisie. If we paid her even part of the cost of a nursing home, Eva was willing to give up her job and look after Maisie full-time. But the crucial fact was that Maisie could not see her way to imposing herself on any of us, which ameliorated but did not eradicate the guilt we all felt at the time.

I had assured her that if she was not completely happy with Beneavin, I would take her out immediately, that very day, not the following or any other day. But to our great relief, far from finding the least fault, she insisted she was completely satisfied with her new accommodation. She was a practical woman who quickly realised that she had her own room—secure, clean, comfortable and warm—with nursing staff at her call day and night. She was no longer living alone in a house filled with memories, having to fend for herself most of the time and always with the threat of a sudden medical emergency or even a break-in at the back of her mind. It helped that, unlike some of the other residents, she had all her mental faculties and could make her way to the dining room and bathroom unaided. It helped even more that she was naturally gregarious and made friends easily and quickly, which meant that she made fewer demands on the staff, who rewarded her with a special regard.

Eileen and Eva were heroic in their attention, ensuring she had a daily visit for a chat and to check that she needed for nothing. She was always happy to see her white-headed boy, especially when I had one of my daughters or my granddaughter with me; she never lost her love of children. Whenever we were alone, we spent most of the time in one of our oldest and most enduring pastimes. I would ask her about her childhood and get her to detail incidents that had passed into family lore.

ON 27 July 2006, Maisie's optimism was vindicated: she reached her ninetieth birthday and we arranged 'a fuss'. Not that this was advertised: in line with family tradition, it had to be a surprise.

A party was organised in the extensive bar of Eva's GAA club and a host of family, relations and friends assembled. Maisie had been informed that Maura and I would collect her from Beneavin and drive her over to Good Counsel for a small family gathering; but I knew her too well to think that she had been taken in by our cover story. She may not have been sure what awaited her but she knew it would not be 'a small family gathering'; on the other hand, she was too much of an old trouper not to know her part and play it. Lookouts had spotted our arrival and there was absolute silence in the bar as Maura and I helped her up the stairs. Then the door was thrown open to an explosion of clapping, shouting and whistling. She was clearly surprised by the extent of 'the fuss' but never, I felt, in danger of fainting from shock.

She was in her element when the party got underway, delighted to have a laugh with friends and but, above all, proudly matriarchal to chat and be photographed with her children and grandchildren.

AS IN the case of Con's death, I suspect my memory of Maisie's, on 6 August 2007, is patchy, almost certainly due to my unwillingness to face the facts at the time. Maisie had an easier end than Con. Despite her mental alertness and unfailing good humour, she knew and seemed to accept that her systems were running down. Maura and I were advised to be on stand-by and eventually the medical staff told us to be prepared. By then there was very little communication with Maisie, who was sleeping peacefully most of the time. The four of us just hung around, Eva and I smoking like chimneys in the open area. A member of staff told us to take a break, that nothing would happen for at least six hours or so, and we went by bus into town. We had hardly arrived when, outside Clerys, somebody's phone rang and suddenly we were urging the taxi driver to go as fast as he could. He did his best but we were too late. Maisie had died peacefully.

Though I cried to think I would never again have a chat with her, I was relieved she was at peace.

The following day the four of us went down to St Canice's church to make the arrangements. In a room I had known as an altar boy, the priest—in tracksuit trousers and trainers—was all-accommodating until Maura mentioned that she and her sisters wanted me to say a few words at the mass. We were all taken aback when the priest shook his head.

'It's no reflection on you—I can see you are a very respectable family— but for the last while we have had a blanket policy of not having eulogies at the mass.'

'Why not?'

'Again, no reflection on you and your family but you will probably have seen on the news that recently we've had a spate of what they call "gangland killings" in the area. Well, on a couple of occasions members of the victims' families have used the pulpit to threaten all kinds of terrible vengeance on whoever was responsible. We could not allow that and so the only option open to us was to ban eulogies altogether. I'm sorry but that's the rule. Your brother can say a few words at the removal.'

I did, standing on the altar where I had often served mass. I simply wished to satisfy the demands of the occasion and say what a great mother Maisie was but I was loath to be hypocritical in the presence of her coffin. Where the customary formula was to find consolation in the fact that Maisie was now happily reunited with Con in heaven, I said something to the effect that 'in our hearts and our imaginations Maisie was up there with her beloved Con'. The priest was obviously irked and in his concluding remarks pointed out that I had been wrong in something I had said. Oddly enough it was not my reference to imagination but to something I had not said (which is probably why I cannot remember it).

Maisie was buried with Con. My only clear memory is of standing over the grave with my nephew Dualta, Eileen's son, as he sang Maisie's song, 'Teddy O'Neill'; I tried to keep up with him but did not stand a chance as my tears hopped off the coffin.

> *Shall I ever forget when the big ship was ready*
> *And the time it was come for my love to depart?*
> *How I cried like a child, 'Oh goodbye to you, Teddy,'*
> *With a tear on my cheek and a stone in my heart.*
> *He said 'twas to better his fate he went roving,*
> *But what would be gold to the joy I would feel*
> *If he'd only come back to me, tender and loving,*
> *Though poor, but my own darling Teddy O'Neill.*

Peadar Bourke led us in 'Slán Libh'.

That evening the four of us got together in Eva's house to be alone together, to have a glass of wine and unwind after the various tensions of previous few days; but we were hardly seated when we all simultaneously erupted, babbling like children surging out the school gate. Such was the clamour that some sort of order had to be introduced, the rule of the poker, whereby only the person holding the poker was entitled to speak.

After the first few tumultuous minutes we settled down to the ritual of reminiscence, each of us recalling and sharing some episode associated with Maisie, generally humorous, very occasionally tinged with melancholy. It was like an old family rosary—one person leading and the others mumbling in agreement, confirming the facts of the story and adding some 'trimmings' of their own—except that it was enacted mostly amid shrieks of laughter, the laughter becoming shriller and the re-tellings more theatrical the more the bottles went round.

We were never as close together as on the night we realised we were orphans.

A SOLDIER'S SONGS

In the presence of God, I, Peadar Kearney, do solemnly swear that I will do my utmost to establish the independence of Ireland, and that I will bear true allegiance to the Supreme Council of the Irish Republican Brotherhood and the Government of the Irish Republic and implicitly obey the constitution of the Irish Republican Brotherhood and all my superior officers and that I will preserve inviolable the secrets of the organisation.

In 1957, almost fifteen years after his death, his nephew Jimmy Bourke (writing as Seamus de Burca) published *The Soldier's Song: The Story of Peadar Kearney*. By then the author of several plays and adaptations, he had begun visiting Peadar on a regular basis in 1932 and seems to have been accepted as official biographer when Peadar gave him his essays on the Irish Republican Brotherhood, the 1911 Abbey Theatre Tour of England, his Personal Narrative of Easter Week and a wide range of reminiscences on the struggle for independence up to his internment.

de Burca's account of Ballykinlar ends (about two-thirds through the book) with a reference to the Anglo-Irish Treaty signed in December 1922; the subsequent—and final—chapter begins with his visits to Inchicore in 1932. There is practically no reference to the intervening decade, to Peadar's involvement in the civil war or to the years that we know from public records were particularly lean for him and his wife and his young sons. Instead we are taken straight into the 1930s and a chapter entitled 'Poet's Den', which presents a portrait of a veteran poet-patriot in serenely contented retirement. Having abandoned his former pastimes of angling and country walks, he spends his time reading and writing. His only excursion—apart from short walks to the local library—was his weekly trip for a chat with his old friend Tom Pugh in Farrelly's pub between 3.00 and 5.30. In the parlour *off* is his wife, referred to as 'the lady'. At his feet is Jess, the elderly Kerry Blue.

By way of context, it is interesting to note that three years later saw the publication of *The Shaping of Modern Ireland*, a collection of essays by leading Irish historians edited by Conor Cruise O'Brien. Absent from the subjects chosen were Michael Collins and Éamon de Valera, arguably the two men who had done most to shape modern Ireland, and it is generally agreed now that they were omitted because they had come to personify the civil war, the bitter memories of which were still alive in 1960; that and the fact that de Valera had recently been elected President of Ireland, an office deemed to be above politics and granting him a degree of immunity from criticism.

Even closer to home, more than a quarter of a century after de Burca's biography, *Mother of All the Behans,* was published in 1984, consisting of the recollections of Peadar's sister Kathleen Behan as recorded by her son Brian. She is candid in her accounts of tenement squalor and human weakness but coy when dealing with her famous brother. He is given full credit for his contributions to the national cause, military and musical, but though his close friendship with Michael Collins is stressed, a veil is drawn over his involvement in the civil war, possibly because while her brother was a Free State prison censor her husband, Frank Behan, was imprisoned as a republican.

Not long after deciding to attempt a memoir of my parents—and of my father, in particular—I realised I would have to look outside the authorised family narrative if I was to get any closer to the actual Peadar Kearney and what follows is based to a great extent on external sources, especially the archives of the Bureau of Military History.

PETER PAUL was born in 1883, the eldest son of John Kearney, who had come from near Ardee, County Louth, to be apprenticed to a grocer in North Earl Street, Dublin, and who by the age of thirty had acquired two grocery shops in Dorset Street. For reasons now unknown, John's business failed: his shops were lost and at the time of his death in 1897 he was reduced to working as an insurance agent and living in a tenement at 47 Dolphin's Barn Lane, between the Liberties and Inchicore.[1] There are hints of mental instability. His daughter Kathleen Behan describes his unhealthy fascination with courts of law:

> At first he went to the courts just to pass the time; then, like everything else, it went too far. He thought he was a judge, and used to spend all his day there in the law courts. He would dress up in a swallow-tail coat, white gloves and a tall black hat.... So my father, who was a rich man and then became a poor one, sentenced himself in the end with his law cases—and he sentenced the rest of us to the poor house. He never went mad—he was very intelligent. He taught us all the national songs and when my sister brought her school books home the first thing he did was rip out the picture of Queen Victoria.[2]

I myself heard that he did not attend merely to observe but was inclined to comment on barristers' arguments and judges' rulings, not always favourably.

Peter—who would in his late teens adopt the Irish form of his name, Peadar—had never been a biddable boy, mitching from school to such an extent that his father removed him from the Christian Brothers School in Marino and set him to work. He took a series of jobs—from mending punctures to 'marking' in billiard saloons—before becoming an apprentice house painter at the age of sixteen.

John Kearney had educated him politically, taking him to places in Dublin associated with the struggle for independence and to the Mechanics' Institute Library to read and to hear lectures by ardent nationalists such as Willie Rooney—whose patriotic ballads James Joyce reviewed dismissively in the *Daily Express* in 1902—but otherwise offered him a poor model of parenthood. Peadar came from a broken home, thanks largely to his eccentric father who had wasted the family fortune and with whom Peadar had never enjoyed a warm relationship. Peadar had just turned fourteen when his father died of pneumonia at the age of forty-three, obliging Peadar's mother to put his sisters into an orphanage.[3]

The 1890s had seen the rise of cultural nationalism, most notably the foundation in 1893 of the Gaelic League with the objective of restoring Irish as the vernacular. Peadar joined and quickly became sufficiently fluent to win first prize in a *Derry People* competition for a short story in Irish. His first literary production had been a 1902 poem in English in *St Patrick's Weekly*—a companion to William O'Brien's *Irish People* which offered young people an alternative to 'degenerate' British publications—and he continued to write for this nationalist periodical until 1906.

In 1901, at the Willie Rooney Branch of the Gaelic League, Peadar met a kindred spirit. Sean Barlow was just as avid a reader and equally keen to develop the life of the mind but his principal interest was the theatre and he would go on to become stage manager of the Abbey Theatre. He and Peadar went cycling and fishing together and they also attended the first performance of Yeats' *Cathleen ní Houlihan* by the Irish National Dramatic Company in Clarendon Street in 1902. In 1904 they were among the first to enter the Mechanics' Theatre, which was about to be reopened as the Abbey by the National Theatre Society. Though never on the permanent staff, Peadar worked on-and-off with the Abbey until 1916, mainly as a property manager available for walk-on parts but also using his painter's skills to 'fill in' designs outlined by Robert Gregory.

Peadar could not make himself available full-time because of his overriding commitment to revolutionary politics. In 1903 he had been sworn into the Irish Republican Brotherhood, a secret society known to its members as 'the organisation' and dedicated to the achievement of Irish freedom by military means. The IRB sought to place its members in influential positions in other nationalist organisations—cultural and political—with a view to bringing them around to its own more radical positions. When required to travel outside Dublin on IRB business, Peadar would resign from the Abbey, knowing that when he returned, Sean Barlow would re-employ him as soon as possible.

Though obviously not democratic, the IRB was egalitarian: regular elections were held and members promoted on the basis of their abilities, irrespective of their educational qualifications or social standing. Peadar was elected to the Supreme Council in the aftermath of 1916, the only high rank he ever achieved. Towards the end of his life, when it had long since ceased to be active, he wrote an incomplete essay on the IRB in which he identifies himself as first and last a member of that clandestine, physical force organisation. He implies rather than advertises a detailed knowledge that could only have come from extensive involvement at the top, keeping the promise he made on taking the oath 'to keep secret the business of this organisation'. And being close to Tom Clarke and Sean MacDermott, the two main drivers on the road to the 1916 rebellion, he had secrets to keep. His unfinished essay is generally detached in expression but there are some flashes of personal feeling, one of them describing Tom Clarke. 'To be admitted into that magic circle, to be one of the chosen company with whom Tom discourses without restraint, was something to be worthy of, and a memory to be proud of.'

(Early in 1912 Peadar and Peadar Macken attended an Irish-language meeting in the Moira Hotel in Trinity Street, Dublin, that was addressed by Patrick Pearse, till then associated with the politics of the Irish language. Peadar was so taken by Pearse's insistence that a rifle should be as familiar as a hurley in the hands of an Irishman that he immediately informed Clarke. Shortly afterwards Pearse was sworn into the IRB; if Peadar was indeed the first to acquaint Clarke with Pearse's new militancy, he played a significant role in the prelude to 1916.[4])

IN 1906 HE played the notorious Major Sirr in an amateur production of *Robert Emmet* in Molesworth Street Hall. The star and main force behind the production was P. J. Bourke, who would marry Peadar's sister, Margaret; one of the soldiers was played by Peadar's friend Paddy Heeney. While threatening to hang Anne Devlin, Major Sirr discovered that he had not brought his rope on stage. With some aplomb, he turned to Paddy Heeney: 'Fetch a rope, poltroon.' When there was no sign of Heeney returning, Peadar improvised further, to the great amusement of the audience, turning to another soldier: 'You, sirrah, you poltroon, go off and see where that other poltroon is and fetch me a rope to hang this wench.'

Peadar had begun collaborating on ballads with Paddy Heeney in 1903, he supplying the words, Paddy the music. In late 1909 or early 1910 they set out to satisfy the need for a stirring song with which young nationalists could assert their dedication to the cause of Irish freedom and the result was 'A Soldier's Song' which, after a slow start, established itself as the anthem of Irish separatism, especially with the foundation of the Irish Volunteers in 1913.[5]

Clubs with patriotic purposes were springing up everywhere, one of which, Cumann na nGaedheal, met in a hall at the back of Walker's tobacco shop on High Street. Members were encouraged to contribute to a manuscript journal that contained 'poetry written by Peter Carney, one of the young fellows with a talent for verse'.[6] The Walkers' daughter Mary achieved fame on the Abbey stage as Máire Ní Shiúlaigh and was in Jacob's factory during Easter Week 1916.

These must have been exhilarating years for Peadar. He was living 'for the cause', teaching Irish and writing songs. He also wrote plays: one was entitled *Wolfe Tone*, another—*The Call to Arms*, based on the life of the Cork Fenian Peter O'Neill Crowley—was produced by the Oliver Bond Club in 1907. In 1910, to improve their Irish (and encourage the local IRB) he and Peadar Macken spent seven months painting the lighthouse on the Irish-speaking Tory Island off Donegal. The following year he joined the Abbey as property master for an English tour, the highlight of which for him was the Shamrock Bar in London's Fetter Lane where he enjoyed the company of his 'own people', including Michael Collins and Sam Maguire who, on being told by Peadar of the death of Paddy Heeney, collected £17 for his widow.

In the census of 1911 Peter Kearney, aged twenty-seven, is living alone in a room in 46 Corporation Buildings in the North Dock ward. When or why he crossed the river is not known. Perhaps it was in order to be closer to the Abbey Theatre and/or to his fellow activists. Sean O'Casey, who also lived in the North Dock in nearby Abercorn Road, had sufficient confidence in his Irish to identify himself, Seaghan Ó Cathasaigh, as 'fear an tighe' (man of the house) and translate his Unionist mother and his British Army brother Michael into Irish for the occasion.

On 25 November 1913, Peadar became a founder-member of the Irish Volunteers. By then, aged almost thirty, he had been smitten by a seventeen-year-old Dublin girl, Eva Flanagan, one of two orphaned sisters who had been born into considerable comfort but were now living in a drawing-room flat in North Great Geeorge's Street.' Peadar and Eva were married on Sunday, 15 February 1914. (His proposal may have been prompted by the availability of a furnished room in 17 Russell Place on the North Circular Road, recently vacated by Paddy Heeney's brother Michael, and the presence of his IRB friend MacDermott in number 15.) There is strong evidence in his songs and letters that they loved each other but she must have known from the beginning that Ireland had first call on him. As with the couple in one of his most popular ballads, their honeymoon was 'a whole afternoon down by the Liffeyside'. Peadar started a painting job the following day.

But neither marriage nor painting was allowed to get in the way of his work 'for the cause'. His importance to 'the organisation' is witnessed by his presence at both illegal importations of arms in 1914, Howth in July, Kilcoole in August. His detailed account of the Howth landing (included in his essay on the IRB) could only have been written by somebody involved in the planning and execution of these episodes but, again, the instinctive reticence of an IRB man gives nothing away.

> Early morning 26 July 1914 found a small party of picked men at Howth Harbour, preparing to receive the white yacht and help to pass her precious cargo into the hands of the Volunteers who would soon be on the march from Dublin. Each man was a member of the IRB.

Despite the shackles of the impersonal mode, the excitement at the docking of the *Asgard* could only be first-hand: 'There are moments in the lives of most of us whose memory time can never erase and for those who stood on the jetty at Howth that morning that was one of them.' From his front row position he described the landing of the arms:

> The landing party boarded her at once, and proceeded—under orders, of course—to smash the cabin lights as the quickest method of getting the cargo ashore.... While the glass was being demolished, a rowing boat came within hailing distance. It contained a party of coastguards, led by an officer, who wanted to know what it was all about. However, the appearance of automatic pistols in the hands of the glass-breakers, who had turned suddenly in his direction, spelt trouble—so he gave orders to back oar and away.[7]

A comparison with Luke Kennedy's Witness Statement, submitted to the Bureau of Military History in November 1948, shows how careful we must be when taking Peadar Kearney at his word.

> The "Asgard" came along in full sail into a berth in the harbour. Myself, Kearney and a number of other men went aboard. The cabin of the ship was packed with arms and ammunition. The coastguards who were stationed at the other side of the harbour came across in a boat to within 2 or 3 boats length of the yacht. I ordered them back. They still came on, so Kearney and myself produced revolvers and ordered them again to get back. They went back and on arrival at the far side they sent up rockets.[8]

More secret agent than boasting soldier, when Peadar Kearney features in one of his own accounts, his self-portraits are anything but heroic.

On 23 May 1915, he was in a group of Volunteers whose parade through Limerick—led by Patrick Pearse—was attacked by a local mob, one of whom tried to take Peadar's rifle away and would have succeeded had a priest not intervened, driving off the assailant and passing the rifle to a policeman. By an extraordinary coincidence, this was a priest Peadar had known on Tory Island.[9]

In his Witness Statement Seamus Daly describes another misadventure involving a rifle.

During the first part of 1915, all our time was occupied drilling and training. We erected a miniature rifle range in Father Mathew Park and this was open to all Companies in the Brigade. We fired as much practice as our ammunition allowed, and the more ammunition one could buy the more practice we could have. We usually spent Saturday evenings on the miniature range and one of these evenings, Peadar Kearney, then fairly unknown to most of us and who was a member of the 2nd Battalion, got wounded accidentally in the knee with a .22 bullet. This threw Kearney out of work. He was a married man then with a young family. At this time 'B' and 'F' Companies of the 2nd Battalion organised a concert in the Clontarf Town Hall to raise funds for arms. For the concert we got a few thousand copies of 'The Soldier's Song' and sold them during the concert at 1d each. The proceeds of the sale of these ballads were allocated in aid of Kearney and at the time we all believed that this was the first occasion on which this song was sung in public.[10]

It is not clear who fired the bullet accidentally. There is no record of the incident in his biography or in the oral tradition of the family. (Nor did either mention the 'young family' Peadar and Eva had in early 1915: a veil of semi-secrecy had been drawn over the short life of Cónal, who had died before the birth of Pearse in May 1916. Before reading Daly's Witness Statement I had never known why Pearse had called his eldest son Cónal.)

In March 1916 he was on another Abbey tour in England when he received word that the Rising was imminent. The tour manager's threat—that he would never work again in a Dublin theatre if he abandoned the tour—made no impression but it is possible that by the morning of Easter Monday Peadar regretted his return. The countermanding order had caused fatal confusion and when a mobilisation order was delivered to the house, he was inclined to dismiss it until Eva asked him 'what if this is the real call?' At which point he dressed and, having joined his brother-in-law Mick Slater in nearby Summerhill, proceeded to St Stephen's Green.

He left a 'Personal Narrative of Easter Week'[11] in which he described his experience in Jacob's factory under the command of Thomas MacDonagh and Dick McKee. He was willing to die for the cause, but only if necessary. Disgusted by the turn-out—one-tenth, he reckoned, of B Company, 2nd

Battalion—he decided to have a pint in the Grafton Bar and when reminded by Mick that anybody taking alcoholic liquor was liable to be shot, retorted that 'the way things are looking we'll be all shot, order or no order, before the night is out', and went in for his pint.

Jacob's was somewhat isolated from the main centres of the Rising. Fighting was sporadic and one group spent their off-duty periods in the top-floor library where they discussed Shakespeare's *Julius Caesar*.[12] Among them were his friends, Tom Pugh and Mick Slater, and Peadar, who makes no mention of it. He did record the finale:

> By Friday every man of common sense realised the end was in sight, but never, until it was officially announced on Sunday morning was the word 'surrender' hinted at. On the contrary, and there are scores still living who can vouch for it, many brains were concentrated on the problem of making the inevitable suc-cess of the British as costly as possible.[13]

Peadar was typically cool and pragmatic, and unimpressed by the order to surrender: 'I had no intention of marching myself to Bride Street to give myself up, as it needed no unusual foresight to visualise the barrack square and the gentlemen of the G Division picking out certain individuals for special treatment.'

Why would a mere Volunteer be singled out by the detectives of G Division? Hardly because he was a senior member of the IRB; many such men had surrendered. Because he had written seditious songs, including 'A Soldier's Song'? Again, unlikely. But Peadar's remark suggests that, apart from taking part in the rebellion, he was linked with some serious offence he has refused to detail and the fact remains that he and Mick Slater were listed as wanted in *Hue and Cry*.[14]

Not for the first or the last time we are left to wonder what Peadar has decided not to tell us and why. He was temperamentally disinclined to beat his own drum and this instinct was encouraged by a political lifetime of clandestine activity in which secrecy was a major virtue and loose talk a weakness that could have disastrous consequences for him and his comrades.

Although Peadar managed to slip across the river to the north side of the city, he dared not risk returning to Eva in 5 Fairview Avenue, which had been raided and was presumably under surveillance; instead, he kept on the move, one step ahead of the security forces, until he managed to rent the basement kitchen of 41 Rutland Street. Here a heavily pregnant Eva brought arms and ammunition that had been successfully hidden in Fairview. Peadar was reduced to scavenging cabbage leaves from outside shops and into this world of fear, destitution and near-despair, their son was born on 22 May and named Pearse in honour of the man who had proclaimed the republic outside the GPO and was the first to be executed on 3 May. Peadar waited outside the Rotunda all night and when, the following morning, a porter told him he had a son, Peadar retorted: 'I'm not interested. How is the little girl?'

Many of those executed in the aftermath of the Rising were not merely commanders and comrades and fellow members of the IRB and the Volunteers. As he wrote in 'Our Dead (Easter 1916)':

> They are not ancient heroes
> From the dim and misty years,
> But the dearest friends we had on earth
> Who shared our smiles and tears …
> Yet we would not bring them back to life;
> In death they're stronger still!

These politically correct lines, in which he suppresses personal emotion in favour of the greater cause, may strike us as too easily achieved; but perhaps they were the only means available to him to assuage what must have been heart-rending grief and to make any sense of his loss. There was no 'treatment' for a man in his position, only more anxiety and fear, and though Eva would have done her best, she had her own problems.

Despite his disinterest at the maternity hospital, the sight of baby Pearse in his 'narrow bed' inspired him to write what seems to be the only poem addressed to either of his sons. (I do not know when he wrote 'Romany Rye', a gipsy lullaby with which Eva used to lull me to sleep, but the physical features described—'your raven hair, and the smile in your dark brown eye'—are not those of the Kearneys.) 'Daddy Boy' is more concerned with the gazing father than with anything that might be happening within the infant's consciousness. There is no conventional depiction of the baby's innocent charms and the father is unusually specific in his hopes for his son.

All my hopes are set on you,
Daddy boy, Daddy boy,
God grant they'll all come true,
Daddy boy, Daddy boy,
When you're big and brave and strong
Ireland's cause you'll carry on
Just like Con and Tom and Sean,
Daddy boy, Daddy boy.

If you live these lines to read
Daddy boy, Daddy boy,
And old Ireland's still unfreed,
Daddy boy, Daddy boy,
There's a solemn pledge implied
You're to try as Colbert tried
Or to die as Colbert died
Daddy boy, Daddy boy.

Was there ever a lullaby in which a father proudly imagined his child emu-lating Con Colbert, Tom Clarke and MacDermott and falling before a firing squad? And there is even sterner stuff to follow.

There's a straight and narrow path,
Daddy boy! Daddy boy!
There's a day of coming wrath,
Daddy boy! Daddy boy!
When by earth and air and sea
Mother Ireland shall be free;
Ah may you be there to see,
Daddy boy!

I would rather see you dead,
Daddy boy, Daddy boy,
In your wee and narrow bed,
Daddy boy, Daddy boy,
Than to think that you should grow
And foregather with the foe

219

They who laid your namesake low
Daddy boy, Daddy boy.

There could be no more striking illustration of Peadar's mind in the after-math of the Rising: he allowed neither the deaths of his close friends nor the survival of his only son to deflect him from what he believed was his primary duty.

IN AUGUST 1916, under cover of a Gaelic League Oireachtas, 'a meeting to reorganise the IRB was attended by Dr Patrick McCartan, Diarmuid O'Hegarty, Martin Conlon, Peadar Kearney, Luke Kennedy, Ó Muirthile and "a patriotic young priest from the North".'[15] There was a general release of prisoners in December 1916, which probably meant that Peadar could breathe more freely and soon he was more actively involved than ever, this time as an IRB organiser in the new military campaign, led by men such as Michael Collins who favoured guerrilla warfare over symbolic gestures. Years later Michael Noyk (legal advisor to Arthur Griffith and Michael Collins and, later, Peadar himself) recalled the revival of enthusiasm in early 1917 when 'the crowd again began gathering in the Bailey and also in Sean Farrelly's public house at the corner of Stephen's Green and Grafton Street. The place was a great centre for Volunteers particularly and a number of men who might be described as "unknown soldiers" used to meet there. Among them were Peadar Kearney, Jack Toomey and Andie "Mocky" Comerford.'[16]

What did he mean by describing these men, all of whom had been 'out' in 1916 and one of whom he identifies as the author of the most famous Volunteer song of them all, as 'unknown soldiers'? Noyk was writing thirty-five years later and was well aware how Peadar Kearney had fared in the independent state he had done so much to bring about. Perhaps he was betraying his awareness that, in the case of Kearney, the extent of his role in 'the organisation' between 1916 and 1920 had never been fully ac-knowledged, partly because he operated undercover, partly because of his instinctive reticence.

Peadar described himself at this time as an organiser, a man chosen by the leadership—in Peadar's case most likely by Collins or McKee—for his trustworthiness, experience, dedication and efficiency, and delegated to dis-tricts where the structure, discipline, morale and training of the Volunteers needed improvement. The best-known account of such activities remains Ernie O'Malley's *On Another Man's Wound*. Part intellectual revolutionary, part gunslinger, he wrote a memoir as exciting as any novel: he never withdrew safely when he could launch an odds-against attack, showed nerves of titanium when entering Dublin Castle in British army uniform in search of a legal permit to buy a pistol, was wounded several times, captured, tortured and threatened with execution before escaping and living to tell the tale.

It is unlikely that Peadar Kearney—or anybody else—could make such claims but there can be no doubt that an organiser lived in constant danger of arrest and torture and being executed 'while trying to escape'. On the other hand, Ernie O'Malley had not left a wife and children at home while he made his way through the valley of the shadow of death.

In the aftermath of the Rising the re-arming of the Volunteers was one of the most vital and perhaps the most difficult of all the tasks facing the leadership. In 1917 Peadar was a founder member of the Arms Committee, which consisted of about six people with Luke Kennedy, Peadar's partner at the Howth gunrunning, as chairman and Michael Collins as treasurer, from whom Peadar received the first cheque for £50. Jack Toomey who, like Peadar, had been in Jacob's with B Company, wrote that when Peadar was excused from company parades it was because 'or so I understood of attendance at more important work. I can verify this because on one and I think two occasions he secured from G.H.Q. £50's for me to pay for arms purchase, i.e. rifles, revolvers and ammunition'. It is telling that even a close comrade could only assume that Peadar operated in a twilight world, an ordinary man (that is to say, not an officer) in the Volunteers who was in close contact with GHQ and involved in the Arms Committee and in other forms of 'more important work' that Toomey knew nothing of. At this stage we are not surprised that the only example of this work that Peadar gave his biographer was a heavily censored account of a spell in Baltinglass in early 1917. In his pension application in 1924, submitted to a board that was aware of his activities leading up to and during the War of Independence, he wrote that 'many of the most active years of my life were spent in connection with the national organisation thro' Ireland and the other side of the Irish Sea.'[17]

Peadar's preferred role was undercover. When he and Mick Slater set off from Summerhill on Easter Monday, Mick was in Volunteer uniform while Peadar wore a sports suit made from Volunteer material. He was probably following the example of Tom Clarke and MacDermott in rejecting the self-identification of a uniform. On the cover of his application for a military pension his rank in both the Irish Volunteers and the Irish Republican Army is 'unknown'. It is hardly surprising therefore that his preferred milieu was a pub in the red-light district.

A CASE could be made for Phil Shanahan's in Montgomery Street (now Foley Street) as the most remarkable pub in Irish history. Shanahan was a Tipperary man who had been in Jacob's in 1916, after which he was interned in Frongoch Camp in Wales. His pub, in the Monto immortalised by Joyce in *Ulysses*, was such a haven for militant republicans that it is difficult to imagine how it survived at all during the war of independence (and the subsequent civil war when it became an 'Irregular' establishment).

Thomas Leahy of the Irish Citizen Army wrote of Phil Shanahan's:

> It was here I got to know Dan Breen, Sean Treacy, Sean Hogan, Seamus Robinson, Peadar Carney (author of The Soldier's Song), Tom Slater and Jim Lawless, who were the driving force in getting things done throughout the country, notwithstanding curfew laws and raids by police.[18]

This was some company. The first four were, after Collins, the most wanted in Ireland, 'hard men' members of the Tipperary Brigade who had come to Dublin to assist Collins' special operations unit, The Squad. When the Dáil Loan was floated in 1920 individual collectors, such as Thomas Leahy, passed the money on to Jim Lawless who was responsible to the minister for finance, Michael Collins.

Phil Shanahan's was also something of an arms depot, with some unusual suppliers. Luke Kennedy stated that 'a lot of British soldiers used frequent Phil Shanahan's public house and it was there most of the contacts were made.'[19] Dan Breen recalled that 'the lady prostitutes used to pinch the guns and ammunition from the Auxiliaries or Tans at night, and then leave them for us at Phil Shanahan's public house'. He was careful to add that 'there was no such thing as payment for these transactions, and any information they had they gave us. The man who composed "The Soldier's Song" frequented Phil Shanahan's. Saints and sinners met there.'[20]

There were good nights in the snug such as those described in one of Peadar'a most interesting songs, 'Down in the Village: Phil Shanahan's Pub,

Dublin, 1918'. 'The Village' was another name for the red-light district and this ballad looks back nostalgically on a specific time, 1918, the year before the outbreak of the war that was to claim many of his close friends.

> *Sad is the theme of my muse and my story,*
> *Gone are the days of the snug and its glory;*
> *Dark are the clouds that are hovering o'er me,*
> *Down in the village we tarried so long.*
> *[Chorus]*
> *Heigh ho! Slán to the revelry*
> *Shouting and drinking and singing so merrily,*
> *Red nights we never again will see,*
> *Down in the village we tarried so long.*

Behind the nostalgia and the cast of strangers, one gets a rare sense of the boisterous friendship that bound these brothers-in-arms. Among the revellers in Phil Shanahan's are IRB men and fellow members of B Company: Dick Stokes, Mick Donoghue, Jack Toomey, Sean Byrne, Peadar Kearney, Tom Pugh and Phil Shanahan himself, all of them 1916 men who were preparing for the next phase of the revolution. With them was Tom Slater, brother of Mick and Adjutant of C Company.

An earlier composition of Peadar's, written in the aftermath of the Rising, had offered an even more detailed description of him and his friends that is consciously at odds with the popularly preferred image of the rebels as men whose lives were as pure as their politics. Here, with some relish, he recalls the low esteem in which his type was held.

> *The poets have chanted their paeans of praise*
> *To the men who were pure of soul;*
> *I tell of a bunch who in different ways*
> *Find a place on the muster roll.*
> *'Tis very low down, still you'll all agree*
> *They have earned their places there,*
> *Tho' their principal pastimes seemed to be*
> *To drink and gamble and swear. . .*
>
> *Oh, a holy crush, not one of us*

223

But of devilment had our share,
We all had our jags on the backs of the book
And most of us some to spare.
We sang our songs and courted the girls
And quaffed the eau-de-vie,
And seldom saw home till the rays of dawn
Shot up from the Irish Sea.
We had no friends 'mong the 'unco guid', [21]
Tho' some of the brave and true
Would grin and say: 'That bunch, we guess,
Are not God's chosen few,'
While the word-spinning hypocrites passing by
Said 'They are the Devil's Crew'.

But these poor, apparently feckless Dublin men were 'the pick of the bunch' when called to assert the independence of Ireland in 1916. Unlike Peadar himself, they obeyed the order to surrender, but

… had the order been 'Carry on!'
I'm telling a thing that's true—
The last shot fired from Dublin's ruins
Would [have] come from the Devil's Crew!

Oddly enough, there is no denunciation of the Saxon foe: though half of the seven verses deal with the Rising, the main energy is derived from class or moral rather than national consciousness and Peadar's contempt is reserved for the snobbish spoofers and 'the canting cowards who preached/ From the depths of an easy chair'. [22]

ON 1 August 1918 my father was born and christened Colbert, after Con Colbert who had been executed for his part in the Rising. On the birth certificate Peadar is listed in English and described as 'Labourer', presumably to attract as little attention as possible. Both sons were named after 1916 martyrs who had been associated with the training of boys, Con Colbert with Fianna Éireann, and Pearse with St Enda's School, where Con Colbert had worked as a drill instructor.

On the day Peadar attended the opening of the First Dáil in the Mansion

House, 21 January 1919, Volunteers attacked and killed two members of the Royal Irish Constabulary (RIC) at Soloheadbeg in County Tipperary. Though unsanctioned by higher authorities the action was soon accepted as the opening shot of a renewed war against British rule and the attackers later found themselves accommodated in Phil Shanahan's as they awaited orders from Michael Collins.

Peadar Kearney told his biographer of an occasion when members of the Tipperary Flying Column were assembled in the upstairs room of Shanahan's. While Peadar was getting drinks to bring up to these mostly teetotal men, he saw four lorry-loads of British soldiers rushing towards the pub and immediately warned the Volunteers, one of whom ordered him to 'get out of this, Kearney; this is no place for you'. Fortunately, the raiders contented themselves with trashing the bar.[23]

It may be true that the Tipperary Volunteer did not consider Peadar suited to a gunfight and perhaps he was right; however, given Peadar's tendency to present himself as an unheroic and unarmed observer, we should not assume this story is the whole truth. Consider his comment that 'only one other man did I know who was as cool and level-headed as Sean Treacy in a tight corner, as able to command men and demand respect, and that was Michael Collins'.[24] How was he qualified to come to this conclusion? Had he been there with them in tight corners? If he was merely deducing from the reports of others, would he not have used 'heard/knew of' rather than 'knew'?

Peadar became particularly fond of Sean Treacy, who combined a rather demure demeanour with utter fearlessness and dedication to the armed struggle. He excelled in close-quarter exchanges, whether rescuing a comrade from a train at Knocklong or escaping from a safe house in Dublin. His end came on 14 October 1920, when surprised and killed by a team of British Secret Service agents in Talbot Street, but not before he had killed two of them. When, years later, his friends decided to make a presentation to Peadar, they commissioned a portrait in oils of Treacy by Sean Keating.

The years 1919 and 1920 were years of all-out war. As Peadar put it:

My wife never knew when she would hear of my death. But it was easy to be shot or hanged—it was hard enough to live ... Twice in my life I left my home never to return to it. Books,

manuscripts, prints, furniture lost. Personal mementoes, auto-
graphs of Tom Clarke, Sean MacDermott and the rest, all destroyed.[25]

But he survived, unlike some of his dearest friends. Had Treacy not been
killed, he would have been part of Michael Collins' most audacious plan to
neutralise British Intelligence in Dublin. On the morning of 21 November
1920—Bloody Sunday—eleven officers were shot by members of The
Squad. Enraged RIC men and Auxiliaries responded by killing fourteen
civilians at Croke Park and hunting Collins' men with a new zeal.

The most painful consequence for Peadar was the loss of two more
close friends, Dick McKee and Peadar Clancy (for whom, along with Sean
Treacy, Peadar would later ask his baby sons to pray). Peadar recalled how,
in Shanahan's on Saturday, 20 November, McKee had insisted on shaking hands with him: 'We see each other often but we never seem to shake
hands.' Then McKee and Clancy headed off to their 'safe house' in nearby
Gloucester Street. But they had been followed by members of the security
forces, who arrested both men and took them to Dublin Castle for inter-
rogation. On hearing they were in the Castle, Peadar had no doubt: 'take
my word for it they are dead'. Which they were, probably tortured to death
and then shot 'while trying to escape'.[26]

Within the week Peadar himself was arrested and taken eventually to
Ballykinlar Camp in County Down. His time there—between April and
November 1921—is the most fully documented of his life, thanks to his
wife Eva who kept his letters. They were written with the censor in mind
by a man in poor health, separated from his wife and children and from 'the
organisation' that had dominated his life for more than twenty years. Few
would be at their best in such circumstances.

BALLYKINLAR WAS a brutal place. Men were shot dead for standing too
near the perimeter wire and poor hygiene guaranteed disease and ill-health
but, anticipating the censor, the letters avoid these matters. Similarly, there
must have been a great deal of political discussion among the internees
but, again, there is no explicit mention of this, apart from some hints of
dissension (following the truce of July 1921) concerning the prospects of a
resolution involving less than an all-Ireland republic. The general tone of
his letters is that of a disciplined soldier:

Let you all keep up your hearts, that's the ticket. Anyhow when you consider what the country is going thro' I know you will all be only too glad to take your own share. No grumbling or lamenting, cheer on the living and pray for the dead and everything will come right in the end.[27]

He applied himself to teaching Irish and learning the violin and also resumed his work as a lyricist. Two of his works show his spirit undaunted. The final verse of 'The Ballykinlar March'—music by fellow-internee Martin Walton—is typical:

> List ye, nations of the world,
> To the message of the free;
> Ireland stands with flag unfurled,
> Sword in hand for liberty!
> Ever shall her voice be heard
> In the councils of the free,
> Ever shall her shining sword be bared
> For truth and liberty.

This rings hollow to our ears today but we can understand the desire of an organiser to raise the morale of others. He wrote an equally bombastic poem to Sean Treacy.

> To you, O Flower of Ireland's Youth!
> Across the grave we send a nation's praise
> Hailing your name—the greatest name of all,
> Young Ireland's pioneers!
> Chanting your courage cool;
> Your deathless love for her,
> Your changeless hate for those
> Who sought her soul to rend
> Those you pursued and slew without remorse
> Those you destroyed and conquered to the end.

He remains a physical force man, fully supportive of Treacy's lethal violence, strikingly suspicious of those he terms 'politicians'.

> I'd give a lot to be able to say and publish what's in my mind, but I'm between two fires here. If I please one I displease the other and vice versa. Once we get into the hands of the politicians we're simply pawns in the game.[28]

Peadar had a contempt for politicians that is common among soldiers. In a letter written on 1 June, he tries to dampen Eva's hopes of a truce and early release: 'But not being a political genius like some of the stiffs that pose as statesmen I may be up against peace "release" and all the rest of it & can't see it.'

There are times when he sounds selfish and unfeeling, complaining of the parcels Eva sends, apparently unconcerned as to her ability to feed and clothe herself and two young children, but when, in late August, she sends up a distress flare (presumably suggesting that he has lost interest in her) he is quick to reassure her: 'My fancy never paints a picture of the future that does not contain you and the lads. The lads occupy a big space in my dreams but without you there would be no picture.'[29]

There are moments of genuine affection and physical desire:

> Do you know it's dangerous to cut loose & write what it is your mind, besides if I told you what I'm thinking about it might shock the censor. No matter, I have an idea we'll have a good laugh yet in the right place, where we had many a good laugh. Don't show this to [your sister] Katie or she'll lose her eyesight.[30]

In a letter to Eva probably written during the Treaty negotiations he finds a visionary consolation that revives his old faith in the revolution:

> At times you feel you would do anything on earth to get home to those you love, but it is a temptation that is put under foot. We internees are not much use to any person or thing, but we can at least be faithful unto death. One thing I wish and that wish will come true: my sons will honour and respect me. I know that & I'm happy in the knowledge. I care nothing about what anybody on this earth thinks while they with your help will remain fit representatives of a great name, to carry on. Swank? But it's true, & mark my words they who live shall see. No matter what the

immediate future may hold this will be some country & there are
tiny lads toddling round who will be some men.[31]

In spite of all vicissitudes, he is convinced of his own place in history: if his
sisters seem to have forgotten 'their poor relations', 'wait till my funeral is
on & they'll all be claiming me as a member of the family'.[32]

There are constant inquiries after 'the lads' and their education: 'I build
great castles as to what I'll teach the lads if God wills I see them again.' One
was the violin, which he was learning himself, and he was insistent that,
voices or no voices, both should be learning songs, presumably the patriotic
variety. Eva depended on support from Maura and Mick Slater and Peadar
suggests that one of their daughters, Máirín, should teach Pearse and Con
Irish.[33]

Given the circumstances—the harshness of the camp, poor health and
growing anxiety about the treaty negotiations—he kept up his spirits and
his sense of humour:

> I was listening to new music today to words I strung together &
> do you know the title? 'My Tolka's Banks'. Oh those were days
> & nights too. 'I'd live the same life over if I had to live again.'
> Now I may grouse sometimes, but in your new home [in Mount
> Brown] I want you to develop an easy mind & be as comfortable
> as you possibly can under the circumstances. You have the lads
> to study & see they have their father's one or two good points
> & remain ignorant to his bad points we heard so much about. I
> suppose they'll hardly be saints but they can be miles better than
> [their] father. (This is the first good laugh I had today.)[34]

Peadar was not enthusiastic about the move from Richmond Parade to
Mount Brown. He had very happy memories of cavorting with Eva on the
banks of the Tolka and it was in a rather small area of the Dublin north-
side—bounded roughly by Amiens Street, Talbot Street, Gardiner Street,
Dorset Street and the North Circular Road—that he and his comrades had
taken on the British Empire and brought them to the negotiating table.

On 25 November 1921 he was released on parole to visit Eva, who was
ill. The sergeant who conducted him to the gate supposed 'if you had me
in Dublin this minute you'd plug me'. Perhaps it was attempted humour;

perhaps the sergeant had access to information about him that Peadar has chosen not to pass on to us. He was due back on 8 December but the Treaty was signed two days earlier, leading to a general release, but not to carefree courting on the banks of the Tolka.

THE MAN who arrived in 79 Mount Brown in late November was in poor health but glad to see his wife and children and look forward to a domestic life that, for all its problems and limitations, would be a welcome relief after the penal squalor of Ballykinlar. Presumably friends and relations assembled to welcome him home but, the party over, he joined his family in grim poverty. There was a pittance in royalties from 'A Soldier's Song'; otherwise they depended on the kindness of those same friends and relations and also on charity, specifically from White Cross, an organisation that distributed American funds to those in distress in Ireland because of the political situation.

Nor did the political situation inspire hope for a better future. Hardly were the signatories back from London when a series of IRA commanders began to repudiate the Treaty. The Dáil had approved it in January 1922 and supporters of the Treaty won 75 per cent of the vote in the June general election but its opponents were not halted by such manifestations of the will of the people. On 28 June the National Army shelled the anti-Treaty occupants of the Four Courts and civil war had begun.

In July Peadar took up the post of Chief Military Censor in Maryborough Gaol (and subsequently in Kilmainham Gaol and the North Dublin Union, which also housed republican prisoners, finishing in January 1924). It was hardly the role he would have chosen in the new state, even at a time of civil war, and shortly after his arrival he must have been relieved when, while visiting the gaol, his old friend Michael Collins—now General Collins, Commander-in-Chief of the National Army and effectively the most powerful man in the Free State—said that 'my job was only a temporary one but I was to sit tight and I would be all right'.[35] But a couple of weeks later, on 22 August 1922, Collins was shot dead at Béal na Bláth, leaving Peadar (and others) to wonder how different life would have been for him and his family had Collins lived to 'look after' his comrade.

It is likely that Peadar's decision to side with the Free State had less to do with the will of the people than with Collins. There must have been some in the Dublin Brigade—based on The Squad—who saw the Treaty as an unacceptable compromise, but such was their loyalty to Collins that almost all followed him, including Paddy O'Daly, former leader of The Squad and now Brigadier in the new National Army, who had led the attack on the Four Courts. Peadar was a big enough 'name' to attract visits from old friends, ladies and gentlemen, who had taken sides against the Treaty.

> [They] were anxious to obtain even my name for anti-Treaty purposes. As I never agreed with them the conversations generally wound up in futile political controversy. One of the things I was asked to do was to write (salary attached) the Irish weekly article for the "Irish World". On my refusal their visits ceased.[36]

His appointment as censor was almost certainly an executive decision by his old friend Jack Toomey, who used his position as commandant of Maryborough Gaol to help an ailing comrade by giving him a job and an income with which to provide for his family. As Peadar would soon discover to his cost, there was no official record of his enlistment or military rank. Such an arrangement may seem strangely *ad hoc* unless we recall that these were men who had just emerged from a guerrilla into a civil war.

Not that this employment solved all his problems. Sometime between July 1922 and the end of 1924 Eva and the boys had been evicted from the house in Mount Brown. If, say, this took place around Christmas 1923, Pearse and Con (then aged seven and five) would have been old enough to share the terror of their mother at being ordered out of their home. Neither of them offered any detailed reminiscences to their children, perhaps because the episode did not reflect well on their father.

Was Peadar away in Maryborough at the time? It seems unlikely that an IRB man of his experience would not be able to dissuade the sheriff, as he had, for example, the coast guards at Howth. Without his protection his sons would have watched as their mother, with nobody to defend her, was put out on the street with them and her belongings.

How had such a catastrophe been allowed to happen? If Eva had been unable to come up with the rent, why not? We know she and the boys were living in great poverty, but could Peadar's sisters have not come to her rescue on this occasion? If Peadar was in Maryborough—less than sixty miles away—why could she not have got word to him to come home immediately with the rent money? Surely she was given a period of notice?

(A likely explanation was offered some fifty years later by a woman who worked as an archivist for Dublin Corporation and who had come into Bourke's of Dame Street, where Con worked, to buy stage make-up or fancy dress. In the course of their conversation Con confessed to a lingering curiosity about what exactly had happened in Mount Brown way back in the early 1920s and the archivist promised to see if there was any record of the eviction. There was, and of a corporation rent collector in the area who had been fired for his illegal and anti-social activities. His scam was to be utterly strict in condemning tenants to eviction: one hour late with your rent and you were gone. Why? Because there was a housing shortage and he had many seeking his favour, which he was happy to grant, for a price. He had evicted the Kearneys in order to accommodate new tenants who paid him not only the corporation rent but a bribe that went straight into his own pocket.)

Peadar was discharged from the army on the release of republican prisoners in January 1924 and, after an unexplained absence of nine months, he returned to his trade of house painting, working in the Post Office Factory between October 1924 and June 1926. He was paid £3 17s. 9d. a week but his time was considerably 'broken' by slackness of work and illness.

HELP APPEARED on the horizon with the passing of the Military Service Pensions Act 1924 to reward those who had rendered active service during Easter Week 1916 and/or the period from 1 April 1920 to 11 July 1921 and who in addition had served in the National Forces between 1 July 1922 and 1 October 1923, which is to say, persons such as himself. The only question was whether the pension had arrived in time to rescue him: his application suggests a man all but crushed by illness, poverty, humiliation and depression, and conjures up an appalling picture of the circumstances in which the Kearney family found themselves when Con was aged between six and eight.

The conduct of the Board of Assessors was at least as bureaucratic and parsimonious as its British predecessor. It approved the payment of pensions to 3,855 applicants; almost a thousand others were described as having prima facie cases but were deemed outside the scope of the Act. The amount payable varied according to the rank held by the applicant in the National Forces/Defence Forces and the amount of continuous service. Easter Week 1916 was counted as four years' service and the maximum possible pension was £350 per annum. The application form was, inevitably, more suited to gauging the contribution of a regular soldier with regular duties in a regular army than to a clandestine 'organiser', but applicants were allowed to nominate referees and submit a personal statement.

To vouch for his claim, Peadar chose IRB friends, almost all of whom had been on the Supreme Council and who had, like him, been close to Collins and had supported the Free State during the Civil War, fighting men rather than politicians. But the tide had begun to turn against the IRB: while a hard core believed it should continue as a clandestine control group within the National Army, there was growing support for the view that a secret society had no place in a democratic state.

To make matters worse for Peadar, his primary referee, Major General Paddy O'Daly (Pádraig Ó Dálaigh), perhaps the most prominent soldier on the Free State side, who had followed the taking of the Four Courts with the 'pacification' of Dublin, Cork and Kerry, had been obliged to resign in March 1924 after the massacre of Republican prisoners in Ballyseedy, County Kerry, the previous year. Why would Peadar choose such a man as his referee? If it was a defiant act of faith in an old comrade, it was—at best—misplaced. More disturbing is the possibility that Peadar was unaware how self-undermining his choice was. O'Daly failed to supply a reference, perhaps in the belief that it would do Peadar more harm than good.

His second referee was Commandant Sean Toomey, who had employed him in Maryborough Gaol, his third, Piaras Béaslaí, a major-general in the National Army who was even then working on *Michael Collins and the Making of a New Ireland* (1926).

There were other referees to cover specific periods, almost all of them high-ranking officers in the National Army, the lowliest being a mere captain. Among them was Lieutenant General Ó Muirthile, a leader of those who wished to maintain the influence of the IRB within the National Army, who had been obliged to resign his commission and who, like O'Daly, failed to produce a reference.

Perhaps the closest of all to Michael Collins had been his cousin and adjutant, Lieutenant General Gearóid Ó Súilleabháin. He too had resigned from the army but redirected his energies to politics and was appointed secretary to the Board of Assessors. It is obvious from a note Peadar wrote to him in Irish that a degree of intimacy existed between them.

Peadar must have thought a decent pension was a *fait accompli*. It was

233

common knowledge among those in the know—including his referees and the secretary to the board—that he had played an important part in the fight for freedom but, obliged to be bureaucratic, the board was not interested in common knowledge: they wanted documented and verifiable facts on a form. Yes, Peadar Kearney had worked as Chief Military Censor and such was his familiarity with the Commander-in-Chief of the National Army, Michael Collins, that he could have a private conversation with him when he visited Maryborough Gaol, but where was the evidence? Look how he answered the questions on the form. What rank did he hold in the National Army? *Chief Military Censor.* Where did he enlist? *July 1922.* When did he enlist? *Went to Maryboro' as Military Censor.* He could not supply an army number or rank because he had never been officially registered with the army even though nobody had objected when he 'messed [took meals] with the officers', presumably because he was a close friend of the commandant.

Nor is it difficult to imagine his soldierly frustration at having his life's work subjected to bureaucratic analysis, or his instinctive recoil when invited, as he would have understood it, to boast of his achievements. And it is clear that—whether through debility or vanity, more likely the former—he resented being required to rehearse for any Board of Assessors what he had done for his country out of a sense of love and duty. His referees were eminent men who had been in the thick of things and were well aware of his clandestine activities: their word should be sufficient. He concluded his application on 29 December 1924:

> Many of the most active years of my life were spent in connec-
> tion with the national organisation thro' Ireland and the other
> side of the Irish Sea. Details of such activities if desirable would
> be difficult to supply at this date. All such activities were really
> aimed at increasing and equipping the IRA and are well known
> to people named herein (i. his referees) and many others. Lieut-
> Gen Gearóid Ó Súilleabháin (Adj-Gen) can vouch for my services
> in Maryboro, Kilmainham and N[orth] D[ublin] U[nion].

From his own point of view this was a reasonable assertion, even if his al-
lusion to the Secretary to the Board was ill considered. On the other hand, his personal statement was almost incoherent.

234

I was one of the original organisers of the Vols. I was a house painter. Mobilised Easter Monday and all the week & at the time of surrender I escaped from Jacob's. I had to lie low after 1916 for nearly 12 months doing no work avoiding arrest [.] rejoined on release of Frongoch men. I was a sort of an organiser I rejoined B Coy. I helped in forming B. Coy [?]. I was organising throughout the country and in Scotland in 1917. I formed first Arms Committee. I got the first cheque for £50 from Gen. Collins to pay for arms. I travelled all round Ireland and Scotland on organising [?] & arming armed patrols & getting arms. Arrested 1920 the time of round up of 1916 men. Released in Jan 1921. When I came back on release was in very bad health. My wife had been receiving money from White Cross. I had a small income from the Soldier's Song of which I wrote the words. At the time of the Four Courts [,] being a very intimate friend of Gen Collins at the end of July or beginning of August 1922 I went to Maryboro as Military Censor. I belonged to no organisation from release from Ballykinlar. I was absolutely [unfit] at the time[.] In Maryboro till Gen Collins called there on his way south he chatted to me and said that my job was only a temporary one but I was to sit tight and I would be all right. I was paid £4 - 4 - 0 a week. I travelled with the soldiers and the officers in the lorries. I was not compelled to do it but when I did I was armed. I might have a .45 in my bedroom. I messed with the officers. Went from Maryboro to Kilmainham then to N.D.U. about January 1924 there was a general demob and release of prisoners … in 6/26. My position in Maryboro Gaol [:] I was an old comrade of Commandant's and whenever he travelled I travelled. I was most [?] in Commandant's confidence. I decoded messages from Irregulars backwards and forwards and I discovered such messages going in and out. The result of close connection with Toomey I always travelled with him armed. One incident was a letter coming through in code from people inside [?]. That letter was brought to Gen Mulcahy. He did not decode it. I decoded it. It related to arms going through. [T]he other two censors were not in this decoding work.

This is a man in such emotional turmoil as to be unaware that he was sub-
verting his own application and risking the loss of money that he and his
family so badly needed. One can understand why he might—in a rage of
resentment or a drunken fury—have written such an incoherent draft, only
to have second thoughts the following morning when he saw the condition
of his wife and children. A more likely explanation is that he was deeply depressed and not so much unwilling as unable to correct what he had written.

(There was, for example, no reference to his role in the Howth gun-
running in his pension application. When, some ten years later, Mick Slater,
who had not taken part in the civil war, applied for a pension, he detailed
his role in the Howth and Kilcoole gun-running. Acting as his referee,
Peadar confirmed Mick's claims and added that Mick had been no ordinary
participant but 'one of the few specially picked men'.)

He was lucky to have influential friends who were aware of his contribution (and of his poor circumstances) and who were willing to intercede on
his behalf (and to make allowances for the shortcomings in his application).
In August 1925 he wrote rather brusquely to Ó Súilleabháin:

> Is fad an lá ó chuireas páipéar an phinsiúin chugat agus ba mhaith
> liom d'fhagháil a bhfuair tú ar aon chor é. Deirtear nach bhfuil
> mé gnóthach go leor mar gheall [ar an bpinsiún] ach is dóigh liom
> féin go bhfuil aithne a ndóthain ar chách orm gan mé ag imeacht
> thart ag nochtaghadh mo sgéil.

> [It is a long time since I sent you the pension form and I would
> like to know if you ever got it. It is said that I am not sufficiently
> active in the matter of my pension but in my own opinion every-
> body knows enough about me without me going around plead-
> ing my case.]

Who was in a position to say that he had not been assiduous enough in
promoting his case? Presumably he had heard this from somebody on the
inside, somebody familiar enough with the system to see that Peadar's sub-
missions were far from adequate, perhaps from Ó Súilleabháin himself.

The slow pace of the assessment process gave him plenty of time to ponder
his situation. On 20 July 1926, he wrote again to Ó Súilleabháin—'Má tá
aon sgéala le fagháil i dtaobh an phinsiúin úd, bhéinn ana bhuidheach díot

dá gcuirtheá chugam é' [If there is any news about the pension I would be grateful if you let me know.]—who replied that his application had been passed on to the Department of Defence. On 20 August 1926 he turned to Diarmuid O'Hegarty, another old IRB friend who had been close to Collins (and who had been at the reorganisation meeting of August 1916) and was now, as secretary to the cabinet, one of the most powerful men in government. Almost two years of poverty and humiliation had unstiffened Peadar's back:

> Tá súil agam nach bhfuil mé ag cur isteach ort ag sgríobhadh an nóta so, ach is cruaidh mo chás, & tá mé cinnte go ndéanfaidh tú aon rud tá ar do chumas ar mo shon. Fuair mé fios raithe[?] ó shoin ó'n Board of Assessors go raibh sgeul mo phinsiúin curtha go dtí an Roinn Cosanta & chualaidh [?] mé nach mbeidh mórán le fagháil ach gidh gur beag bídeach é tá sé ag teastáil go géar agus go tapaidh. Tá an tsláinte go dona agam féin, agus tá mo bhean ina luighe. Ní maith liom mo stát a nochtughadh ach tá beirt buachaill á choinneáil ar sgoil & biadh & éadaigh a sholáthar dóibh. Más féidir leat rud ar bith a dhéanamh chun an pinsiún a bhrostaghadh déanfaidh tú an rud is fearr a rinne tú ariamh do shean chara.

> [I hope I am not putting in on you by writing this note but I am in a difficult situation and I am certain you will do anything you can on my behalf. I was informed a while back by the Board of Assessors that the matter of my pension had been sent to the Department of Defence and I heard that I will not receive very much but however trifling it is needed badly and quickly. My own health is bad and my wife is bedridden. I find it hard to speak about my own circumstances but there are two boys to keep at school and to be fed and clothed. If you can do anything to expedite the pension you will do the best thing you ever did for your old friend.]

To his credit, O'Hegarty immediately wrote to the Army Finance Officer that Mr Ó Cearnaigh was 'very badly in need of funds' and asking him to ensure that 'no avoidable delay would occur in the payment of any pension that may be awarded to him'. It is likely that O'Hegarty was responsible for getting Peadar a grant of £35: on 22 October 1926, he showed great consideration by phoning the Department of Defence to inform them that the grant was from a special fund and was 'not to be recovered' from his pension.

In October 1926, almost two years after his application, Peadar was informed that he had been awarded an annual pension of £30 16s. 8d., backdated to 1 October 1924. This would have been a very useful supplement to an income but, as a painter in poor health, he was lucky to work for half the year. He had not given 'the most active years of my life' with a view to payment but, now that the government had decided to measure and reward such contributions, it must have seemed a paltry amount to a broken man struggling to feed his family. On the other hand, given his inability to satisfy the legalistic demands of the bureaucracy, he was lucky to have been designated a non-commissioned officer who had been discharged in March 1924 (two months later than he himself had claimed), for which he had influential friends to thank.

ABOUT A year later Peadar submitted a memorandum to his solicitor, Mick Noyk, which provides the context for his *ask-me-arse* rejection of Joe McGrath's greeting that young Con witnessed with such amazement. McGrath had been an accountant before he joined the IRB, fought in 1916, served time in prison and became a close friend of Michael Collins. During the War of Independence he had specialised in raising funds by robbing banks and, like Peadar, he was interned in Ballykinlar, where he was elected Commandant. McGrath was a minister in the first and second Executive Councils of the Free State but resigned in April 1924 in protest against what he—and many others including, presumably, Peadar Kearney—felt was the cabinet's abandonment of nationalist ideals and neglect of those who had fought for them. In 1925 he became an adviser to the German company, Siemens Schuckert, who were building the Ardnacrusha dam, the first step in a famously successful commercial career.

McGrath had always taken a special interest in distressed Volunteers and, according to Peadar's memorandum, approached him

> ...and gave me the impression that he was very anxious to fix
> me up, and when eventually I asked him to get me fixed up he

238

told me I would never have to work again, that he was looking after a small annuity and that as a matter of fact a cheque for a substantial sum (I heard £250) was actually drawn in my favour and was awaiting signature. Acting on Mr McGrath's advice I borrowed a considerable amount from a mutual friend who was aware of the promises made. . . I believe I am entitled to some little consideration and my own friends can hardly credit I am penniless and go so far as to say that it serves me right for taking things so quietly but all my life I have detested publicity and sincerely hope this matter will be settled in peace and decency. Peadar Ó Cearnaigh 24/8/26

There was no written proof of McGrath's promise and no evidence that he gave any explanation 'of the extraordinary position in which he placed not only me but himself'. Apart altogether from hurt feelings, Peadar was deep in debt: 'It would take at least £150 to entirely clear me of debts which have accumulated since the beginning of my internment'.[37] Only a lender who was himself a friend of McGrath and convinced of 'great expectations' would have allowed an ailing house-painter into such a debt but for some unknown reason the promise was not fulfilled, which would explain Peadar's behaviour at the removal.[38]

THE MEMORANDUM to Noyk seems to be related to Peadar's campaign for recognition of his rights arising from 'A Soldier's Song'. The pain and humiliation of the pension application had the minimal virtue of being confined to himself and his family. The next affront to his dignity was played out in public and over a longer period. If his IRB activities were known only to a clandestine few, he was more widely identified as the man who had written the words of what was *de facto* the national anthem.

Because the Irish Free State was a dominion of the British Empire, the new government did not immediately nominate a national anthem although the National Army—consisting mainly of those who had sung it when they were Volunteers—tended to play 'A Soldier's Song' on special occasions and in 1924 the President of the Executive, W. T. Cosgrave, had declared himself against 'replacing it'. This failure to take more positive action led to the tune of Thomas Moore's 'Let Erin Remember' being used at several events abroad, including the 1924 Olympic Games in Paris, and the lack of an official anthem prompted the Dublin *Evening Mail* to organise an unsuccessful competition to find a suitable anthem. While nationalists continued to use 'A Soldier's Song', unionists continued to sing 'God Save the King' and eventually, to prevent this, the government decided hugger-mugger to adopt 'A Soldier's Song' as a national anthem in July 1926.

Despite this and despite 'A Soldier's Song' being played from 1926 onwards at the end of programmes on national radio and from 1931 onwards at the end of cinema programmes, Peadar Kearney received no royalties and was forced, together with Michael Heeney, brother of the dead Paddy, to sue the government. Eventually, in July 1934, with de Valera's Fianna Fáil in government, the Department of Finance bought the copyright on behalf of the state, paying them £490 each (almost twice what Peadar in the memorandum to Noyk described as 'a substantial sum').

IN A homemade scrapbook entitled *The Soldier's Song* Peadar pasted newspaper cuttings relating to the controversy from 1926 until 1936. These included both criticism from such eminences as Count John McCormack as well as letters he himself had written to the press, making his case for compensation and threatening to sue those who infringed his copyright, among them the Catholic Truth Society and the managers of the Royal and Gaiety theatres.

He is generally described in the press as 'a humble house-painter' living 'in humble circumstances' in Inchicore. He is photographed in painter's overalls and it is difficult not to notice in the criticism of 'A Soldier's Song' as national anthem a snobbish disdain that the work of such 'humble' men as Kearney and Heeney should represent the aspirations of their social and cultural superiors in the new establishment. Even lower than 'humble' was complete anonymity: a 'special representative' of the *Daily Express*, who interviewed Peadar in Inchicore in December 1930, described him as 'the man who has written the best-known song in Ireland and yet who is totally unknown'.

In December 1927 'Carbery', a journalist with the *Cork Examiner*, visited him at work in Rathmines and left an invaluably detailed physical description of

> a rather frail-looking man, in a mechanic's paint-stained coat,
> wielding a brush deftly. His face is anaemic and pale, he is clearly

a victim to the ills of his trade, aggravated by long spells [*sic*] of prison hardship. Yet his eyes are blue and bright, though sad betimes. This is Peadar Kearney—poet, soldier, house-painter—writer of many stirring ballads, including that inspiring 'Marseillaise' of the Irish Volunteers, now played all over the world as the Irish National Anthem—'The Soldier's Song'.

By 'the ills of his trade' Carbery is most likely referring to poisoning from lead-based paints which caused damage to the nervous system, to the kidneys, to muscles and joints, leading to a range of discomforts from head and stomach aches to irritability and memory loss. House painters were not generally expected to last into extreme old age.

THERE HAVE always been objections to 'A Soldier's Song' on musical and textual grounds, perhaps the most hurtful that expressed in the Dáil Finance Committee Debate on 22 November 1933 by Senator MacDermot:

> Leaving out sentiment, I must confess, from both a literary and a musical point of view, I would regard the 'Soldier's Song' as, shall we say, a jaunty little piece of vulgarity, and I think we could have done a lot better.

The hurt would have been the greater had it not come from the colourfully Anglophile MacDermot (Downside and Oxford, British Army major and youngest son of the Prince of Coolavin) and no doubt Peadar found some consolation in the response of the Fine Gael deputy for Leix-Offaly, Dr Tom O'Higgins Snr:

> National Anthems come about, not because of the suitability of the particular words or notes, but because they are adopted generally by the nation. That is exactly how the 'Soldier's Song' became a National Anthem in this country. It happened to be the Anthem on the lips of the people when they came into their own and when the outsiders evacuated the country and left the insiders here to make the best or the worst of the country. It was adopted by the people here before ever it was adopted by the Executive Council.

In a story characterised by omission, perhaps the most amazing is the lack of any allusion to the windfall that was Peadar's half of the purchase price of the national anthem, the equivalent of at least €50,000 today, and proportionately more to a poor family. If there was a celebration, it did not pass into the family folklore. My inquiries have produced not a single word on the effects of such a bonanza on a family that had known little but poverty and humiliation. What is perhaps even more baffling is the absence of any mention of it in de Burca's biography.

de Burca made regular visits to Inchicore between 1932 and Peadar's death in late 1942, which is to say he had been on intimate terms with Peadar for two years when the purchase of the rights to the national anthem had been approved by the Dáil. Imagine a biography of Rouget de Lisle that did not include the government's acceptance of 'La Marseillaise' as national anthem in 1795 and then wonder what happened between de Burca and Peadar Kearney.

It is not clear at what stage Peadar accepted his nephew as his authorised biographer and, by giving him his manuscripts and his extensive reminiscences, his literary executor. What is beyond reasonable doubt is that de Burca's lack of coverage of Peadar's life between his release from Ballykinlar and, say, 1935 was not because it was lacking in interesting elements—such as Peadar's campaign for his rights arising from 'A Soldier's Song'—or because he was unaware of such elements. It was not unusual in the Ireland of that time to skirt around matters relating to the civil war, which might explain his near-silence on Peadar's participation on the Free State side and his subsequent pension, especially when by then Peadar had withdrawn his support for Cumann na nGaedheal, but that would hardly explain the refusal to allude to the official recognition of his rights by Fianna Fáil in 1934.

DE BURCA'S portrait of the artist as serenely contented veteran is striking for a variety of reasons, not least for his assertion that he 'would live the same life over if I had to live again' and for the lack of any vestigial hostility or resentment. His life had been divided in two. Up till Ballykinlar he had followed his dream of an independent Ireland that he shared with equally dedicated comrades; afterwards he had known only the nightmare of civil war and the back-to-earth of a civilian life of illness and poverty during which he must have asked himself if the Irish Free State had been worth the lives of so many brave friends.

The Peadar Kearney of the portrait is probably a composite but the prevailing tone is valedictory: he has abandoned his old pleasures—angling and taking long walks into the countryside—and spends most of his time at home, reading and writing, apart from a weekly trip into town for a chat with Tom Pugh. This composite must have been heavily weighted towards the very end of Peadar's life for there is a good deal of evidence that contradicts this monastic regime.

His own compositions suggest a man who enjoyed convivial drinking. The principal pastimes of 'The Devil's Crew' were 'to drink and gamble and swear'. 'Sweet Cork Hill' (1917) celebrates the snug of McMahon's public house, 4 Cork Hill, when Sean Farrelly was manager.

> With many a ditty and story witty,
> Each with the other in friendship vied,
> While at a glib rate the pumps would vibrate
> And refilled tankards were passed inside.
> No thought of sorrow or of the morrow,
> No thought of trouble or woe or ill
> Disturbed our dreaming, while we saw gleaming
> The foaming tankards on sweet Cork Hill!

The 'red nights' remembered in 'Down in the Village' involved 'shouting and drinking and singing so merrily'. Written in 1935, during the period of the Poet's Den, 'Lament for Kearney' suggests more than the once-a-week tipple with Tom Pugh. The fictional speaker, who is trying to locate the ghost of the recently deceased Kearney, concentrates his search on a number of pubs, including The Cuckoo's Nest in Tallaght and one in Ballyfermot known as My Aunt's.

> No more he'll bless the Cuckoo's Nest
> Nor gambol in Old Bawn;
> The Dodder trout may venture out,
> Their poaching foe is gone;
> No more he'll gush poetic slush
> While tortured tipplers moan,
> By book or crook, he's slung his hook,
> And left for parts unknown.

Eventually the search is concluded because

> *. . . each one says, that knows his ways,*
> *If Kearney wants a jar,*
> *There's not a doubt, his ghost hangs out*
> *Inside the Grafton bar.*

Where Sean Farrelly, formerly of Cork Hill, is now in charge. One gets the impression that even when out on his rural rambles—fishing or simply walking the roads—he frequented the local pubs, entertaining the other customers with recitations of his verses.

It could be argued that despite its date 'Lament for Kearney' refers to an earlier phase in his life but at least one of his neighbours in O'Donoghue Street would not have agreed. Con never gave me any reason to believe his father was a heavy drinker but he did recall for my sister Eileen an incident in the immediate aftermath of Peadar's death in November 1942. On hearing the news a crowd had gathered outside the house and as Con was making his way through he heard one woman whisper to another that 'it was the drink that killed him'. Con recalled being stung by the remark but he did not—at the time or when talking to Eileen—dismiss it as a baseless slander.

On another occasion, while we were enjoying our pints in The Willows, the conversation turned to his mother and I asked him the specific cause of her death. Staring at the table, he replied 'poverty and neglect'. I was taken aback and was about to ask him who had neglected her but the old telepathy advised that the less said the better and I held my tongue, afterwards wondering what grim scenes he had witnessed and had no desire to relive.

Again, it could of course be argued that he was blaming the Irish Free State for its inadequate treatment of his father and the disastrous consequences for his mother but if, as I am still inclined to believe, he was letting slip that his father had somehow neglected his mother, what could he have had in mind? That in his devotion to 'the cause' Peadar Kearney had failed to take adequate care of Eva? Peadar had claimed that 'without her sympathy and courage' he could not have given his years to 'the cause'.[39] Had Con, who had always put his wife and family above everything else, come to conclude that his father had made a wrong choice? If so, it was the only time I have ever heard him come close to criticising his father.

As a child I had seen how well Eva had got on with my mother when we returned to Inchicore and they shared the house and their beloved Con, and over the years I had realised that, unlike Eva, Maisie had never espoused or preached the gospel of nationalism or worshipped at the shrine of Peadar Kearney. I knew better than to ask her about him while Con was alive—she would never have wanted even to be thought to contradict him on such matters—and so it was several years after his death when I asked her how she had got on with Peadar. She responded with enthusiastic praise of Eva and, having let her have her say, I repeated my question. She fell silent for a few seconds, then shrugged and muttered: 'Sure he was never there.'

Although I was perplexed and curious, I couldn't find a form of words that would elicit the clarification I wanted without embarrassing her. Did she visit O'Donoghue Street when Con knew his father would not be there? Did Peadar absent himself when he knew Con was bringing her over to meet his mother. Did Maisie, daughter of a Dublin Fusilier, suspect that Peadar did not approve of her lack of 'national feeling'? Had she ever mentioned anything like this to Con? Looking back, I suspect she was going as far as she dared: she would have done anything for me, except offend Con's spirit by betraying their unspoken agreement to protect the great name of Peadar Kearney. But protect him from what?

Among the Seamus de Burca papers in the National Library of Ireland is a copybook containing, among drafts of various literary projects, an account of a conversation with Eva. It is impossible to transcribe it with confidence or to date it other than after Peadar's death. He suggests to Eva that Peadar was 'the true artist, sacrificing everything for his art'. She seems to reply with a statement that is followed by a question mark: 'Yes but it was wrong'? [*sic*] A slight emendation would make sense: 'Yes, but was it wrong?'

> In that moment a light seemed to pass across her face, the light that had a sadness [?] in it. Perhaps in a sudden the ghost of the hardships, the [illegible], the insults even, that she had shared with her patriot husband, but I [illegible] there was any regret [?]. Nay, I firmly [?] believe she would have gone through it every minute [?] again if only for the [illegible] of the [illegible], happy hours when nothing mattered but both of them to each other and Ireland since Ireland meant so much to him. She was a patriot.[40]

It is difficult to avoid noting that de Burca's belief is benevolently subjective and based on his sense of Peadar as a great man, while Eva's doubt arises from close experience. On another occasion, when somebody had assured her that she had been 'married to a genius', Eva is said to have replied: 'If that was genius, God preserve us from it.' Again one wonders: preserve us from what?[41]

(The most telling comment on their union was made by one who was best placed to observe it: Pearse told his son Cónal that 'Peadar Kearney should never have got married'.)

If de Burca was aware—as he clearly was—of the hardships and insults Peadar and Eva had borne, why did he not include them in his biography? Presumably for the same reason that he reduced Peadar's drinking to a weekly two and a half hours with Tom Pugh. His task, as he saw it, was to preserve the memory of a great man, not a detailed warts-and-all biography, more a hagiography.[42] His book was a literary version of the oral tradition preserved within the family where nothing was ever mentioned that might detract from his greatness.

THANKS TO the Bureau of Military History we almost certainly know a great deal more about Peadar Kearney post-Ballykinlar than de Burca did. Not as much as Eva, Pearse and Con, of course, but for the most part they kept their counsel. By his own account he was a broken man, in poor health, who must have been further sickened by the degradation of the fight for freedom into the savagery of civil war. Even if the struggle to which he had dedicated his life had yielded a happily unified and independent Ireland it is unlikely Peadar Kearney would have escaped what we now term Post-Traumatic Stress Disorder, common among those who have been in combat. The most obvious symptoms are difficulty in readjusting to civilian life, nightmares and flashbacks to traumatic incidents, panic attacks, survivor's guilt and depression, proneness to anger and irritability.

Peadar recalled for de Burca the eve of Bloody Sunday when Dick McKee insisted on shaking hands with Peadar before leaving Phil Shanahan's. When Peadar made light of the formal gesture, McKee had replied: 'we see each other often but we never seem to shake hands.' Shortly afterwards McKee was arrested and taken to Dublin Castle. As soon as he'd heard of the arrest Peadar had known he would never see his friend again, anticipating his torture and brutal death. This was only one of many bloody incidents that would have haunted a friend who survived.

It takes no great effort to imagine him suffering from PTSD, to picture Eva's shock at the change in the man who had been arrested in Richmond Cottages, or the confusion of Pearse and Con at the return of the father they were in many ways encountering for the first time. If they had been awaiting a doting dad who would hug them and teach them Irish, they would soon assume that he was not that kind of a father: it wasn't that he wouldn't teach them Irish, more that he couldn't. Some fifty years later Pearse, in a conversation with his son Peadar, recalled that when he was a very young child his father had spoken Irish to him 'continuously', which suggests that before Ballykinlar Peadar had sought to create an Irish-speaking environment in their home, an experiment that was not resumed on his release.

If he displayed such symptoms as wild panic attacks or sullen periods of silent depression he would have been understood as 'suffering from his nerves' and every effort made to conceal his condition—popularly considered shameful—from the outside world. There was no treatment—pharmacological or psychiatric—available to such men, many of whom self-medicated with alcohol, itself a depressant and counter-productive. And *if* he drank excessively in his post-Ballykinlar years, that too would have been a failing his family and friends would have preferred not to publicise. It might also explain, for example, the veil of secrecy thrown over the national anthem bonanza of 1934, initially welcomed but soon seen as a mixed blessing for a disappointed man with a drinking problem.

IRRESPECTIVE OF the storms or doldrums in which he found himself, Peadar Kearney never wavered in his dedication to the ideal of an independent and united Ireland. He took the Free State side in the civil war largely because he believed in Collins and the freedom the Anglo-Irish Treaty gave them to achieve full freedom. His support did not last much longer than the death of Collins and failure of the Cumann na nGaedheal government to respect his entitlement to a decent pension and recognition of 'A Soldier's Song' as national anthem. Unfortunately I can only remember snatches of satirical verses Con quoted in which his father mocked members of the government: W. T. Cosgrave (President of the Executive Council), Ernest Blythe (Minister for Finance) and Patrick McGilligan (the Minister for Industry and Commerce, who had replaced Joe McGrath in 1924). He did not transfer his support to Fianna Fáil, even when, shortly after coming to power, they bought the rights to 'A Soldier's Song'. In 1935 he addressed a public meeting called to protest against the Fianna Fáil government's suppression of the IRA and no doubt his antipathy was increased when they declared it illegal the following year.

Long after 'the organisation' had ceased to exist he remained an IRB man, faithful to the oath he had taken in 1903 committing himself to the achievement of a 32-county republic by whatever means necessary, not excluding armed violence. Not only did he approve of the IRA campaign, he also adhered to the principle that my enemy's enemy is my friend. Con remembers him marking on a map—and rejoicing in—the German advances in the early stages of World War II. Germany was not an ally of long standing but, in its favour, it was opposed to the British Empire. The United States, on the other hand, had long been a source of support for the fight for Irish freedom—and was crucial in the foundation of the IRB—but they were allies of the British which was why Peadar celebrated the attack by the Japanese on the American fleet in Pearl Harbour in December 1941. Again my recall of the verses Con quoted is slight but I remember the opening:

> *There's a certain [something] gentleman*
> *Whose name is Uncle Sam;*
> *His pedigree is doubtful,*
> *Whether Japhet, Shem or Ham....*

I also remember the gleeful tone with which he—the house-painter who had taken on the British Empire—described how the little man surprised the major power:

> *But the little slant-eyed yellow man,*
> *He didn't given a damn*
> *And he hit him with a hammer in Manila.*

Within a year Peadar was dead and spared the defeat of Germany and Japan.

WE HAVE seen how Peadar had welcomed the birth of Pearse in the aftermath of the Easter Rising:

> *All my hopes are set on you,*
> *Daddy boy, Daddy boy,*

248

> *God grant they'll all come true,*
> *Daddy boy, Daddy boy,*
> *When you're big and brave and strong*
> *Ireland's cause you'll carry on*
> *Just like Con and Tom and Sean,*
> *Daddy boy, Daddy boy.*

Though Pearse and Con inherited and transmitted to their children the 'national feeling' epitomised by their father, neither emulated him—or Con Colbert, Tom Clarke and MacDermott—in joining the armed struggle. For all their reverence for their father's involvement in the fight for an independent and united Ireland, neither joined the IRA.

Unlike their cousin Brendan Behan—five and seven years younger than Con and Pearse respectively—who, having served his apprenticeship in the junior branch, Fianna Éireann, was sworn into the IRA in 1939 and shortly afterwards, without official sanction, travelled to Liverpool to join the bombing campaign against English cities. He was quickly arrested and served two years, initially in Walton Gaol and then, as a young offender, in a Borstal Institution. (From Walton he wrote to Peadar, noting the similarities between his arrest and that of Peadar's friend, Tom Clarke, in London in 1883 for possession of explosives.) Of a turbulent nature, months after his return from confinement he fired shots at the police outside Glasnevin Cemetery, for which he served another four and a half years. He was in Mountjoy Gaol when he heard of his uncle's death; refused parole, he wrote a letter of condolence to Pearse.

> I know that you will understand that I have lost a very dear friend—merely being my uncle would not have caused the deep affection in which I held him—after all you choose your friends but you can't help your relations—But my uncle Peadar was the one, outside my own parents, who excited the admiration and love that is friendship. . . I was proud that the same blood ran in our veins.

Prior to his solo expedition to Liverpool he had been a regular visitor to Peadar who clearly approved of the only member of the extended family to follow his political example.

There is no evidence that Peadar thought the less of his own sons, who joined the Irish Army at the beginning of what was called the National Emergency in 1939, or that his sons harboured any resentment at his admiration for their young cousin. For as long as they lived, Pearse and Con remained fond friends of Brendan, with whom both worked as painters at various stages.

Con's service in the army had been brief, most likely because it separated him from Maisie Brady with whom he was in love and hoping to marry. They both wanted a family and it would not be surprising if the family Con contemplated was different from what he himself had experienced. Even before she married him in 1914, Eva knew that for Peadar 'the cause' came before everything else, including family. Neither Pearse nor Con had ever agreed to such an understanding. They had not experienced the carefree cavorting Peadar and Eva had enjoyed on the banks of the Tolka. All they had known was the price the family had paid for Peadar's dedication. They were their mother's as well as their father's sons, their mother who, according to Con, had died of 'poverty and neglect'. Amid much that must remain hypothetical one fact is irresistible. For all his reverence for his father as patriot, Con would not accept him as a model husband or father: Con's wife and family would take precedence over everything else.

But though he chose not to repeat his failings, he never saw Peadar as a failure, rather as a victim of history, who had given his early life for an Irish republic, had known the exhilarating danger of the fight which had claimed the lives of so many of his friends, then been humiliated by the politicians—was there a tradesman among them?—who had come to power on other men's wounds. Though he rationed the details in accordance with my age, he could hardly have helped transmitting to me his general sense of his father and, for as far back as I can recall, it seemed to me he had two fathers: the stern patriot neglected by the state he had brought into existence and the jovial spirit who composed 'The Devil's Crew' and 'Down in the Village'. The Peadar Kearney I warmed to was the wordsmith. My idea of heaven was a family get-together when Con and Pearse revelled in rollicking anti-English satires such as 'Whack-fol-de-Diddle', 'It's a Grand Ould Country' and 'Sergeant William Bailey' and we all joined in the chorus. They were never so ebulliently proud of him, even if, after a silent pause and a shake of the head, they muttered the strangely antiphonal 'me poor father'.

My favourite turn—and maybe Con's too—was Pearse's rendering of

'It's a Grand Ould Country', for the final verse of which he'd go down on his knees and semi-speak the lines, miming religious piety—

> *Now we'll spend the time in praying*
> *While we're waiting for the day,*
> *And we'll pray for Mother England*
> *Till we're bald and blind and grey;*
> *We'll pray that dying she may die*
> *And drowning she may drown—*

and then, standing up and returning to full song—

> *And if ever she chances to raise her head*
> *We'll pray to shove it down!*
> *[Chorus] For it's a grand ould country every time,*
> *With its trees and rivers, rocks and soil and clime;*
> *We're God's own people and we shout from tower and steeple:*
> *It's a grand ould country every time!*

Following Con I learned all the popular Peadar Kearney songs and could identify quotations from 'The Devil's Crew' and 'To a Dog'.

Peadar Kearney is generally considered a writer of songs and ballads and humorous verses but in an interview with the *Daily Express* in 1930 he had identified himself as 'a house painter by trade and a poet by choice'. Two years previously the Talbot Press had published *The Soldier's Song and Other Poems* and shortly after his death—probably in 1945—his friend Martin Walton published *Songs, Ballads & Poems by Famous Irishmen: Peadar Ó Cearnaigh*.

Filling in his death certificate in November 1941 Con gave his father's occupation as 'painter'. Almost two years later, on his own marriage certificate, he described him as 'Poet'. We will never know what prompted the change but, as well as being less distraught than immediately after the loss of his father, he'd had two years to consider what his father's real occupation had been and possibly concluded that the single thread throughout his life from adolescence to his last days was the writing of songs and verse. Was this image of his father as a neglected poet, obliged to earn a living as a house painter, what sparked his instantly intense interest in the Ó Rathaille poem that night in The Willows? Like the Kerry poet two centuries before

251

him, his father had once enjoyed the respect and affection of his leaders but had lived to share their downfall, reduced to the level of an outcast with no hope of assistance from the gang who had replaced them.

> *Cabhair ní ghairfead go gcuirtear mé i gcruinn-chomhrainn*
> *Is dar an leabhar dá ngairfinn níor ghaire-de an ní domhsa;*
> *Ár gcodhnach uile, glac-chumasach shíl Eoghain,*
> *Is tollta a chuisle 'gus d'imigh a bhrí ar feochadh.*

> *[I won't call for help till I'm put in the narrow coffin*
> *And, my oath, if I did, there's no chance I get it;*
> *Our strong-handed commander-in-chief, true heir of Eoghan,*
> *His artery is opened and his life-force withered away.*

From Ballykinlar Peadar had written to Eva that internees could not effect much 'but we can at least be faithful unto death'. Con had seen his ailing father keep that faith—his pride in doing so strengthened rather than weakened by his poverty—loyal to the end to what he believed was a timeless value that linked him to the great men of the past.

NOTES

1 *The Soldier's Song: The Story of Peadar Kearney* (Dublin: P. J. Bourke, 1957), 26ff. Future references to SS.

2 *Mother of All the Behans* (London: Hutchinson, 1984), 28f.

3 SS 27.

4 SS 91-94.

5 SS 24-57.

6 Bureau of Military History Witness Statement 848, 10. Future references to WS.

7 SS 97f.

8 WS 165, 4.

9 SS 61. *The Old Limerick Journal* (Winter 2003) www.limerickcity.ie/media/Media,4148,en.pdf

10 WS 360, 15.

11 SS 113-29.

12 WS 312, 9.

13 SS 126f.

14 SS 132.

15 Leon Ó Broin, *Revolutionary Underground: The Story of the Irish Republican Brotherhood 1858-1924* (Dublin: Gill & Macmillan, 1976), 175.

16 WS 707, 13.

17 Peadar Kearney application in Bureau of Military History (1916-1923) Pension Archive.

18 WS 660, 13.

19 WS 165, 16.

20 WS 1739, 36. It is interesting that Breen seems to have Peadar represent the saints.

21 'The Rigidly Righteous' of Robert Burns' 'Address to the Unco Guid'.

22 The quotation was a favourite with Pearse and Con, which suggests they had often heard their father declaim it.

23 SS 154f.

24 SS 162.

25 SS 220.

26 SS 164.

27 *My Dear Eva: Letters from Ballykinlar Internment Camp 1921* (Dublin: P. J. Bourke, 1976) 15. Future references to MDE.

28 MDE 26.

29 MDE 25.

30 MDE 31.

31 MDE 37.

32 MDE 36.

33 MDE 33, 37, 15. Con is variously Con, Conn and Colbert.

34 MDE 38f.

35 Pension application.

36 Family Archive.

37 Family Archive.

38 I still doubt if Con was aware of McGrath's broken promise.

39 SS 231.

40 NLI MS 39, 123/1.

41 Even as a child I wondered why, in 'The Three-Coloured Ribbon', his ballad of Easter
    Week dedicated *To Eva*, the female narrator sings the bravery of her 'true love' who
    is killed in the fighting.

    The struggle was ended, they brought me the story,

    The last whispered message he sent unto me:

    'I was true to my land, love, I fought for her glory,

    And gave up my life for to make Ireland free.'

    Now I cannot help wondering if he, however unconsciously, recognised that as far as
    Eva was concerned, he had died 'for the cause'.

42 For a broader, historiographical account of the context in which
    de Burca wrote, see Fearghal McGarry's 'Hard Service: remembering the Abbey The-
    atre's rebels' in *Remembering 1916*, edited by Richard S. Grayson and Fearghal McGarry
    (Cambridge: Cambridge University Press, 2016).

INDEX

25, 26, 29, 31, 83, 201, 202, 203, 204
Griffith. Mamie 33